D0778750

CALGARY PUBLIC LIBRARY

941.
443
GIB

Gibb, Andrew.
    Glasgow, the making of a city / Andrew Gibb. --
London : Croom Helm, c1983.
    197 p. : ill. ; 23 cm. (Croom Helm historical
geography series)

    Includes bibliographical references and index.
LC: 83125531 ISBN: 0709901615 : $24.60

1. Glasgow (Scotland) – History. I. Title.

944

HUMANITIES
PRODUCED IN CANADA BY UTLAS Inc.
6812 CPLA
0100 84OCT31 95455220
PRODUIT AU CANADA PAR UTLAS Inc.

⸴ GLASGOW ⸴
The Making of a City

CROOM HELM HISTORICAL GEOGRAPHY SERIES
Edited by R. A. Butlin, University of Loughborough

The Development of the Irish Town
Edited by R. A. Butlin

The Making of Urban Scotland
I. H. Adams

The Fur Trade of the American West, 1807-1840
David J. Wishart

The Making of the Scottish Countryside
Edited by M. L. Parry and T. R. Slater

Agriculture in France on the Eve of the Railway Age
Hugh Clout

Lord and Peasant in Nineteenth-Century Britain
Dennis R. Mills

The Origins of Open-Field Agriculture
Edited by Trevor Rowley

English Country Houses and Landed Estates
Heather A. Clemenson

The Medieval English Landscape
Edited by C. M. Cantor

-GLASGOW-
THE MAKING OF A CITY

Andrew Gibb

CROOM HELM   LONDON

© 1983 Andrew Gibb
Croom Helm Ltd, Provident House, Burrell Row,
Beckenham, Kent BR3 1AT
Croom Helm Australia, PO Box 391,
Manuka, ACT 2603, Australia
Reprinted and first paperback edition, August 1983

British Library Cataloguing in Publication Data

Gibb, A.
   Glasgow (Strathclyde) — History
   I. Title
   941.4'43   DA890.G5

   ISBN 0-7099-0161-5
   ISBN 0-7099-1169-6 (paperback)

The publisher acknowledges subsidy from the Scottish
Arts Council towards the publication of this volume.

Book design:©1983 Kate Kelly

Typeset by Gray & Dawson Typesetters Ltd., Glasgow
Printed and bound in Great Britain by
Biddles Ltd, Guildford and King's Lynn

CONTENTS

To the city and people of Glasgow, if they will forgive the presumption.

And especially to those closest to me.

FIGURES, PLATES, TABLES & GLOSSARY

List of Figures

List of Plates

List of Tables

Glossary and Periodical Abbreviations

Street- and other place-names have changed their spelling over time, and in early periods consistency was never a keynote. Wherever possible, contemporary spelling has been used in the text, and this accounts for variations in certain names, especially the following:

Argyll; Argyle Street
Briggait; Bridgegait; Bridgegate
Candlerig; Candlerigs St.; Candleriggs St.; The Candlerigg Street, etc.
Ducat; Dowcat; Ducal Green

St. Tenus; Thenew; Thenaw; Tenaw; Enoch (Gait and Square)
Tronegait; Trongait; Trongate
Waulkergate; Saltmarket.

Most terms are explained in the text, but the following items may be unfamiliar:

Baillie: town or city magistrate

Burgh: urban settlement holding a charter granting trading, tenurial and organisational privileges

Burgh Muir: common grazing land — not necessarily moorland

Burn: stream

Close: varied meanings: as in 'Cathedral close' — the area in the immediate vicinity of the Cathedral; in relation to burgage morphology – a narrow alley giving access along the plot; in later contexts – a common entry giving access to upper storeys of tenement buildings.

Court: open area behind tenement frontage, usually surrounded by buildings

Feu Duty: annual sum payable to feudal superior in respect of ground rent

Gait or gate: major street

Loan: lane or track leading to arable and pasture lands

Manse: minister's or other ecclesiastic's dwelling place

Police burgh: urban unit empowered by Act of Parliament (after 1850) to levy rates, maintain services including a police force, and elect a town council

Port: town gate or gateway

Vennel: minor street

Wynd: narrow alley or street

S.G.M. — Scottish Geographical Magazine

S.H.R. — Scottish Historical Review

T.G.A.S. — Transactions of the Glasgow Archaeological Society

ACKNOWLEDGEMENTS

In the construction of this book, all sins of commission and omission must be placed firmly at the author's door, but if there are any qualities of value, these must owe a great deal to the individuals and institutions who gave unstintingly of their time and expertise. Sections of the manuscript were read and constructively commented upon by colleagues in the University of Glasgow. Eric Talbot of the Department of Archaeology, Ian Cowan of the Department of Scottish History, Anthony Slaven and John Kellett of the Department of Economic History, Jean Forbes of the Department of Town and Regional Planning, and Robert Price, Arthur Morris and James Henderson of the Department of Geography contributed their expertise, and I am grateful to all of them for their kindness and always useful suggestions. Special thanks must go to my friend and colleague, Charles Docherty, Principal Teacher of Geography in St. Pius Secondary School, Drumchapel, for a truly heroic effort in reading the entire manuscript. For their technical advice and expertise in matters photographic and cartographic. Ian Gerrard, Leslie Hill, Michael Shand, Yvonne Wilson, Andrew Newman, David Barbour and students of the Diploma of Cartography course at the University of Glasgow have more than earned my thanks. Kate Kelly's artistry in cover design, internal layout and artwork speaks for itself, and disproves the adage about raw materials for silk purses.

The staffs of the Mitchell Library, Glasgow, Strathclyde Regional Archives, the Scottish Records Office and the map room of the National Library in Edinburgh provided efficient and courteous access to invaluable materials. I am especially grateful to the guardians of the Special Collections of the Library of the University of Glasgow, who patiently endured all my questions and rendered me great assistance, and to Elspeth Simpson, of Glasgow University Archives for her interest, expertise, and infectious enthusiasm. I am grateful also to the following organisations and individuals who kindly gave permission to reproduce photographs or adapt illustrations. Gerald Eve & Co. for Fig. 7.v; J. Menzies for Fig. 1.i; Aerofilms Ltd. for Pl. 7.i; Annan & Sons for Pls. 2.iii, 5.i and 6.ix; B.K.S. Surveys for Pl. 7.vii; Old Glasgow Museum for Pls. 5.iii, 6.i, ii, iv, v, and vi, and the cover photograph; Strathclyde Regional Archives for Pl. 6.x; and the Carnegie Trust for the Universities of Scotland for a grant towards the cost of illustrations.

Finally, I must reserve a special note of gratitude for my head of department, Professor Ian B. Thompson, for his unfailing support, practical advice and constant encouragement, without which this book would never have been completed.

Andrew Gibb
June, 1982.

PREFACE

A book which takes as its subject matter the historical geography of a single city may seem an indulgence, providing an account of interest to only a few. At the same time, the extension of the period of examination up to the present may seem to negate the term 'historical'. However, every city is unique in site, situation, and detailed form, and the processes which produced that form are by no means universal, or clearly defined, therefore detailed study of a single urban unit may help to refine those definitions. At the same time, the broader processes which shaped Glasgow's urban structure and its social distributions are strongly related to the mainstream of British urban development, and as a case study Glasgow therefore offers both uniqueness and the opportunity for comparison.

Although development processes may be perceived as finite in time, a range of processes operating simultaneously over part of their duration may functionally affect one another. River improvements involving canalisation helped create available building land along the banks of the Clyde as the areas between jetties became infilled, and the locating power and needs of industry ensured that this land became devoted to industrial use. Earlier processes, their energy spent, may provide the structural frame for future developments. In this way, for instance, the spatial arrangement of streets, plots and buildings designed for eighteenth century residential use came to contain and constrain central business functions. Sets of evolutionary linkages of this kind carried the city's development forward to the present, and provide an explanation of the existing palimpsest of the urban landscape.

The choice of Glasgow as a focus for study is far from arbitrary, since in the scale, rapidity, range and effects of urban change, it stands out among British, let alone Scottish, cities. From being a small medieval trading burgh with a population of a few thousands, it grew through the centuries on the basis of European and Atlantic trade, and its pioneering achievements in industry in the nineteenth century. At the height of its Edwardian greatness, it was home to one million people, seeing itself as the second city of the British Empire, and through its decades of decline, it remained the largest and most important city in Scotland. In its present weakness, stricken by the full virulence of urban diseases, its gap sites and empty buildings the scars and sores of debility, its pulse is still strong.

This book is essentially an outline of change, taking as an organisational framework the major dynamic processes which have fuelled urban growth at various periods. It is neither an economic history, nor a complete social geography of Glasgow, but a selective examination of aspects of the city's historical geography which the author considers illuminating and important. It does not attempt to resolve the debates on the role of the cotton industry or the growth and integration of shipbuilding, for instance, leaving those aspects to economic and other historians better equipped to discuss them. It focuses on the structural components of the townscape, its streets and houses, markets and mills, canals and railways, and at its centre, the River Clyde and its improvements. Within this framework, population is examined from a viewpoint of growth, migration, and the relationships between people, their urban environment, and public health.

Each chapter has its own emphasis, based on those elements which seemed to be most important in any particular period. Thus after a brief scene-setting, Chapter 2 examines the medieval foundations of Glasgow in terms of its landscape elements. Chapters 3 and 4 focus on the importance of trading extension into a widening geographical sphere, and the mercantile expertise, capital accumulation and industrial investment developed on that basis. The first major spatial expansion of urban growth, synchronous with the first great phase of industrial growth, is discussed in Chapter 5, while Chapter 6 attempts to look more closely at the living conditions of the people who produced Glasgow's Victorian wealth. Finally, Chapter 7 looks at planning and the built environments created since the end of the First World War.

1. ENVIRONMENT AND URBAN ROOTS

In the historical geography of a city, deep tap-roots may draw their sustenance from the environment of its site and setting, as well as from the pre-urban activities of human beings, and consideration of these influences provides a framework within and upon which, later development may be examined. In the case of Glasgow, attention naturally focuses upon the River Clyde, as barrier, routeway and provider at the local scale, and as the unifying element and core of a wider hinterland. Two contrasting facets of its lower valley strongly influenced the early development of the city. From Lanark downstream to a point where the Molendinar Burn joins the Clyde (Fig. 2.i) the freshwater river is relatively narrow, and could be crossed by ford or bridge at numerous points. Immediately downstream of the Molendinar confluence, a ford lies next to what was for many centuries the lowest bridging point on the river, and the upper limit of tidal reach. Below Glasgow bridge, the salt waters of the Clyde broaden into an estuary giving access to a suite of long, deep sea-lochs which penetrate the mainland of Argyllshire. These two facets symbolise the background to Glasgow's early growth, as the market centre for an agricultural hinterland, and as the head of navigation of a western area of fishing and sea-borne trade. On its course to the sea, the Clyde flows across a range of rock types and rock structures which provided the city with sandstone for building, coal for domestic and industrial fuel, and iron ore for its foundries, while confluent streams flow to their junctions across glacial till and through drumlin swarms whose surfaces supported agriculture and provided dry settlement sites for early man. At all scales, a wide range of natural assets awaited the exploiting mind and hand of man, allowing him to lay the cultural foundations upon which a great city might arise.

Geology and geomorphology

The Clyde Valley is itself a facet of the western portion of the great Midland Valley of Scotland, and it embodies many of the features of geology and geomorphology common to its parent. Lying between the Highland and Southern Uplands Boundary Faults, the Midland Valley is an extensive down-faulted rift, whose floor of Old Red Sandstone is overlain by sedimentary rocks of the Carboniferous series, broken in places by igneous extrusions. The Carboniferous rocks differ in their stratigraphic sequence from those of England and Wales[1], with oil-shales and cementstones making up for the absence of thick Limestone strata. The important coalbearing strata, however, are well represented in the Coal Measures and the Carboniferous Limestone Series. At the base of the sequence, the rocks of the Calciferous Sandstone Series in the Glasgow region lack the economically useful oil-shales characteristic of their eastern extensions, but above them the rich organic fossils of the Limestone Coal Group of the Carboniferous Limestone Series more than compensate for this deficiency, with blackband ironstone high enough in carbonaceous contact to permit smelting without charcoal or coal[2]. Above all, their coal seams, relics of the swampy environment whose Lepidodendroids are preserved in the Fossil Grove in the west of Glasgow at Whiteinch[3], yielded a rich return to miners. The succeeding Millstone Grit, while devoid of fossil fuels, embodies seams of refractory fireclay, of sufficient thickness and extent to be of considerable economic value.

At the top of the sequence lie the Coal Measures, whose surface Barren Red Measures give way to the lower Productive Measures, up to 400 metres in thickness, with numerous workable seams. Though the effects of local faulting often made exploitation difficult, the character of the coal made it worthwhile. The greater part of the deposits was bituminous, with 80-90% carbon content, with some localised metamorphic anthracite in the vicinity of igneous intrusions. The igneous rocks of the Carboniferous Series complete the geological picture, with their exposed volcanic vents and resistant lava flows providing the high ground which almost encircles the site of Glasgow to the north, south and west, thus producing the major differentiation of topography within the western sector of the Midland Valley. Smaller scale topographic features, some of localised, and others of wider significance, owe their origin and form to the effects of glaciation.

The geological skeleton was clothed by the deposits of the Devensian glaciation, during which ice from the Highlands, reaching the Glasgow region by way of the Gareloch, Loch Lomond and the Strathblane Gap, first blocked the flow of the Clyde to the sea, forming a large pro-glacial lake, 30 metres deep, in the Clyde Basin. Sands, silts, gravels and clays were deposited on the bed of this lake, to be moulded by the eastward-advancing ice into drumlins, numerous on both sides of the river. The melting ice of deglaciation swelled post-glacial seas, permitting marine transgression c.13,000 B.P.[4] with the formation of deposits of silts and clays of considerable lateral extent within the basin. Isostatic readjustment elevated these to around eight metres O.D., providing a series of gently-sloping low-lying surfaces. Between these raised marine terraces, backed by their drumlin swarms, the Clyde flowed west, through the gap between the lava plateaus, to empty into its broad estuary, itself

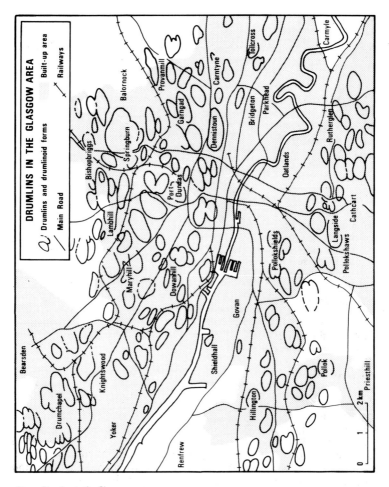

1.i   Drumlins in the Glasgow area

giving access to a suite of long, deep sea-lochs, extending their fingers into the south-west Highlands.

On a smaller scale, the landforms which most dramatically characterise the local topography are undoubtedly the drumlins. The present built-up area of the city covers over 180 of these whalebacks[5] (Fig. 1.i), some two-thirds of which lie north of the river, and the remainder to the south. Their higher, steeper faces are aligned roughly north west, with the gentler slopes of the tails pointing south-east, echoing the direction of glacial advance through the valley. They display wide variation, both in areal extent and in height from base to crest, with over 50% being more than ten metres in height, and a significant number from 25-30 metres, with one north-western outlier reaching 37 metres. In their original form, the drumlins must have been even larger, since an estimated four to five metres of till has been removed from their surfaces by periglacial mass movement[6]. The uneven hilly land surface which they produce has had significant effects on the alignment of roads and railways, which largely avoid crossing them, and often make detours following the valleys between them[7], while from Victorian times onwards, numerous sections of the built-up area have been contoured around their slopes.

The development of Glasgow took place within a rich and varied geological and geomorphological framework, affording a range of possibilities to its inhabitants at different technological stages. In medieval times, the fording point on the Clyde, the possibilities of fishing locally and further afield, and farming on the heavy clay soils developed on the glacial till provided both a natural focus for trade, and the commodities to support the growth of a burgh and its market. Fast-flowing streams and abundant soft water within the region gave power and progress to the early textile phase of the Industrial Revolution, while the local coal and iron ores provided fuel and raw materials for its subsequent phases, which saw the structures of the city march north, south, east and west along the alluvial terraces and over the drumlins.

Early man in Glasgow: prehistoric to early Norman

From the early Post-Glacial period onwards, access via routeways from the Forth and Tweed valleys in the east and south-east, Ayrshire and the Solway Lowlands in the south-west, and along the broad highway of the River Clyde itself, gave a nodality to the basin of the Lower Clyde and attracted human settlement. The low-lying, sheltered basin, with its mild, moist climate, would have been thickly wooded in prehistoric times, and the marshy lowland flats or haughlands along the river would have provided a rich source of food for early hunter-gatherers, although the incursion of the Post-Glacial sea removed probable sites of Mesolithic activity.

Neolithic farmers and Bronze Age metallurgists left numerous traces of their presence, ranging from artifacts such as polished stone axes found at St. Enoch Square and Sauchiehall Street, copper and bronze axeheads found at Spean Street, Cathcart, and York Street, Anderston, to dugout wooden canoes from numerous locations, including Stockwell Street, London Road, Glasgow Cross, the Drygate, Springfield Quays, and St. Enoch Square[8]. Dating of these latter artifacts is imprecise, since their use covered many millennia, but the last-mentioned, discovered during excavations for the foundations of St. Enoch's Church in 1780, contained a polished stone axe of Neolithic type, dating back over four thousand years. Early structural traces are limited to sepulchral monuments of the Middle Bronze Age, comprising cist cemeteries discovered at Victoria

Park, Whiteinch; Greenoakhill, Mount Vernon, and Springhill Farm, Baillieston, just east of the city, and a possible late Neolithic henge monument at Shiels Farm, Govan[9]. In the immediate vicinity of Glasgow, traces attributable to the Iron Age are rare, but in the wider context of the lower reaches of the Clyde, the presence of Celtic tribes is indicated by a number of hillforts. Foremost among these by virtue of its size and possible function is the OPPIDUM of Walls Hill in Renfrewshire, the probable tribal centre of the Damnonii, whose relationships with the Roman military occupation forces were to be of considerable significance for future developments in the region. Within the Glasgow area itself, finds of coins, bowls, glass, metalwork, and a leather sandal, attest to the presence of outposts of Roman civilisation, which from the first century A.D. brought the possibility of urban life to the Clyde[10].

Following earlier and more temporary occupation, the second century A.D. witnessed the construction of the Antonine Wall, with its accompanying sub-structures of roads and forts. From Bridgeness on the Forth to Old Kilpatrick on the Clyde, the Wall followed the lines of the Carron and Kelvin Valleys across the narrow waist of Scotland, sealing off the great massif of the Scottish Highlands and the rich eastern coastal plain, with their large and dangerous populations. To the south of the Wall the Romans once again exercised control over four major Celtic tribes, the Novantae, Selgovae, Votadini and Damnonii, and varying policies towards these tribes, based on the earlier Agricolan formula, created legacies of territorial dispositions and political institutions fundamental to subsequent developments. The territory of the Selgovae was gripped tightly within a grid of roads and forts, whose western section effectively isolated the Novantae in Southern Ayrshire, Dumfriesshire and Galloway. In contrast, the Votadini of the Lothians, and probably the Damnonii of Renfrewshire and Dunbartonshire, entered into some kind of treaty arrangements with the Roman armies, whereby they retained a measure of control over their own affairs.

Few Roman installations intruded into the territory of the Damnonii, and it is possible that the tribal lands progressed through being a Roman protectorate to the status of a federate, or treaty, state. The territory which was later to become Strathclyde therefore lay in an intermediate position, spatially, politically and culturally, between the urbanised area of the Civil Zone of southern Britain, and the barbarian lands beyond the Roman frontier. A crucial aspect of that culture was the early Christian Church, established in North Britain on a diocesan basis, and surviving the withdrawal of Roman authority. It is possible that the native principality of Strathclyde to some degree overlapped spatially with a sub-Roman diocese[11], and that some recognisable focal point within the principality was the seat of the bishop. Glasgow and Govan emerge as principal contenders, and a convincing case can be made for each site, or indeed for both at different times, and the importance of such a function in post-Roman Europe, where former ecclesiastical centres acted as focal points for urban foundation in many cases, is an obvious one.

For some writers, the identification of Glasgow with the episcopal centre poses no problems, its role and status being closely linked with the personality of Kentigern, later the patron saint of the city. Kentigern lived in the late sixth and early seventh centuries A.D., with his death recorded in the 'Annales Cambriae' at 612 A.D.[12] He founded a monastery at Glasgow on the site of an ancient cemetery formerly consecrated by St. Ninian[13] and which later became the site of Glasgow Cathedral. That monastery was the seat of a bishopric whose bounds were coterminous with those of the Brythonic Kingdom of Strathclyde. The development of a cult centred upon Kentigern enhanced the importance of Glasgow, and indeed Kentigern gave his name to the settlement. The name of Glasgow was "probably explained by the occurrence of 'Glas' for church", in conjunction with the first syllable of the Brythonic Celtic version of the saint's name, 'Cunotegernus'[14]. Over time, 'Glas-cu', the church of Kentigern, hardened into 'Glasgow'.

Govan on the other hand, has no such deep and enduring roots, and probably represents a newer foundation of the post-Columban church, during the period of reconstruction following Norse depredations in the west. At this time the relics of Saint Constantine, to whom the church at Govan is dedicated, were possibly moved from a site in Kintyre overrun by the Vikings, to a safer location far upstream on the south bank of the Clyde, opposite its confluence with the River Kelvin, where a new monastery was founded. Weight is added to this argument by the large collection at Govan of sculptured memorial stones, among which there is not a single example attributed to before C.900 A.D.[15] An alternative view is that Govan was a more anciently-established ecclesiastical site, becoming a monastic centre between 635 and 663 A.D., as the influence of the Columban church spread in the Scottish Lowlands[16]. Under later Northumbrian influence, it may have become a 'monasterium' or minster, with a resident clergy in a central church serving a large district, as part of the early development of the parochial system in medieval Scotland[17]. This argument finds a reflection in the extremely large size of the parish of Govan, which survived down to recent times (Fig. 1.ii), and given its existence, it is unlikely that an equally large and important church flourished contemporaneously just across the river at Glasgow. The spatial translation of ecclesiastical centres in the medieval period is known from a number of examples, among them being Muthil to Dunblane, Mortlach to Aberdeen, and Tain to Fortrose, and it is possible to view the roles of Govan and Glasgow in that successive manner. However, there still remains the question of why there should have been a translation of site, and an examination of the historical processes affecting the area from the sixth to the eleventh centuries A.D. may help to provide an answer.

The later sixth, and the early and middle seventh centuries saw the expansion into Strathclyde of the Celtic church[18], while in the later part of the century following the Synod of Whitby in 663 A.D., Anglian usage became dominant in the area, with the Bishop of Durham, and the Archbishop of York, claiming ecclesiastical sovereignty. Troubled centuries followed for Strathclyde, with pressure from Picts and Scots,

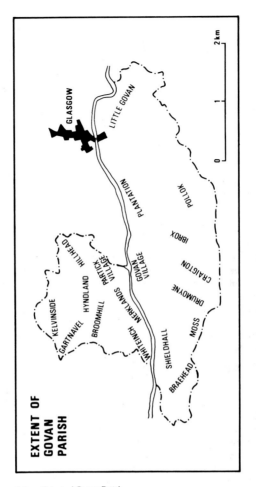

1.ii   *Extent of Govan Parish*

Angles and Norse, at varying times. Dumbarton was burned in A.D. 780, and sacked by the Norse in A.D. 875. In A.D. 945, Edmund of Wessex overran the kingdom, later ceding the lands to Malcolm the First, King of the Scots[19]. Strathclyde then swiftly threw off Scots overlordship and remained independent until the death of its ruler Owain in 1018 A.D., when it was unified with the expanding Scottish kingdom, busy consolidating its hold on territories previously Anglian and British. Thus by the eleventh and twelfth centuries, the Glasgow region lay within a politically unstable western frontier zone in which military, political and ethnic difficulties were exacerbated by a complex religious history. To the young kingdom of the Scots, these complexities embodied claims by external forces on their territories, as well as the seeds of internal insurrection, and special measures may have been necessary to ensure security. Therefore whatever the argument for and against Glasgow or Govan, the recognition in the twelfth century of Glasgow as the seat of the metropolitan may have been for political and military, rather than purely ecclesiastical, considerations, involving deliberate state fostering of the cult of Kentigern, and therefore elevation in status of the seat of that cult. Reduction of Celtic influence in the west, with its Gall-Gael connections, may have been a motive, while the removal of the claims of the metropolitan of York[20] to jurisdiction in ecclesiastical matters in Strathclyde may also have been politically motivated.

In the first quarter of the twelfth century[21] David, 'prince of the Cumbrian region', later to become David the First of Scotland (1124-53), caused an inquest to be undertaken into the possessions of the church of Saint Kentigern, the findings of which established or re-established the diocese of Glasgow, "co-extensive with his Cumbrian territories"[22]. The enquiry secured considerable endowments for the church at Glasgow, later enhanced by grants of lands, rents, and churches by David the First as king, and by succeeding monarchs. There can be no doubt about the importance of the diocese of Glasgow, whose great extent, including most of Cumberland and Westmorland before 1133 A.D.[23], special position and numerous endowments found physical expression in the series of cathedrals erected over the shrine of its cult-figure, Kentigern. At the same time, the gradual, pervasive influence of the Normans in Scotland intensified under David the First, with the granting of portions of the royal demesne to incoming knights. In Strathclyde it is possible that these grants conformed to existing territorial units of lordship, but whatever the case, by the end of the twelfth century, under Malcolm as well as David, some of the lands listed in the Glasgow inquest had been taken from the church and used to endow Flemish knights[24]. This feudal colonisation of the Clyde Valley may be seen as "a deliberate and forcible stroke of royal policy"[25], bringing the area into the expanding sphere of Norman organisation, creating a more secure frontier zone between the eastern heartland of the Scottish kingdom and the troubled and turbulent islands of the western seas, and creating a settled political and military climate in which urban life, in the form of burghs, could be erected and encouraged to develop.

REFERENCES

1. George, T. N., 1958. 'Geology and Geomorphology of the Glasgow Region', in Miller, R. and Tivy, J. (eds.), *The Glasgow Region*, p.28.
2. George, 1958, *op.cit.*, p.35.
3. MacGregor, M. and Walton, J., 1972. *The story of the Fossil Grove*, 3rd edition, p.15.
4. Price, R. J., 1975. 'The Glaciation of West Central Scotland — a review'. *S.G.M.*, 91.2, p.142.

5. Menzies, J., 1976. 'The Glacial Geomorphology of Glasgow with particular reference to the drumlins'. University of Edinburgh, unpub. Ph.D. Thesis.
6. Dickson, J. H., Jardine, W. G., and Price, R. J. P., 1976. 'Three late Devensian sites in west central Scotland'. *Nature*, 262, pp.43-44.
7. Elder, S., McCall, R. J. S., Neaves, W. D., and Pringle, A. K., 1935. 'The Drumlins of Glasgow'. *Transactions of the Geological Society of Glasgow*, xlxii, p.287.
8. Duncan, J. D., 1883. 'Note regarding the Ancient Canoe Recently Discovered in the bed of the Clyde above the Albert Bridge'. *T.G.A.S.*, 2, 121-30.
9. Maxwell, J. H., 1937. 'A Bronze Age Cemetery at Springhill Farm, Baillieston, near Glasgow'. *T.G.A.S.*, New series 9, pp.287-302.
10. Scott, J. G., 1966. *South-West Scotland*. Regional Archaeologies Series.
11. Thomas, C. 1971. *The Early Christian Archaeology of North Britain*, fig.2, p.16. Laing, L. 1975. *The Archaeology of Late Celtic Britain and Ireland*, fig. 9, p.297.
12. Radford, C. A. R., 1970. *Glasgow Cathedral*, p.9.
13. Radford, C. A. R., 1967. 'The Early Church in Strathclyde and Galloway'. *Medieval Archaeology*, xi, p.112.
14. Russell, Miss, 1890. 'The Name of Glasgow and the History of Cumbria'. *British Archaeological Journal*, XLVI, p.43.
15. Radford, C. A. R., 1960. 'The Early Christian Monuments at Govan and Inchinnan'. *T.G.A.S.*, N.S., xv(4), p.188.
16. Cowan, I. B., 1975. 'Early Ecclesiastical Foundations', p.18 in McNeill, P. and Nicholson, R. (eds.) *An Historical Atlas of Scotland, c.400-c.1600*.
17. Cowan, I. B., 1961. 'The Development of the Parochial System in Medieval Scotland'. *S.H.R.*, x1, p.46.
18. Radford, C. A. R., 1970, *op.cit.*, p.8. Cowan, I. B., 1975. *op.cit.*, p.17.
19. Barrow, G. W. S., 1973. *The Kingdom of the Scots*, p.143.
20. Shead, N. F., 1969. 'The Origins of the Medieval Diocese of Glasgow'. *S.H.R.*, xlvii, p.221.
21. Pryde, G. S., 1958. 'The City and Burgh of Glasgow', p.134. in Miller, R. and Tivy, J., (eds.) *op.cit.*, dates the inquest to 1115 A.D. Cowan, I. B., 1974. 'The Post-Columban Church'. *Records of the Scottish Church History Society*, xviii, p.248., gives 1116 A.D. Duncan, A. A. M., 1975. *Scotland: The Making of the Kingdom*, p.257, dates it to 1123 or 1124 A.D.
22. Renwick, R., and Lindsay, J., 1921. *History of Glasgow*, vol.1, p.34.
23. Barrow, G. W. S., 1973, *op.cit.*, p.143.
24. Duncan, A. A. M., 1975, *op.cit.*, p.257.
25. Barrow, G. W. S., 1973, *op.cit.*, p.291.

2. THE MEDIEVAL TOWN: 1175~1560

The routes whereby the embryonic proto-urban units of Scotland emerged into the light of history as burghs have been ably and succinctly charted by Adams in his seminal work on urban Scotland[1]. Whatever the relative roles of the existence of church or castle, the benefits of topographic advantage or demesne centre function in the development of pre-urban nuclei, one consistent historical fact defines the appearance of the burgh, and that is the granting of a charter of erection. The burgh, as a basic tool of feudalism, is but one of a range of organisational devices through which the Norman world was ordered, and the regular, disciplined, and clearly defined hierarchy of rights and obligations was maintained. Its charter conferred legal existence, status and functions, not merely on the settlement unit, but on its inhabitants, and especially upon those actors whose roles came to dominate the medieval stage, the burgesses. A further, and crucial, concomitant of the regularising powers of the charter may have been a physical reflection in the landscape of the town, manifested in an orderly layout of streets, burgage plots and ports, whose form was a reciprocal of burghal function. Upon these general considerations an examination of the specific case of Glasgow may be based.

Between 1175 and 1178 A.D. William the Lion issued a charter to Bishop Jocelin and his successors in which Glasgow was granted burghal status, with the right to hold a weekly market on Thursdays. Soon after, probably between 1189 and 1198, authorisation was given to hold a fair, for eight full days from the seventh of July[2]. Significantly, the first charter did not define the territory within which customs and tolls could be levied, nor did it specifically grant any lands, but Glasgow was to enjoy all the freedoms and customs which any of his burghs throughout his whole land possessed. In addition Glasgow was granted the King's peace, a special privilege from which considerable advantages accrued, and by which Glasgow's favoured status was assured from the beginning. From the last quarter of the twelfth century, therefore, the legislative conditions for burghal growth were in existence, and attention must now turn to the manifestation of those conditions in terms of the appearance of physical units of the urban landscape.

Development of the townscape

Accurate reconstruction of the morphological development of medieval Glasgow is rendered difficult by the sparse and fragmentary nature of surviving records and structures, and diverse viewpoints on the sequence and direction of urban growth have been expressed by historians and geographers. After centuries of evolution, the town plan of medieval Glasgow resembled a cross of Lorraine[3], whose axis ran north-east from the fording-point below the Molendinar confluence (Fig. 2.i), to the precincts of the Cathedral. From two crossing-points, radiating streets formed the bars of the cross, with Rottenrow and Drygate close to the Cathedral in the north, and Trongate and Gallowgate close to the river in the south. (See Fig. 3.ii, p.47, for street names). Around these crossing streets, twin nuclei developed as the cores of the town, and it is the relative roles of these nuclei which have given rise to controversy. From the eighteenth century onwards, the dominant role of the upper, ecclesiastical nucleus has been stressed.

> "From . . . about the year 1350, the town in its progress, seems to have extended gradually from the high ground, on which the cathedral and most ancient part of the city stands, towards this bridge (across the Clyde) . . . what chiefly gave rise to the extension of the town towards this bridge, was the establishment of the college by Bishop Turnbull in the year 1450."[4]

This description of downhill growth from the Cathedral area, induced by a desire to secure an outlet to the river and the sea, became accepted by the majority of commentators[5]. An opposing, and less popular, viewpoint reversed the sequence, stressing the importance of the lower nucleus as the earliest market core of the town, from which urban growth gradually led outwards, west and east in extensions of Trongate and Gallowgate, and north towards the Cathedral, along the uphill track later known as High Street[6]. A re-examination of the datable evidence for building activity, in relation to the physical characteristics of the site, and especially the indications of colonisation of a broad fringe belt lying between the market and the Cathedral, would seem to lend support to the latter hypothesis rather than the former.

Site characteristics and pre-urban nucleus

The site of medieval Glasgow sloped uphill from the north bank of the River Clyde. Above the flood-plain of the river, the gentle gradient of the Post-Glacial raised beach commences about halfway up the present Saltmarket, giving way to a steeper slope from about mid-way up the present High Street to just below the line of Rottenrow-Drygate, whence a

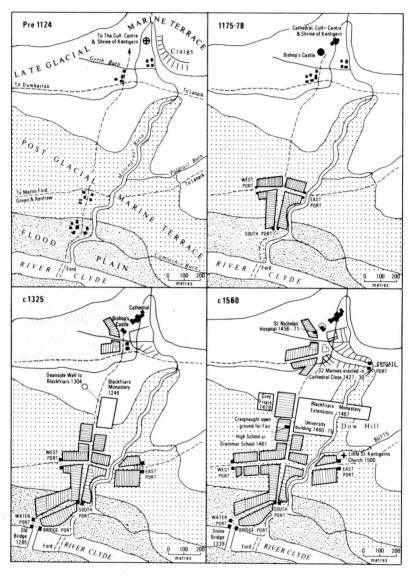

2.i   *Medieval Glasgow: conjectural restoration*

relatively flat surface formed on the Late Glacial marine terrace in turn gives way to a thick covering of till, interspersed with drumlins, stretching to the north. The rock outcrop of the Craigs (the Eastern Necropolis) forms higher ground to the east of the Cathedral, and is separated from it by the deeply incised gorge of the Molendinar Burn, flowing south and pursuing a winding course across the marine terraces, joined by a number of other small streams. From the west, just below the site of the Cathedral, it is joined by the Gyrth Burn, while lower down the slope, the Poldrait and Camlachie Burns flow into it from the east (Fig. 2.i).

There are a number of indications of at least one pre-urban nucleus in the town plan, and while there may have been others, only this one has left a substantial imprint. The earliest recorded building traces on the site of Glasgow are the early foundations of the Cathedral, a much smaller building than the present edifice, which is at least the third on the site, and is the inheritor of a tradition of religious occupation of the site deeply rooted in time.

The difficult site, sloping steeply down to the gorge of the Molendinar and necessitating the raising of the main floor of the Cathedral on the undercroft, testifies to the strength of religious tradition. Excavation of a number of ecclesiastical sites in western Europe has given some indication of the sequence of structures likely to have existed on the site[7]. Tradition has it that during the late sixth century A.D., Kentigern established a monastery of the Celtic type on a site above the Molendinar, possibly consecrated some centuries earlier by Ninian as a burial ground. In the succeeding centuries after the death of Kentigern, the structures of the early religious community would come to consist of a group of buildings, with one or more small churches, and other buildings for the monks to live and work within. The main church may well have been built over the grave of the founder, with its altar close to his remains. The whole series of structures would be enclosed by a wall or 'vallum' of stone, earth or turf.

As Kentigern's importance as a cult-figure in the medieval Church grew, his resting-place became a shrine, whose enclosing church, possibly built of wood at first, was later reconstructed in stone, then extended several times as a cathedral. The cult-centre, as was the case throughout western Europe, would attract pilgrims, whose religious needs were served by a growing community of ecclesiastics. Their presence, together with the structures in which they lived, worked, and worshipped, accounts for the pre-urban nucleus on this spot, and probably encouraged the development of a small, unofficial market which served clerics and pilgrims alike.

Charter and burgh

Glasgow's first burghal charter is not dated, but on the basis of the known life-span and activities of its signatories, can be assigned to the years 1175-1178, and if layout of the plot units of the burgh was indeed a function of, and therefore subsequent to, the issuing of this charter, then the process must have been well under way by the period 1179-1199. Between these dates, Bishop Jocelin gave to the abbot and convent of his former church of St. Mary at Melrose, "that toft which Ranulph of Hadintun built in the first building of the burgh"[8]. Apart from the intriguing possibility that the aforesaid Ranulph may have been invited to Glasgow to contribute experience gained in Haddington to the layout and organisation of the burgh, a process parallelled elsewhere in Scotland, the location of his toft is of some significance. It apparently lay either on the north, or the south side of Trongate, the street leading west from the lower junction near the river, and if this was the case, then this area must have been the first focus of plot layout and building in the burgh. That important part of the burgh, formally demarcated and laid out under the auspices of the charter, therefore lay on the gently sloping area of the Post-Glacial marine terrace.

Fig. 2.i. indicates some of the broader topographic features of the site already described, together with the possible routes of two east-west tracks traversing the site. The upper track runs along the Late-Glacial terrace above its break of slope, and probably carried traffic between Dumbarton in the west and Lanark in the east, important centres in the Kingdom of Strathclyde, then possibly on towards Edinburgh. The lower track, along the Post-Glacial terrace above the river flood plain, may have had the same eastern destinations, but led to Partick in the west, and thence across the river by the Marlin Ford to Govan, Renfrew and Paisley. A third track may have run north from the ford across the Clyde to Kentigern's shrine, intersecting the other two tracks.

Settlement would probably be limited to irregular clusters of houses near the river, and perhaps in the vicinity of the cult-centre of Kentigern, close to the pilgrim tracks. In the wake of the granting of the charter of 1175-78, delineation of the first plot units may have produced a T-shaped street plan, with the crossbar of the 'T' aligned along the southern track, and its shaft following the line of the north-south track. The town gates, or ports, marked the limits of the streets and plots, with the East Port at the end of a short length of street and on the west bank of the Molendinar, giving added security to the eastern approach. The South Port was probably located some distance short of the river bank, above the confluence of the Camlachie burn with the Molendinar, on ground less liable to flooding. The position of the West Port is less certain, though the regularity of burgage plots makes the junction of the present King Street/Candleriggs with Trongate a likely candidate. The streets thus created focused the life of the town, with Waulkergait broadening northward from the south port to its junction with the streets later to be named Trongate and Gallowgate, thereby opening on to, and creating, a market place. The earliest built-up area of the burgh was therefore of limited extent, measuring no more than c.300 metres east to west, and c.350 metres north to south. Up the gentle then steeper slopes to the north, a walk of c.800 metres led through open farm land to the Cathedral and associated buildings.

By c.1325 A.D. there is evidence of expansion in several directions. The first reference to a bridge over the River Clyde dates to 1285[9], being a wooden structure built c.100 metres downstream of the long-used Horse Ford, which debouched on the north bank of the Clyde at a point c.250 metres from the South Port. Construction of this bridge may have encouraged plot development between its northern end, and the south port, along the line of the later Bridgegait. There may also have been some feuing out of plots in the lower part of Fishergait, since details of the sale of a burgage in this street accompany the first mention of the bridge. Support for this early activity in the Fisher-gait is provided by the fact that the Knights of St. John had a tenement in Stockwell Street. This order inherited many of the holdings of the disgraced and disbanded order of Knights Templar, who had a tenement in the burgh, and whose demise took place from c.1307 onwards. Gallowgait is first mentioned in 1325[10], and plot extensions eastwards across the Molendinar may have taken place about this time, along both sides of the track to Lanark. There is a distinct change in alignment of the street east of the Molendinar, and this may mark the stretch of c.180 metres, to the site of the later Gallowgait Port, along which plot development took place, with the Poldrait burn possibly forming the northern plot boundary.

Activity is also documented in the open farmland between burgh and cathedral. In 1246, the Dominicans or Blackfriars came to Glasgow, and were granted an extensive tract of land for the erection of their conventual buildings[11]. In 1304 they were given the Meduwel on Deanside, from which fresh water was led to their domestic quarters. The grant of other lands in the vicinity, such as that to the sacristan of Glasgow of a vacant piece of land which seems to have adjoined that of the Dominicans on the north[12], lends credibility to the picture of agricultural land, stretching in a crescent from St. Enoch's burn, west of the burgh, eastwards between burgh and cathedral over the Molendinar and down past the Poldrait and Camlachie burns to the Clyde. There is no direct evidence for the feuing of plots in this area, but later references to plot extensions may indicate some northward development along the track to the High Kirk, perhaps as far as Old Vennel, or even Blackfriars Wynd on the east side, and a similar distance on the west side. The same inference holds for the opening of building plots in Rottenrow. One such plot, with its buildings lying on the west side of Fishergait, later Stockwellgait, and fronting on St. Tenus' Gait was described in 1551 and 1567 as a tower, with a fortalice or fortified house, houses, yards, orchards and other tenements. The orchard alone has been calculated as c.3,000 sq. metres in extent, and together with the elements of this holding, implies all the aspects of an extra-burghal aristocratic residence[13].

The two centuries after 1325 witnessed building activity in all three sections of Glasgow, the burgh, the intervening fringe, and the cathedral close. In the burgh, there was probably some westward extension of plots in St. Thenew's Gait. Producing a change of street alignment, the West Port was re-sited c.250 metres to the west on the line of Old Wynd, which ran south to Bridgegate and Goosedubs Lane. Westward of this point, the already discontinuous building line petered out, giving way to fields, orchards, and the occasional house. On the east side, the chapel of St. Mungo without the walls was founded in 1500 A.D. on the Dow-hill, a little beyond the East Port, indicating that there had been no extension of Gallowgait by this date. On the south, a new eight-arch stone bridge replaced the earlier wooden structure in c.1410 A.D., enhancing the effectiveness of the crossing-point for trade, but not, apparently, having a great effect on the spatial extension of the built-up area. However, in the centre of the burgh, a charter of 1490 granted the right to have, and thereby created the physical entity of, a tron, a public weighbeam used to assess duty on all marketable produce. The first location of this machine was west of the market cross, on the south side of St. Thenew's Gait, whose name now became Trongait[14]. On the northern edge of the market-place stood the Tolbooth, first erected at an unknown date, but certainly used for a Michaelmas head court of the burgh in October 1508[15]. These structural manifestations of the growing regularisation of trade focused attention on the market area of the burgh, and it may be that, as in Haddington or Montrose, the tolbooth structure, like its surviving successor, aided this process by partially closing exit and entry to the market-place via the track to the High Kirk.

Identification of the line of this track with the later High Street of Glasgow has been the source of some semantic confusion. The 'High Street' of many towns in Britain is the main trading street, often the oldest built-up street in the settlement, and the focal point of many aspects of town life. In Glasgow, a number of streets, or sections of streets, changed their name over time and the appellation 'High Street', for the routeway between the Tolbooth and the Cathedral was neither early nor consistent, with other streets being described as 'High Street' over a long period. In July 1641, in a disposition of lands, St. Enoch's (St. Thenew's) Gait was referred to as 'high street'[16], with the absence of capitalisation denoting an adjectival rather than a locational description. In a similar case, in January 1628, the Town Council ordained that

> "the calsey fra the croce down the Salt Market be pull out and laid als neir as can be to the buithes on baithe the sydes of the gaitt to mak the high street braid"[17].

Even such a distinguished and prolific scholar as Sir James Marwick indexed this entry in his editing of Extracts from the Burgh Records of Glasgow as a widening of the High Street[18]. In earlier references, the street or track is anonymous. In a charter of 1418, which includes the first direct reference to Glasgow Cross, there is a note concerning the conveyance of property in the street which extends from the cathedral to the market cross[19], while in 1433 further property was conveyed "lyand in the gat at strikes frae the market cors till the Hie Kirk of Glasgow"[20]. While there is no evidence as to whether or not these properties had been built upon, grants of lands for institutional uses requiring open ground were made around the middle of the fifteenth century. On the east side of the later High Street, some time before 1454, a tenement and grounds lying north of the Blackfriars' holding together with lands extending across the Molendinar on to Dowhill, were given to the Blackfriars, and then in 1460 to the University, founded nine years previously. In 1467 an additional tenement and land, lying north of the University property and extending to the Molendinar, was given to the Faculty of Arts[21]. On the west side of the street in 1460/1, a tenement was granted for the founding of the Grammar School[22], but slightly later in the century, there is evidence that the upper section of the street, below the break of slope leading to the Cathedral precincts, was being built upon.

> " . . . the provost, bailies and community, with consent of the prior and convent and also of the bishop, feud to Thomas Kerd, burgess, and his spouse, two roods of land described as lying on the east side of the High Street, upon the Friars' fore and west walls, between the lands of John Rankyn, Smith, on the south, and unbuilt lands on the north. . . . On 24th March, 1470/71, Thomas Kerd acquired additional ground which was described as lying near the cemetery, extending from his house at the entrance to the cloister, between seven aspen trees, on the north, and the enclosure at John Rankyn's building on the south. Other sales are recorded, including one of unbuilt lands conveyed, in 1478, to Robert Forester, who bound himself to construct, under his building, a gate and passage to the Friars' church."[23]

It would seem that demand for a High Street frontage was inducing the feuing of land from the edge of the Blackfriars property, thus extending the northward march of the building line. On the west side of the street, a similar extension of properties may be inferred from the location of the Franciscans or Greyfriars, when they arrived in 1473-1479. A charter of James III described a monastery with gardens attached, reached from the west side of High Street by a lane known as Greyfriars Wynd. Their small property was extended slightly to the west in 1511, and the convent was demolished at the Reformation in 1560[24]. Adjoining their convent was a piece of open ground known as Craignaught, upon which the Fair was held, and there is a record of 1574 of the burgh court being held there on the eve of the Fair. These activities may have been set back some distance from the High Street because that frontage was already built up, or at least plots had been feued out.

The Cathedral Close

In the upper part of the town, centred around the Cathedral, the keynote of change between 1325 and 1560 was the rise to overwhelming

2.i   *Glasgow Cathedral and the Bishop's Castle*

dominance of ecclesiastical holdings, and their associated buildings, the Cathedral itself, the Bishop's castle, St. Nicholas' hospital, and the manses of the prebends (Pl. 2.i). In the Cathedral, the major building works were completed in the fourteenth century, by which time the edifice had reached its present scale. Fifteenth and sixteenth century work consisted of alterations and additions, principal among them being the Blacader Aisle running south from the transept[25], and adding to the curious asymmetry of the building which dominated the upper town (Fig. 2.ii). The Palace, or town residence of the Bishop, was a fortified structure, testimony to the uncertainty of medieval life, even for prelates, and especially to the endemic strife between the political and religious factions

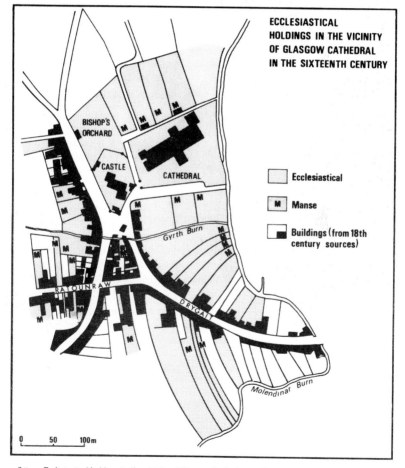

2.ii   *Ecclesiastical holdings in the vicinity of Glasgow Cathedral in the sixteenth century*

of Scotland, spawned by regencies and minorities, and the inexorable progress to Reformation. It lay to the west of the Cathedral, and consisted of a large central keep, or tower-house, with a vaulted kitchen, banqueting hall, and apartments above. It was surrounded by the ditch of an earlier earthwork castle, crossed on its northern side by a drawbridge, while beyond that again, a stone curtain wall with flanking towers and gatehouses completed the defences. That there was no superfluity of defence works is indicated by the fact that the castle was attacked in 1516, 1517, 1544, 1560, 1568, and 1570[26], by which time it had been so badly battered that it no longer functioned as a fortress. The Bishop also held a large portion of ground, lying to the north of the castle's curtain wall, variously described as an orchard or gardens.

Beyond the Cathedral and the Bishop's ground to the north, west and south, lay the residential manses of the clergy. Some controversy surrounds the actual dates of construction of these buildings, and while some local historians adhere to the theory that they were initiated by Bishop Cameron, c.1427-30, when he insisted that each prebend must build a manse near the Cathedral, it is unlikely that there was such a massive single event of construction. More tenable is Renwick and Lindsay's hypothesis that

> "these churchmen, bound to give attendance at the cathedral during a considerable part of each year, must always have had suitable residences in Glasgow, and it is probable that the arrangements proposed in 1266, whereby the bishop then to be appointed was required to provide such additional space as might be required for the erection of manses, was substantially carried into effect at the time."[27]

Whatever the case, it is probable that by c.1440, there were 32 prebends, each with a manse in the cathedral area, and whether or not the structures were all two-storey stone buildings with staircase towers, wooden balconies, and extensive gardens[28], they certainly combined with the cathedral and castle to overwhelmingly dominate and set the tone of the upper town (Pl. 2.ii).

Other buildings near the cathedral included the house of the Vicars of the Choir, a common residence erected on a piece of ground north of the cathedral, between a lane called Vicars' Alley on the west and the manse of the precentor on the east. In c.1471, a tenement, chapel and hospital, the latter two dedicated to St. Nicholas, were erected on ground south-west of the castle, bordering on the north bank of the Gyrth burn. This hospital was intended for the accommodation of twelve poor men, and was presided over by a priest[29]. Part of the hospital still survives, in the form of Provand's Lordship, as an enduring monument to those medieval ecclesiastics who made this part of Glasgow almost exclusively their own. The exclusion was not total, however, since the surviving records show transfer of property title among burgesses of the town, and also among the lesser nobility, who may have found the rarefied atmosphere of the

2.ii ˙ *Provand's Lordship*

cathedral precincts more to their liking than the noisy, noisome bustle of the lower town.

The burgh lands

The territory of the medieval burgh of Glasgow was not confined simply to the built-up area, but extended considerably beyond that into the rural fringe. In his book on burgh organisation in Glasgow[30], David Murray defines three principal classes of burghal lands or territory, distinguished on the basis of tenure and land use. The Terra Burgalis comprised the houses and gardens of the town proper. The Terra Campestris was the arable land held by the burgesses in sections, and the Terra Communis was the commonty, or unimproved wasteland held jointly by the burgesses (Fig. 2.iii).

Terra Burgalis

In the first category, there was no tenure in the feudal sense, or holding of land or property, of or for an overlord[31]. Burgages were held in

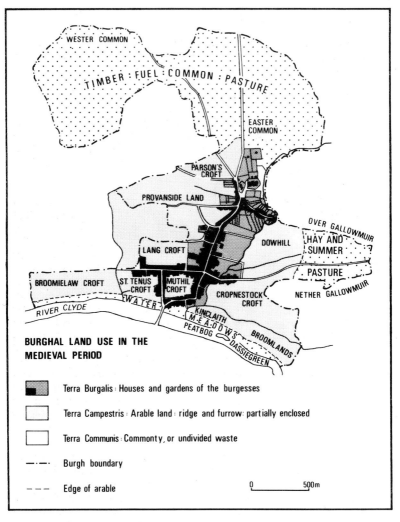

WESTER COMMON

TIMBER : FUEL : COMMON : PASTURE

EASTER COMMON

PARSON'S CROFT

PROVANSIDE LAND

OVER GALLOWMUIR

DOWHILL

HAY AND SUMMER

LANG CROFT

PASTURE

BROOMIELAW CROFT

ST. TENUS CROFT

MUTHIL CROFT

CROPNESTOCK CROFT

NETHER GALLOWMUIR

RIVER CLYDE

WATER

KINCLAITH MEADOWS PEATBOG

BROOMLANDS

DASSIEGREEN

BURGHAL LAND USE IN THE MEDIEVAL PERIOD

- Terra Burgalis : Houses and gardens of the burgesses
- Terra Campestris : Arable land : ridge and furrow : partially enclosed
- Terra Communis : Commonty, or undivided waste
- —·—·— Burgh boundary
- — — — Edge of arable

0   500m

2.iii   *Burghal land use in the medieval period*

absolute ownership, subject to a small, fixed annual payment to the King or Lord and the performance of certain duties such as policing the town. Since there was no 'holding', there was no service due to a feudal superior, nor did heirs have to pay dues on succession to burgage property. The burgages were not only heritable, but alienable, once they had been offered to the selling burgess's kindred and heirs at three head courts, and the purchase of a burgage had to be approved by the community, represented by their elected or appointed officials, since burgage ownership implied burgess qualifications, such as entitlement to use the burgh tillage and pasture, and to draw wood and water, from the waste, as well as trading and legal privileges. Burgh property was not wholly owned by resident burgesses, since considerable portions belonged to barons, bishops, and religious houses, such as the Blackfriars and Greyfriars. However, the burghal character of the tenement was not altered by its ecclesiastical or aristocratic ownership. It remained burgage, and as such subject to the legal jurisdiction of the burgh. The sum of this property, the tenements and tofts, houses and gardens, made up the 'biggit' or built land of the burgh, the Terra Burgalis, which contained wide variation in land use and building type.

The spatial pattern of land use and its reflection of social status patterns within the built-up area was governed largely by the basic unit of land of the burgh, the plot, referred to under a range of names. The term tenement, originally referring to the plot, subsequently came to describe the multi-storeyed structure erected at the head of the plot. Similarly, toft originally described a house, and later was applied to the portion of the plot upon which a house was built. The most comprehensive and least ambiguous term for this long strip of ground is burgage plot, which has a 'head' fronting the street, and a 'tail' ending on the back lane, wall, or some natural feature such as a crag or stream. Internal subdivision gives it a fore-part and an after-part. While the proportions of burgage-plots vary among Scottish burghs, many of the earlier foundations exhibit degrees of internal uniformity in the width and length of plots[32]. This uniformity may have been based upon a predicted demand for frontages on the market street, and demarcated using a standard width of plot[33]. This process of measurement is clearly documented for a number of burghs including Glasgow, in which the laying out of plots at the West Port in 1589 is recorded[34].

Social status patterns within the preindustrial city were a function of the socio-spatial mobility of elite and non-elite classes. The low technological levels of the medieval period meant a reliance on animal and human traction for transport, making central locations attractive from the point of view of movement of goods and people. At the same time, the need for an elite group to maintain itself by ensuring access to the centrally located institutions of government and religion, provided an even stronger centralising force[35] (Fig. 2.iv.a). In the Scottish burgh, a distinct zonal arrangement of land uses was apparent (Fig. 2.iv.b). At the open core was the market place, the functional *raison d'être* of the burgh. Its locating power focused the dwellings and booths or shops of the burgesses around its perimeter, and attracted the public administrative buildings such as the Tolbooth and Tron-house, as well as the Collegiate Church of St. Mary and St. Anne. In the zone beyond this, the burgh craftsmen maintained their dwellings and workplaces, while the outer zone was devoted to less intensive uses such as gardens and orchards. Individual street pattern and plot series alignment gave real spatial structure to this model, and reflected themselves in the arrangement of building type, density, height and mode of construction, both outward from the focal point of the market cross, and rearward along the length of individual burgage plots (Fig. 2.iv.c).

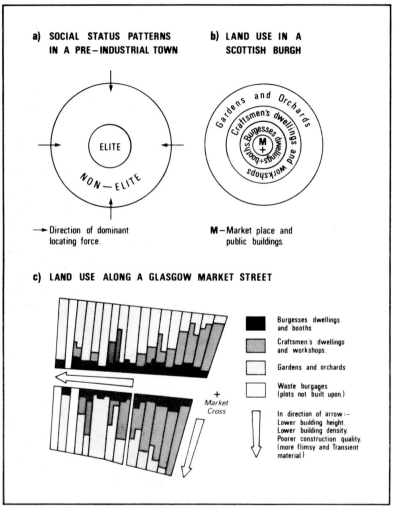

2.iv.a   Social status patterns in a pre-industrial town
2.iv.b   Land use in a Scottish burgh
2.iv.c   Land use along a Glasgow market street

Building types and materials

The range of structures erected upon these plots varies considerably in terms of both function and building material. In Glasgow, apart from public buildings, dwellings, workshops, stores, barns, kilns, yards, and even fortified tower-houses are recorded[36], while frequent mention is made of bark-houses, bark-lofts, bark and lime-holes, and other structures associated with the important early industry of tanning[37]. House-types existed in such a variety as to defy architectural classification[38], ranging from spacious, free-standing mansions, through narrow or multiple-gabled tenements often forming long continuous frontages (Pl. 2.iii) and giving access by pends, closes and wynds to packed warrens of structures on the back lands, to one or two-storey cottages of rural character. Building frontages did not conform rigorously to a building line, prompting later ordinances on the subject of regularity[39], while at street level, open stone or timber stairways giving access to upper storeys, and projecting timber galleries on upper floors, further distorted the ordered layout. Building materials added further variety to this kaleidoscope, with stone being rarely used, at least in the earlier medieval periods, and confined to ecclesiastical and public buildings, and the mansions of the aristocracy and superior burgesses. Slate and tile as roofing materials were similarly restricted, and ordinances in favour of their use point clearly to their previous absence[40]. More prominent in the townscape were flimsy, transient, and above all combustible, materials, such as timber, woven wattle, and thatch, not just on the backlands and outskirts, but in the centre of the burgh. The effects of combustiveness of material combined with contagiousness of density in the core of the medieval burgh are well documented in the great fire of June 1652, which destroyed the greater part of the built-up area of Saltmarket, Trongate and High Street.

> "It pleased the Lord, in the deep of his wisedom and over-fulling providence, so to dispose, that upon the 17th of June last 1652, being Thursday, a little before two of the clocke in the afternoone, a sudden and violent fire brake up within a narrow alley upon the east side of the street above the crosse, which, within a short space, burnt up six allies of houses, with diverse considerable buildings upon the fore-street. And . . . the wind blowing from the north-east, carried such sparks of the flame as kindled, unexpectedly, some houses on the west side of the Saltmarket, where the fire so spread, that it did over-run all from house to house, and consumed, in some few houres, what came in its way, not only houses, but goods also. . . . This fire, by the hand of God, was carried so from one side of the street to the other, that it was totally consumed on both sides, and in it the faire, best, and most considerable buildings, in the town, with all the shops and warehouses of the merchants that were therein, and from that street the flame was carried to the Tronegate, Gallowgate, and Bridgestreet-gate, in all which streets a great many considerable houses and buildings . . . were burnt to ashes . . . the

2.iii   *Old houses, 131 Gallowgate*

dwellings of almost a thousand families were utterly consumed . . . the fire broke out anew (on the Saturday) in the north-side of the Tronegate . . . destroyed diverse dwelling houses, and occasioned the pulling downe of many more."[41]

In a letter dated 17th April, 1653, 24 signatories, including Cromwell and the Earl of Pembroke, attested to the scale of the damage. A third of the town, and almost all the shops and warehouses, together with the residences of the merchants, was consumed, together with 80 warehouses, causing damage amounting to £100,000 Sterling. The aftermath of this fire saw a range of ordinances aimed both at subsequent fire prevention and at regularisation of layout and structure. Though not the first major fire in the city[42], nor despite these efforts the last, the enormous scale of this holocaust prompted vigorous response. Quartermasters were appointed in every street to assess damage and allocate surviving resources and accommodation, with powers to remove inhabitants and squatters, and especially those who had other houses beyond the fire-damaged zone, so that their unburnt houses within the zone might be used by the homeless[43]. Destruction and damage were so overwhelming that the town's masons and other building craftsmen were manifestly unequal to the mammoth task of reconstruction. Citizens who required rebuilding work were therefore licensed to employ such craftsmen as were needed from anywhere in the country[44].

Conditions attached to grants of compensation for property destroyed in the fire placed emphasis on wholly or partly rebuilding in stone[45], and this encouragement was continued in later decades of the seventeenth century by grants of extra land, defrayment of rent arrears and discharge of feu duty in return for stone construction[46]. The fire gave the opportunity to put an end to obstruction of the streets by projecting building facades and stairways, and an ordinance of July 1652, referring to the rebuilding of properties in the Saltmarket proclaimed that, "it is statute and ordainet that nae manner of personne be sufferis to come farder out then another, and that all houssis on both sydes of the gait be buildit conform to ane straight lyne and none to come farder out then another"[47]. In an effort to reduce the risk of further fires, it was made unlawful to build smithies within the burgh, unless the whole tenement belonged to the smith, or the other occupants gave their permission[48]. However, these changes were not total, and relict wooden structures remained in the townscape to provide fuel for future conflagrations.

Nor did all reconstruction take advantage of municipal blandishments or incentives. In the closes off Saltmarket (removed under the 1866 Improvement Act, and probably built shortly after the fire of 1677), were recorded houses whose lower floors were built of stone, with projecting wooden walls with facings of vertical boarding carrying up to the second and third storeys, and unglazed windows with sliding wooden shutters[49] (Fig. 2.v). Municipal intervention was not of itself sufficiently effective to prevent the recurrence of severe outbreaks of fire, and in 1669, a sudden fire east of Gallowgait burn destroyed barns full of hay,

2.v   Wooden houses in close no. 77 Saltmarket

together with stackyards, prompting the Council to order the covering of all candles used in threshing barns, and the manufacture of 100 leather buckets for emergency firefighting[50]. In 1677, a fire destroyed 136 houses and shops[51], including houses in Saltmarket and adjoining streets, and two well-furnished booths with their merchant wares belonging to James Gilhagie, a wealthy Glasgow merchant. This began a catalogue of disaster for the unfortunate man which ended in his application to Parliament for financial relief[52]. After a further outbreak in 1684, a tanner had to be recompensed for wet hides taken out of his tanning-holes and spread over the wooden sides and thatched roofs of buildings in the Gallowgait to prevent the spread of fire[53].

Change over time therefore saw an increase in the use of stone and slate, with a consequent reduction in the use of more flammable and transient building materials, allied to a regularisation of building-lines which often obscured earlier frontages. At the same time, peripheral growth enveloped and brought into the burgh fabric a wide range of structures, from towers and mansions to thatched cottages, barns and kilns, hospitals, churches, friaries, mills and inns (Fig. 2.vi). The late-medieval and immediately post-medieval townscape of Glasgow therefore remained one of considerable variety in style, layout and structure.

Terra Campestris

Burgess status included the right of access to the arable or tillage lands of the burgh, the Terra Campestris, which belonged to the community as a body and in which portions were allocated to individuals for use. The basic unit was the rig (or ridge), a long narrow strip of ground, sometimes referred to as a rood, and when these strips were periodically re-allocated to give equal access to lands of different quality, the process was known as run-rig. Rigs were separated by furrows, and groups of rigs set apart by baulks of earth or turf, while a number of groups made up one unenclosed or partially-enclosed field or croft (Fig. 2.iii). A normal rig length was a furlong or c.200 metres, each rig being c.5m. wide, while a group of four would make up an acre, or 0.4 hectares. Access from the burgh to the arable lands was gained by means of a loan, and the strips of land normally ended on this footpath. Where they ended at right angles or so to another strip or set of strips, or in other words abutted on to it, they were known as butts. Descriptive adjectives were also added where the shape of the field led to truncated rigs, known as great, cut or curt, and short rigs, and similarly great and short roods, meikle (great), middling and small acres[54].

Most burgesses had several rigs in their allocation, and these were not normally grouped into unitary holdings, but scattered throughout the

2.vi   *Thatched malt kiln, foot of Mitchell Street*

different burgh crofts, singly or in multiples. The terms 'contigue' and 'discontigue' applied to strips which were, or were not, contiguous. Murray[55] quotes numerous examples of holdings, including that of Michael Chisholme, Vicar of Cadder, who in 1567, sold to Margaret Rantyn, a rood in Cropnestock Croft, a half acre in Cropnestock, separate from the former, three half-acres and a rood, all lying in different parts of Kinclaith (Fig. 2.iii). He sold to other buyers two half-acre roods and one acre rood, also lying discontigue in Kinclaith, together with three separate parcels in the Broomielaw Croft[56]. These, and many similar recorded transfers of land indicate that the periodic re-allocation which characterised run-rig had ceased by a very early date, at least in the western crofts of Langcroft, St. Tenus' Croft, and the Broomielaw Croft, which had become wholly transferred to individual ownership. However, this was not the case with the eastern crofts where parts of Dowhill, Cropnestock, Kinclaith and Broomlands remained in the community until late in the sixteenth century, though some rigs were conveyed to private ownership. Parson's Croft on the north-west of the town implies arable land by its name, and its ownership, together with the adjacent lands of Provanside, by prebendaries of the cathedral, may have arisen by a similar process or transferring property rights to individuals, or to groups.

In the latter category come the religious institutions of the city, whose holdings embraced large sections of the tillage land. St. Nicholas Hospital, for instance, held two acres of Broomielaw, one acre in Kinclaith, and one acre in Cropnestock, plus various roods and rigs[57], which were leased to rentallers, while the chapel of Little St. Kentigern's was endowed on its foundation in 1500 with several acres of land in Dowhill, Gallowmuir and Provanside[58]. At the time of the Reformation, c.1560, the tillage lands of Glasgow were unconsolidated, unenclosed, and in appearance, striped by ridge and furrow, as seen in many of Slezer's seventeenth century engravings of the environs of Scottish towns[59].

Change over time saw not only the development of individual land-holding on the crofts, but intensification of use, in two directions. Firstly, a growing population in the sixteenth and early seventeenth centuries demanded more foodstuffs, and valuable standing crops were jealously guarded against the intrusion of unsecured domestic animals, and rapacious neighbours, a contemporary ordinance ruling that, "na wife, hussy, or ither persoun, gang amang growand stuff to scheir only"[60]. Gardeners obtained a Seal of Cause in the early seventeenth century, becoming one of the Incorporated Trades. Henceforth all garden produce sold in the market had to be grown within the burgh by a freeman of the craft, and market gardens proliferated throughout the burgh lands. Secondly, as the land passed into private ownership, the alignment and dimensions of the rigs acted as the frameworks for new streets being laid out on the periphery of the old town, a story which will be taken up in a later chapter.

Terra Communis

The third section of burghal land was the Terra Communis, or commonty, comprising the unappropriated waste land, held by the burgesses in common, and used by them principally for pasture, but also for the gathering of fuel, in the form of peat and small timber such as broom and whins, drawing of water supplies, quarrying of building stone, and digging of turf for dyking. A tripartite division of the Glasgow common lands to some extent echoes the character of the major landforms upon which they lay. Bordering the Clyde, the water meadows of the Old or Ducal Green, Linninghaugh, Peatbog and Dassiegreen occupied the flood plain of the river, their swampy sedge-grown character enhanced by the waters of the Molendinar and Glasgow (St. Tenus) burns which emptied across them to their confluence with the main stream. Of low quality as pasture, these lands probably supplied hay for winter fodder. To the east of the burgh, the Gallowmuir lay on the gently-sloping and well-drained Post-Glacial marine terrace, and produced a regular flush of grass for mowing, as well as nourishing summer pasture for dairy cattle. At a higher altitude, stretching north from the Late-Glacial marine terrace to the plain of till studded by drumlins, the Wester and Easter Commons were the principal sources of timber and fuel, and provided extensive common pasture of mediocre quality on the cold, till-derived, poorly drained soils.

Access to these lands, with their range of uses, was of considerable benefit to the burgesses, but as in the case of the tillage lands, the passage of centuries brought change in the tenurial arrangements, involving the transfer of portions of the commonty to private individuals. This process was under way even before the Reformation, with the Collegiate Church of St. Mary gaining 16 acres of the Gallowmuir in 1529[61], and another six roods of the same common going to private ownership in 1553[62]. However, it was in the post-Reformation period that alienation of the common lands took place on a considerable scale, and not without opposition from some sections of the community.

In 1568 it was agreed by the whole community, that is the council, and deacons of the merchants and craft guilds, that portions of the common muir unsuitable for pasture should be feued in half-acre lots[63]. The council exceeded its remit by disposing of a number of areas of good pasture, bringing sharp reproof in 1574 and 1576, with the craft deacons remonstrating that the common moor remaining would scarcely serve the township's needs, and pleading that, "we want the pasturing of guddis for the sustening of our babies", to which the council's response was a moratorium on further feuing[64]. The need to raise £600 to acquire the mill on the Kelvin for the town in 1588 prompted another cycle of feuing, which proceeded with great rapidity. On the 18th of December, 1588 it was agreed that the lands of Peatbog, Milldam and Greenhead, and Dassiegreen were to be visited to consider feuing them, and on 2nd January 1589, the public roup or auction of 24 roods of common land was held in the Tolbooth, with successful bidders including a surgeon, a maltman, and a steel-bonnet maker[65]. The feuing in 1595 of a large section of the northern moor to Sir John Stewart of Minto brought further protest, to which the council's belated reply was that the requests of great men "can nocht weill be refusit"[66], and that administration of the common lands carried numerous burdens and nuisances anyway.

Certainly the records abound with disputes relating to the uses of the common land, ranging from complaints about too much turf being removed[67] to ordinances against the shooting of doves kept in a dovecote on the green[68]. By far the largest number of entries relate to the pasturing and tending of cattle, with the unfortunate John Hogisyarde, fined for allowing his cow to get into James Flemying's corn[69], representative of a multitude of cattle owners whose beasts found the unenclosed croft lands, adjacent to their pasture, all too tempting. Town herds were appointed in 1576, and stray cattle could be impounded if found on the tillage land[70]. The gradual alienation of these important and useful lands in the 150 years following the reformation had two major effects. On the one hand, it deprived the lower ranks of burgesses of an anciently-held and valued privilege, and on the other (in company with fossilisation of run-rig and the growth of permanent holdings on the tillage lands), it placed in the hands of private owners, blocks of valuable land on the periphery of the old town. Through this land expansion had to take place, and upon this land the streets of a new Glasgow began to be laid out.

REFERENCES

1. Adams, I. H., 1978. *The Making of Urban Scotland*, pp.11-30.
2. *Registrum Episcopatus Glasguensis*. Maitland Club (ed. Cosmo Innes), 1843, pp.36-38. (Henceforth, 'R.E.G.').
3. Miller, R., 1958. 'The Geography of the Glasgow Region' in Miller, R. and Tivy, J. (eds). *The Glasgow Region*, pp.5, 6.
4. Gibson, J., 1777. *The History of Glasgow*, p.73.
5. Gregory, J. W., 1921. 'Glasgow and its Geographical History'. *S.G.M.* 37.i., p.8. Murray, D., 1924. *Early Burgh Organisation in Scotland: as illustrated in the history of Glasgow and some neighbouring burghs. Vol. 1. Glasgow*, pp.72-4. Pryde, G. S., 1958. 'The City and Burgh of Glasgow, 1100-1750' in Miller and Tivy (eds.) *op.cit.*, pp.136-137.
6. Renwick, R. and Lindsay, J., 1921. *History of Glasgow*, Vol.1, p.65.
7. Thomas, C., 1971. *The Early Christian Archaeology of North Britain*. Chapter 3 'Cemeteries and Chapels', pp.48-90.
8. Marwick, J. D., 1894. *Charters and other Documents relating to the City of Glasgow.* A.D.1175-1649, i.pt.ii., p.5. (Henceforth 'Charters').
9. *Registrum Monasterii de Passelet, A.D., 1163-1529.* Maitland Club edition 1832 (reprinted 1877), pp.339-401.
10. *Liber Collegii Nostre Domine: Registrum Ecclesia B.V. Marie et S. Anne infra Muros Civitatis Glasguensis, 1517-1549.* Maitland Club edition 1846, ed. J. Robertson, (Henceforth, 'Liber Coll').
11. Liber Coll, 1846, *op.cit.*, xxxviii.
12. R.E.G., *op.cit.*, No.254.
13. Playfair, E., 1981. A fortalice in Stockwell Street. *Glasgow Archaeological Society Bulletin.* N.S. 11, 1-3.
14. Renwick, R. and Lindsay, J., 1921, *op.cit.*, p.267.
15. Charters, 1 (Appendix 1434-1648), pp.478-481.
16. Charters, 1, p.86.

17. Marwick, J. D., 1876-1908. *Extracts from the Records of the Burgh of Glasgow* (Henceforth 'G.B.R.') 1, p.363.
18. G.B.R., 1, p.86.
19. Primrose, J., 1913. *Medieval Glasgow*, p.255.
20. Liber Coll., 1846, *op.cit.*, pp.166-7.
21. Mackie, J. D., 1954. *The University of Glasgow, 1451-1951*, p.46.
22. Marwick, J. D., 1911. *Early Glasgow*. p.55.
23. Renwick, R. and Lindsay, J., 1921, *op.cit.*, p.239.
24. Marwick, J. D., 1911, *op.cit.*, p.47.
25. Radford, C. A. R., 1970. *Glasgow Cathedral*, p.22.
26. Primrose, J. 1913, *op.cit.*, pp.163-7, 192-6, 221-6.
27. Renwick, R. and Lindsay, J., 1921, *op.cit.*, p.196.
28. Kellett, J. R., 1969, *Glasgow*, in Vol. 1 *Historic Towns*. ed. M. D. Lobel, p.3.
29. Gemmell, W., 1910. *The Oldest House in Glasgow*, p.35.
30. Murray, D., 1924. *Early Burgh Organisation in Scotland. Volume 1. Glasgow.*
31. Murray, D., 1924, *op.cit.*, p.36 and footnote 2.
32. Whitehand, J. W. R. and Alauddin, K., 1969. The Town Plans of Scotland: some preliminary considerations. *S.G.M.*, 85.2, p.114.
33. Dodd, W., 1972. Ayr: a Study of Urban Growth. *Ayrshire Archaeological and Natural History Society Collections*, 10, p.318.
34. G.B.R., 1, p.131.
35. Sjoberg, G., 1960. *The Preindustrial City: past and present.*
36. Playfair, E., 1981, *op.cit.*
37. Murray, D., 1924, *op.cit.*, p.56.
38. Stell, G., 1980. Scottish Burgh Houses, 1560-1707. pp.1-31 in Simpson, A. T. and Stevenson, S. (eds.) *Town Houses and Structures in Medieval Scotland: a seminar.* Scottish Burgh Survey, 1980.
39. G.B.R., II, p.233.
40. G.B.R., IV, pp.283-4.
41. Gibson, J., 1777. *The History of Glasgow*. Appendix xxii, pp.314-317.
42. G.B.R., I, pp.223-4. (Recording a fire of 1601 which did considerable damage, and for which a smith and his workers were not to be held to blame by the citizens.)
43. G.B.R., II, p.229.
44. G.B.R., II, p.233.
45. G.B.R., III, pp.158, 248-9; IV, p.119.
46. G.B.R., IV, pp.44, 45-6, 66.
47. G.B.R., II, p.233.
48. G.B.R., III, p.16.
49. Donald, C. D., 1899. Wooden Houses in Close No.28, Saltmarket. *The Regality Club*, 1st Series, pp.26-30.
50. G.B.R., III, p.114.
51. Cleland, J., 1828. *Statistical and Population Tables Relative to the City of Glasgow*, p.2.
52. Act. of Parl. Scot., 1698.
53. MacGeorge, A., 1880. *Old Glasgow: The Place and the People*, p.78.
54. Murray, D., 1924, *op.cit.*, pp.110-112.
55. Murray, D., 1924, *op.cit.*, p.113.
56. Murray, D., 1924, *op.cit.*, p.117.
57. Marwick, J. D., 1911, *op.cit.*, p.240.
58. Renwick, R. and Lindsay, J., 1921, *op.cit.*, pp.282-3.
59. Slezer, Captain John, 1693. *Theatrum Scotiae*. 2nd edition, Edinburgh, 1874, various.
60. G.B.R., I, p.17.
61. Charters, II, p.109.
62. Renwick, R. (ed.) 1894-1900. *Abstracts of Protocols of the Town Clerks of Glasgow, A.D. 1530-1600*. No.151A.
63. Marwick, J. D., 1911, *op.cit.*, pp.151-2.
64. G.B.R., I, pp.50, 51, 52.
65. G.B.R., I, pp.124, 126.
66. G.B.R., Vol. I, pp.167, 205, 206.
67. G.B.R., I, p.17.
68. Tweed, J., 1872. *The History of Glasgow*. (Glasghu Facies) p.52.
69. G.B.R., I, p.61.
70. G.B.R., I, p.52.

3. REFORMATION TO ACT OF UNION

The Growth of a Mercantile Burgh: 1560-1707

In 1560, the Catholic Church in Scotland, having failed to achieve Reformation from within, was removed from its prominent position in Scottish affairs. This event marked the beginning of a period of change in the government of Glasgow, of which the increasing degree of council direction of fabric change in the burgh, considered in the previous chapter, was but one manifestation. The Bishops and Archbishops of Glasgow had been temporal as well as spiritual overlords, with the right to exercise control over the appointment of the provost and baillies of the town. Within a wider sphere, the national and sometimes international stature of the Bishops, with their important royal connections, helped the ecclesiastical sector of Glasgow to flourish, drawing large incomes from richly-endowed and widely distributed benefices, and holding considerable property within the town. At the same time, the practice of endowing individual ecclesiastics and religious orders with incomes from town properties meant that portions of Glasgow were held by non-residents, such as the monks of Paisley, Melrose, Kilwinning and Newbattle. With the Reformation, these lands, properties and incomes were removed from ecclesiastical hands and conveyed to the representatives of the town, greatly strengthening their control over Glasgow's affairs through their ability to control structural change within, and on the periphery of, the town. This alienation of Church property was a crucial step towards a period of mercantile growth and prosperity.

In the century and a half following the Reformation, the fabric of the Cathedral area declined along with the fortunes of the Church, although a little further down the hill, the College entered a new period of vitality on the basis of income from previously ecclesiastical lands and property. In contrast to the upper section of the town, the lower section flourished, as the merchant community took over the direction of Glasgow's future. The accident of geographical location affected the town's fortunes in two ways. During the turmoil of the religious and civil wars of the seventeenth century, the traditional marching-routes and battlegrounds of invading armies lay to the east, sparing the town the devastation suffered by other settlements. On the other hand, its outlook to the west provided Glasgow with a potentially rich series of trading hinterlands, in west-central Scotland, the western Highlands and islands, Ireland, and the Americas. The exploitation of these resources was undertaken by a class of adventurous, far-sighted, and hard-headed men, who formed the Glasgow merchant community, and whose business acumen took Glasgow from a lowly rank in the hierarchy of Scottish towns to a position second only to that of Edinburgh by 1672.

The merchant community and the growth of trade

In an illuminating series of studies of Glasgow in the late sixteenth and seventeenth centuries, T. C. Smout traced the quickening fortunes of the merchant community, and examined the extension of its influence into many aspects of the town's life[1]. Three stages of development began with the period from the Reformation to c.1600, when Glasgow became established as the main commercial centre of western Scotland, and extended her trading contacts across the Irish Sea. During this time, Glasgow was characterised in the description by Bishop Lesley in 1578[2], as an entrepôt of trade, handling butter, cheese, herring and salmon, cattle, hides, wool and skins, corn, ale and wine. With the exception of the latter commodity, this range of produce was derived mainly from the local western hinterland and Ireland, and the rich waters of the Firth of Clyde and the Irish Sea.

The inclusion of wine in the list of commodities obviously hints at Continental trade, and sporadic references support this. In 1552, 'Jeens Wilz', a Glasgow merchant, is reported at Middleburg[3], while in 1564, herring fishing in which Glasgow played so important a part dispatched 20,000 barrels of herring to Rochelle alone, apart from other French and Baltic ports[4]. Salmon also figured in foreign trade, shown by complaints, from merchants having salmon to transport to France and other places, about the captain of Dumbarton charging them for passage through his section of the Clyde[5], evidence of the strong and enduring rivalry between Glasgow and Dumbarton over the lucrative trade of the estuary. Given the limited size of Glasgow's merchant fleet, extensive maritime ventures were not possible. The burgh records for April and May in 1597 list six local ships, together with two from Pittenweem, one from Aberdeen, and one from Dundee[6]. However, these vessels, in combination with chartered ships based at Dumbarton[7], would be sufficient to conduct a vigorous trade in local sheltered waters in the Firth of Clyde, as well as venturing to the visible coasts of the Western Isles and Ireland.

British and Continental trade

During the first six decades of the seventeenth century the trading sphere of Glasgow widened considerably, while its trading contacts became at once more varied and more regular. In some seasons at the beginning of the seventeenth century, up to 900 boats reaped a rich harvest of herring from the inland waters of the Firth of Clyde, taking their catch to Greenock, where Glasgow merchants bought the fish to transport to the curing and packing houses of Glasgow, thence to be exported abroad[8]. Fat cattle, from the surrounding lowlands at first, then by the 1630s as far afield as the pastures of Islay[9], followed the drove roads to the Glasgow market and slaughterhouses, some to meet the needs of a growing population, some to fuel the export trade as barrelled salt beef. The trade with Ireland continued, despite its aspects of illegality, with an Act of the Privy Council of 1601/2 fulminating against certain persons in Glasgow and Irvine for having carried on trade with the Irish rebels[10]. The Scottish Plantation of Ulster forged contacts conducive to trade, and between October 1618 and October 1619, customs books record around 40 voyages from the Clyde to Ireland[11]. Following the Union of the Crowns of England and Scotland in 1603, sea-borne trade with England may have been a little slow to develop, with occasional Glasgow ships appearing in the Thames only in the 1620s[12], but overland trade intensified, with linen and woollen drapers, commonly known as 'English merchants', carrying their wares by packhorse to the English markets in the south. Of 64 of these men who carried on the trade between 1600 and 1736, "many became sea-adventurers afterwards"[13]. The harbour of Glasgow was busy with shipping from the coastal waters, and "divers and sindrie schipis, barkis, and boitis from Irreland, Hylandis, and sindrie vthir pairtis repairs and cumis with wictuell werie freqentlie"[14].

Trade with the Low Countries had clearly intensified by an early date. Matthew Turnbull, first Dean of Guild of Glasgow in 1605, traded to Holland and France[15], while in 1605 and 1607, Dutch skippers brought cargoes of salt and timber to the Clyde[16]. A threat to a lucrative aspect of Glasgow's trade was posed in 1610, when representatives from Glasgow conferred with those from other burghs over audiences of Dutch ambassadors with the King in London, seeking permission to fish in Scottish waters[17], and no doubt seeking the great herring shoals which had deserted Baltic waters. The memorandum book of James Bell, merchant and Provost in Glasgow in 1643, records numerous transactions with the Dutch in 1621[18], while Gilbert Alcorn left his native Glasgow in 1656 to be factor in Rotterdam for his fellow townsmen[19]. Commerce with France was also a mainstay of the burgh's trade. Up to eight ships a year went to Biscay ports in 1618/19, 1620/21 and 1625/1626[20], and this trade grew with the century. Scottish furs, linens, skins, tartans and other small manufactures were exchanged for French salt and, more especially, wine[21]. Glasgow merchants did not restrict themselves to these two areas in Europe, but ventured into the Baltic. In 1655, the Treasurer of the Town Council of Glasgow was authorised to pay 50 merks to help transport the son of a merchant, William Cunningham, to Danzig[22], possibly to act as factor in a similar manner to Gilbert Alcorn in Rotterdam.

William Simpson was another Glasgow merchant who succeeded in sea trading in the first half of the seventeenth century.

" . . . the great projector of trade, was William Simpson, born at St. Andrew's, about one hundred years ago, (i.e. c.1636) he built two ships at the Bremmylaw, and brought them down the river the time of a great flood. The place of our shipping in those days was the bailliary of Cunninghame and sherifdom of Air, he traded to Flanders, Poland, France and Dantzick."[23]

This account provides an interesting insight into not only Glasgow's European trade, but the condition of the river, so unsuitable for navigation that ships built upstream had to wait for a flood to carry them over its shoals and down into deeper and better harbour waters, on the Ayrshire coast. Perhaps the fullest description of Glasgow's trade at this period comes from Thomas Tucker's report in 1656 on the settlement of the revenue of excise and customs in Scotland.

"The inhabitants, all but the students of the college which is here, are traders and dealers — some for Ireland with small smiddy coales in open boats from four to ten tonnes, from whence they bring hoopes, ronges, barrel staves, meale, oates and butter, some to Norway for timber, and everyone with theyr neighbours the Highlanders, who come hither from the Isles and westerne parts . . . and soe pass up in the Cluyde with pladding, dry hides, goate, kid and deere skins, which they sell, and purchase with theyr price such comodytes and provisions as they stand in need of . . ."[24]

Of trade beyond Europe, there are merely tantalising references. The burgh records for 1654 contain an entreaty for help by Marion Young, for the relief of her son James Morrison, "out of the slaverie he is now in at Barbados"[25] and Tucker's report mentions some who have adventured as far as Barbados, but stopped going because of losses sustained. While this in no way implies regular trading contact with the Caribbean, at least one product of the Americas was available in the Glasgow market. In 1636, two merchants were granted licences for retailing tobacco[26], while in 1646, an agent was appointed to go to Dumbarton to make disposal arrangements for a "bargain of tobacco" brought in by a stranger ship[27]. This was obviously a lucrative item of trade, since wine and tobacco were expressly exempted from the excise tack given to a Glasgow merchant[28], and in contentious dispute, attempting to produce a commission to try the matter in Glasgow, "many of the town's people were summoned to go to Edinburgh anent the Inglishman's tobacco", in June 1652[29]. Glasgow's growing importance as a trading centre shows clearly in the customs dues quoted by Thomas Tucker[30] for the eight excise-registered Scottish ports in 1655/56. As table 3.i. shows, Glasgow ranked second equal with Bo'ness (Burrostones), behind the massive lead of Leith.

Table 3.i. Customs and Excise: Scottish Ports, October 1655-October 1656

Port	Contribution	% of Total	Rank
Leith	£4526	42.5	1
Burrostones	£1440	13.5	2=
Glasgow	£1438	13.5	2=
Dundee	£967	9	4
Aberdeen	£828	7.7	5
Burntisland	£666	6.25	6
Ayr	£434	4	7
Inverness	£342	3.2	8

Source: Marwick, J. D. (ed.), 1881. *Miscellany of the Scottish Burgh Record Society*, p.35.

Across the Atlantic

The period 1660 to 1707 was one of further expansion and intensification of Glasgow's trade at all scales, national, international, and inter-continental. Within Scotland, the growing attraction of the Glasgow grain market broke through the east-west independence and isolation, and the demands of her growing population together with requirements for brewing brought grain from Caithness by the dangerous northern route, through the treacherous Pentland Firth and the more sheltered waters of the Minch, round the stormy Mull of Kintyre to the haven of the Clyde. From 1689, the Panmure and Kellie estates in Angus sold regular and substantial shipments of grain to Glasgow merchants[31]. The pattern of European trade became a little more complex with the outbreak of the war between Britain and the Dutch in 1664. Glasgow equipped several privateers to raid Dutch shipping, and triumphantly brought in several prizes to the Clyde, including a shipload of salt, and one of their own 300-ton vessels laden with Spanish wine, which had been captured by the Dutch and re-taken by Scottish subterfuge[32]. This shipload of wine may have been a mixed blessing, since in 1663 a shipload, bought at Calais, failed to meet the expectations of its buyer and was offered for disposal to the burghs of Glasgow and Dumbarton[33]. Spanish salt also found its way to the Clyde in 1695, in the hold of a London ship[34] and doubtless disappeared into the insatiable maw of the herring and beef packers. Walter Gibson of Glasgow began his merchant career with herring, and in one year freighted a Dutch ship, the St. Agat, with 3,600 barrels of the silver fish, and at St. Martin in France was able to exchange each barrel for a barrel of brandy and a crown. On these handsome proceeds, he bought the ship, and two others, and traded to France, Spain, Norway, Sweden and Virginia[35].

From this time there is firm evidence for expansion of trade into and across the Atlantic, with a consortium of Glasgow men building and outfitting ships to exploit the rich fishing grounds off Greenland[36], while "another great company arose undertaking the trade to Virginia, Carriby-islands, Barbados, New England, St. Christophers, Monserat, and other colonies in America", which company amounted to 107 individuals[37]. Tobacco figured prominently in this trade, being bought in indirectly from Edinburgh and Liverpool in 1677 and 1691[38], and directly from a ship arriving at Glasgow in January 1674, offering 40 hogsheads of Virginia leaf tobacco, with 12 barrels of "roll and cutt", together with eight casks of cassnutt sugar, 4,000 pounds of ginger and a ton of logwood[39]. This direct importation may have been in response to expansion of Glasgow's interest in the tobacco trade, since in 1672, a Council officer was dispatched to Edinburgh to discuss the government impost on tobacco imported into Scotland[40], a levy which must have been inhibiting development.

In the wake of their trade with the Americas, Glasgow merchants also involved themselves in colonising ventures. Walter Gibson advertised for "such persons as are desirous to Transport themselves to America, in a ship belonging to him, bound for the Bermudas, Carolina, New-Providence and the Carriby-Islands, and ready to set Sail out of the river of Clyd, against the 20 of February in this instant year, 1684"[41]. For those who could pay for their passage the government in Carolina was willing to grant 70 acres of land to Masters, with the same for every child and servant taken over with them, at a rent of one penny per acre, to begin only in September 1689. After four years of service, servants were to have 50 acres on the same terms. Those unable to pay for their passage, so long as they were tradesmen, past their apprenticeship in any handicraft, could indenture themselves to Walter Gibson for three years, during which time they would be fed and clothed, and at the end of which they would receive 50 acres of land on the same rental terms described above.

A similar venture advertised in the same year for tradesmen, husbandmen, servants and others "willing to transport themselves unto the Province of New-east-Jersey in America, a great part of which belongs to Scotch-men, Proprietors thereof"[42]. The broadsheet painted a rapturous picture of the new colony.

"The Woods and Plains are stored with infinite quantities of Deer and Rae, Elcks, Beaver, Hares, Cunnies, wild Swine, and Horses, etc., and wild-honey in great abundance. The trees abound with several sorts of Wine-grapes, Peaches, Apricoks, Chastnuts, Walnuts, Plumbs, Mulberries, etc. The Sea and Rivers with Fishes, the Banks with Oysters, Clams etc."

Twenty to thirty-fold increases could be expected in yields of wheat, rye, oats, peas and beans, while Indian corn increased 150- to 200-fold on sowing. Sheep never missed having two lambs at a time, and most often three. Winter lasted only two months, and one man's labour could maintain a family of ten or twelve. There were no savage beasts except wolves, which were only enemies to sheep, and "The Natives are very few, and easily overcome, but these simple, serviceable creatures are rather an help and an incouragement, then any ways hurtful or troublesome".

Glasgow and the Darien Scheme

These idyllic descriptions, coupled with the undoubted success of the new colonies, may have formed part of the motivation behind the raising of a subscription to a Scottish Company trading to Africa and the Indies, which opened its subscription books in Edinburgh on 26th February, 1696, with a separate book opened in Glasgow on the 5th of March. The governors chose the disease-ridden, insect-infested, Spanish-dominated Isthmus of Darien in Panama as the site for their colonial venture, and over the next three years shiploads of hopeful colonists set sail westwards from the Clyde to build a new life beyond the grey Atlantic wastes. Disease, starvation, and Spaniards cruelly decimated them, while of those who fled from the horrors of Central America, many perished on the way home. In December 1700, John Lawson, the Surveyor-General of North Carolina, set out from Charleston on a journey among the Indians. On the large and desolate Dix's Island he encountered an hospitable Scotsman whose house was well furnished with flotsam from the 'Rising Sun', a Scottish ship fleeing from Darien, commanded by Captain Gibson of Glasgow, who went down with his ship and over one hundred souls off the bar of the Ashley River in September, 1699[43].

Glasgow had invested heavily in the venture, with over £12,500 subscribed on the first day, and a total of almost £50,000 overall. The General subscriptions list, together with the Glasgow subscriptions list, contains the names of 169 individuals subscribing for themselves or their guilds, sometimes several times. Subscriptions were entered on behalf of the Magistrates and Council of the Burgh, the merchants' house, and the Incorporations of Hammermen, Wrights, Tailors, Coopers, Baxters, Masons and Cordiners, together with groups of partners in business. The Principal and Regents of the College subscribed, as did numerous gentlemen of means, officers in the garrison, and individual craftsmen. Sixty eight merchants subscribed over 53% of the total, their contributions averaging c.£390 in comparison with an average of £230 for non-merchants[44]. The council minutes of March 1696 had stressed the great advantage to Glasgow of sharing in the affairs of this trading company[45], but to later historians, this scheme was responsible for the loss of Glasgow's ships, and the city was not to have its own vessels again until 1716[46]. The financial losses of Darien, however, were more than offset by the success of Glasgow's other trading ventures, and by the time of the Act of Union of 1707, its merchant community had secured a geographically wide trading base. The commercial expertise which they had developed gave a foundation for expansion of trade during the eighteenth century, while a large proportion of the capital accumulated was invested in the development of early industry in the town.

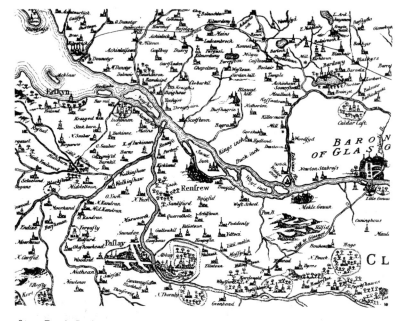

3.i.a   *Timothy Pont's map of the River Clyde: Blaeu's Atlas 1662*

3.i.b   *John Watt's map of the River Clyde: 1734*

River improvements and port facilities

Environmental perils and hazards to navigation impeded the movement of shipping in the waters of the upper Clyde, and the merchants and Council of Glasgow, with the latter body always containing a sizeable component of the former, made strenuous efforts to improve the river and its harbour facilities. The spectre of strangulation of trade by a steady silting-up of the only outlet from the town would have lurked constantly in their minds, sharpened by the example of their erstwhile outport at Irvine whose harbour was clogged by 1656, and "almost choked with sand"[47], reducing her seaborne commerce to a trickle. Timothy Pont's map of the River Clyde, published in Blaeu's Atlas of 1662 (Fig. 3.i.a) shows that the channel from Erskine to Glasgow bridge was narrowed considerably by ten islands or 'inches', forming only the most obvious of the impediments to deep-draught vessels, to which the visible islands were less hazardous than the numerous submerged shoals and bars.

The complaint by Ayr to the Convention of Royal Burghs in 1602, prompting an injunction to Glasgow, Dumbarton and Renfrew to see that the river and its banks were kept clean and unpolluted with matter harmful to fishing[48], referred not just to harmful effluents derived from tanning and curing, but to the slovenly practice of dumping ballast at any convenient point[49]. In 1610, Glasgow requested financial support from the other Scottish burghs in removing the sands which prevented ships from reaching the town[50]. The next two years saw a flurry of effort, with an expert from Culross being brought in to advise on methods of improvement, and 40 workmen provided with iron chains, towropes, cables and barrels striving to remove the 'great stones' from Dumbuck ford[51]. Further efforts in 1631 and 1652[52] made little impression on the obstructions, and in 1656, Thomas Tucker could still write of Glasgow that "The scituation of this towne in a plentifull land, and the mercantile genius of the people, are strong signes of her increase and groweth, were she not checqued and kept under by the shallownesse of her River, every day more and more increasing and filling up"[53].

The fact that attempts to improve Glasgow's port facilities were largely negated by the condition of the river encouraged the development of outport facilities downstream, and throughout the seventeenth century, the two processes operated synchronously. The Broomielaw area was in use as a landing place for cargoes from the sixteenth century, and Council edicts made it clear that boats intending to market their cargoes should proceed upstream to Glasgow bridge, since there was to be no marketing at the Broomielaw itself[54]. Early in the seventeenth century a quay or pier must have been constructed, since both terms are used in burgh records describing measuring of goods for custom, and the dumping of ballast, and boatloads of timber and herring are recorded as being sold there[55]. This quay must have been an extremely modest structure since it was proposed in 1662 to build at the Broomielaw "a little quay ... for the moir commodious laidening and landing of boats", and in the next year stone and timber were sought to make it even higher[56].

Far downstream, on the shores of the Firth, the Council paid the laird of Kelburne for the right to build a pier near Wemyss Bay in 1631[57], for the use of the merchants of Glasgow, but a port closer to the town was obviously desirable, and after Dumbarton's rejection of Glasgow's request for use of port facilities, the Council began to acquire land in the Greenock area. By 1667, the lands of Kilbirnie embracing Inchgreen Bay had been bought[58], and in 1683/4 Glasgow acquired the offices and store-houses of the Royal Fishery Society in Greenock[59], but attention was being concentrated upon the Bay of Newark, one mile upstream, and topographically much more suitable for development. Its use as a sheltered roadstead is recorded as early as 1576[60], and a commission was appointed in 1659 to examine the harbour[61], which Thomas Tucker described as

> ". . . a small place where there are . . . some foure or five houses, but before them a pretty good roade, (i.e. anchorage) where all vessels doe ride, unlade, and send theyr goods up the river to Glasgow in small boates"[62].

In January 1668, Glasgow feued a piece of land for the loading and handling of her ships, and the building of a pier, and in April 1668 the name Newport Glasgow was first mentioned for the place where houses and storehouses were under construction, using a shipload of timber bought from Glasgow merchants[63]. Through the next decade, development of the site continued, with sea marks and 'perches' or poles fixed in the shallows to prevent grounding of vessels, accommodation for skippers and their men, and attractive leases offered to any person who would build there[64]. A smithy was made over to the King's Custom and Excise men, and a new one built, and a commission sent to Waterford in Ireland to obtain 400-500 oak trees to extend the harbour at which all loading or unloading of vessels by Glasgow merchants now had to take place[65]. In the 1680s and 90s a coalyard and saltpan were added, together with a new dock and apparatus for diverting water into it, and a hulk against which ships could be careened[66]. Its harbour facilities thus greatly improved, and its population growing, discussion in 1694 centred on supplying 'Port' Glasgow, with a minister[67]. Glasgow had thus created a flourishing outport for the maritime trade which made the fortunes of her merchants, and created the capital upon which early manufactures were based, and which manifested itself in the new streets and buildings of the seventeenth-century town.

Industry and the townscape

Glasgow merchants in the seventeenth century instigated a relationship between commerce and manufacturing which was to be crucial in carrying the city through the vicissitudes of interruption of vital raw materials by foreign wars and trading disputes in the next two centuries. They did not merely provide the loan capital whereby entrepreneurs were enabled to set up factories, but in fact were the entrepreneurs themselves, taking active roles in guiding the progress of their infant industries, and with their hard-won mercantile knowledge and financial expertise, always alert to the need to diversify their processes and their products. The backlands of the medieval town had long contained an industrial population, and the formation of the various crafts into 14 Gilds or Incorporations had given these artisans a voice in Glasgow's affairs, but although blacksmiths, gold-, silver-, and copper-smiths, armourers, saddlers, weavers, skinners, joiners and many others practised their arts in their small workshops, there were no large industrial buildings or concerns in the city before the seventeenth century. In the establishment of such concerns, as in the inauguration of so many aspects of the life of the city, the merchant-dominated town council played a seminal role.

In 1635 they acquired an old manse in the Drygate for the purpose of establishing a woollen manufactory, which was incorporated three years later into a larger retail and manufacturing concern[68]. Some success must have attended this venture, since another manufactory run by an English clothier was set up in the same street in 1650, after careful study of similar enterprises in eastern Scotland, and the purchase of equipment from Holland[69]. In the next few years, considerable attention was lavished on the works, including the purchase of the best Spanish wool and enlargement of the mill-lade and other facilities, while careful arrangements for marketing the cloth were organised[70]. Control of this operation passed into the hands of the Incorporation of Weavers in 1660[71], and by 1700, three joint-stock companies had been formed for the weaving of woollen and linen cloth, one of them employing 1,400 people, and greatly surpassing in scale and complexity the early manufactories[72]. In 1670 the council encouraged a silk weaver to set up by freeing him of all public burdens for at least five years, and in 1682, set up a workhouse for silk dyeing[73]. Candlemaking, outlawed from the vulnerable parts of the town in 1652, prospered on the Langcroft, with four works in operation in the Candleriggs by 1658[74].

The direct relationship of merchant venturing with manufacturing becomes apparent in an examination of the origins of soap-making. In 1667, according to later histories, nine Glasgow men formed a company, built four ships, probably for whaling, and thus procured the raw material for soap-boiling[75]. However, there is some confusion between the contemporary council records and the later histories on the topic, and it is probable that soap-making had more humble origins, with one Francis Muire, soap-boiler, being granted a licence to make and sell soap in the burgh in 1668[76]. In 1673, John Anderson of Dowhill applied for permission to build a 'soaperie'[77], and since his name figures among a list of the nine stockholders, the later concern may have been set up at this time.

The most enduringly successful efforts of the mercantile joint-stock companies were in the field of sugar refining. As part of the post-Restoration efforts by the government to stimulate home industries, sugar boiling and rum distilling developed directly from Glasgow's trade with the West Indies, and between 1667 and 1700, four sugar-houses were built in the town in peripheral situations in Candleriggs, King Street, Gallowgate and Stockwell Street, because of the fire hazard[78]. The waste molasses from sugar-boiling was used for distilling rum, and the loaf and powder sugar, candy and some molasses was marketed mainly in the Glasgow area. Dutch expertise in sugar refining made their product highly competitive with that of Glasgow, and the Glasgow merchants employed a Dutchman as master boiler, and imported copper vats, iron drip-pots, clay moulds and other impedimenta from the Low Countries. The profits from this industry must have been considerable, since the quantities refined were never great, and it was claimed that the first fortunes in Glasgow were made on sugar[79]. Completing the list of industrial concerns established around the periphery of the town were a ropeworks, built on part of the Old Green in 1696[80], a glassworks set up in 1700 just north of the Broomielaw[81], small hardware and earthenware manufactories, and the tanneries located along the Molendinar. In a period of 70 years, with the greatest activity in the last 40, Glasgow had been transformed from simply a trading town to a centre of trade-inspired industry, with her enterprises inspired, financed and directed by her thriving merchant class.

New streets and new buildings

All of this activity inevitably found expression in the fabric of the townscape, albeit on a small and localised scale and involving no dramatic alteration to the town plan of Glasgow, either in the form of peripheral expansion on any scale, or notable internal change of layout. Rather, those same pressures of population growth, which had encouraged more intensive use of the town's arable lands, together with the requirements of growing trade and embryonic industry, brought the beginnings of building encroachment on the croft lands of the burgh, a forewarning of a much accelerated process to come in the eighteenth century. In 1573, Sir David Lindsay of Kittochside acquired a large portion of Mutland Croft[82], that section of arable land lying south of Trongate and west of Saltmarket, the two most populous streets of the burgh.

He began to lay it out for building, and formed two streets, subsequently known as Old Wynd and New Wynd[83], running south from Trongate to debouch on Bridgegate. For over a century, these remained the sole intrusions into Mutland Croft, and indeed, even the further streets in 1678-1689 were less encroachments on the 'Terra Campestris' than use of the plots of the 'Terra Burgalis' bordering the Croft. Fire provided both the initial reason and the opportunity for the creation of Gibson's Wynd, running west from Saltmarket. The outbreak of 1677 had alerted

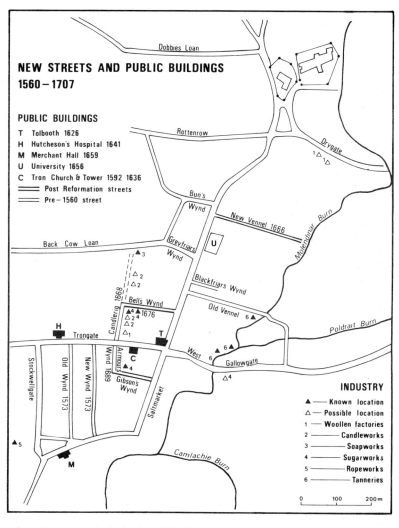

NEW STREETS AND PUBLIC BUILDINGS
1560 – 1707

PUBLIC BUILDINGS

T   Tolbooth 1626
H   Hutcheson's Hospital 1641
M   Merchant Hall 1659
U   University 1656
C   Tron Church & Tower 1592 1636
═══   Post Reformation streets
──   Pre – 1560 street

Dobbies Loan

Rottenrow

Drygate

Bun's Wynd

New Vennel 1666

Molendinar Burn

Back Cow Loan

Greyfriars Wynd

U

Blackfriars Wynd

Candleriggs 1668

Bells Wynd

Old Vennel

Poldrait Burn

1676

H

Trongate

T

West

Gallowgate

Stockwellgate

Old Wynd 1573

New Wynd 1573

Armour's Wynd 1689

C

Gibson's Wynd

Saltmarket

Camlachie Burn

M

INDUSTRY

▲── Known location
△── Possible location
1 ── Woollen factories
2 ──── Candleworks
3 ──── Soapworks
4 ──── Sugarworks
5 ──── Ropeworks
6 ──── Tanneries

0   100   200 m

3.ii   *New streets and public buildings, 1560-1707*

the council to the need to make a fire-break in the congested back-lands between Saltmarket and Trongate, and in December 1679 council officers were empowered to buy suitable land for the creation of a street[84]. They bought Robesoune's land, on which all property had been destroyed by the fire, and in 1680 the street or 'leane' was begun[85]. Entry to Gibson's Wynd was through a close in Saltmarket, and the success of the street is demonstrated by the council's deliberations over the size of the entry, in 1688[86], and its decision in 1689 to purchase half of a shop in Trongate, to make a broad entry to another street, running south from Trongate, to form a right-angled junction with Gibson's Wynd[87]. The land was purchased from James Armour, and the street took his name, becoming Armour's Wynd (Fig. 3.ii).

North of the Cross, the later part of the seventeenth century also witnessed building activity on both sides of the High Street. In 1664, the council purchased a rig of land lying north of the College grounds, and running east from High Street to the Molendinar burn[88], for the formation of a common vennel, opened in 1666[89], and known as New Vennel. In the ground on the western side of High Street, and north of Trongate, two further important streets were opened, forming a right-angled junction in the same manner as Gibson's and Armour's Wynds to the south. Once again, fire played its part as a creative, as well as a destructive, element. In the aftermath of the holocaust of 1652, a nervous council outlawed dangerous manufactures from the built-up and vulnerable area of the burgh. Candle-making, with its need for fire in processing, received the order to depart, and re-located west of the town. The council encouraged this process in its ordinances, setting in feu lands at the back of the Trongate fleshmarket for those who were willing to build candle-houses there[90], at the same time encouraging the fleshers to take advantage of this location by erecting their slaughter-houses on this land.

Their blandishments were obviously successful, since in 1668 they ordered the demolition of the town's tenement on Trongate at the fleshmarket, so that "ane fair and commodious entrie be made ther to the Candle rig"[91]. While this entry may have been opened on to nothing more than a handful of industrial buildings in 1668, by 1679, a petition was drawn up by inhabitants of the "new street", to the effect that their feu duties were too high[92], and in 1692, a mason acquired ground on the west side of the Candleriggs Street to build a house with a "decent stone front", for which his outstanding feu duties were to be remitted[93], as a contribution to fire prevention. The demand for access to the Candle rig prompted the council in 1675 to look for the best place above the cross to make an entry from High Street[94], and in 1676 lands were acquired for the purpose of making a "common street, lone, or vennel", known thereafter as Bell's Wynd[95]. The junction with Candlerigg Street was a success, with ground being feued on the north side of Bell's Wynd in 1680 for the building of three-storey houses with slate roofs[96].

It is interesting to note that, after the private initiative of Sir David Lindsay in the sixteenth century, the growing authority of the town council

3.i   Merchant's House and steeple, Briggait

3.ii   *College facade, High Street*

is more strongly reflected in this seventeenth-century activity of acquiring land for the express purpose of creating new streets, and, by offering financial and other inducements, actively promoting the settlement of these streets. It is justifiable, therefore, to look to the latter part of the seventeenth century for the beginning, albeit on a small scale, of the role of the municipal corporation in creating the townscape of Glasgow, a theme to which return must be made in more proximate centuries, and with far greater emphasis. Acquisition of parcels of land both within the burgh and beyond its bounds was an important aspect of growing municipal control over Glasgow's affairs. Within a few years in the 1660s the council bought parts of Linningshaugh, Kinclaith, Crooks of Milldam, Peitbog and the Langcroft, while land purchase beyond the burgh began with the Barony of Gorbals in 1649, continued with the estate of Provan in 1667, and crucially, the acquisition in 1649 of Ramshorn and Meadowflat[97], valuable arable and grazing lands long in the hands of the Hutcheson family and their descendants of Lambhill[98].

Within the finer mesh of urban fabric, a range of structures in new architectural styles appeared in the townscape. While the greatest part of the increasing population was crammed into the ramshackle buildings on the back lands of the burgage plots, the wealthier members were replacing their fore-tenements with fine new edifices, built in a grander style, and of a higher quality, than their predecessors. Houses were built in Trongate, Stockwell, Saltmarket and Bridgegait, in the early part of the seventeenth century, following the Edinburgh principle of tall, narrow facades, sometimes topped with gables and arcaded on the ground floor[99], though generally smaller than their contemporaries in the capital. In the latter part of the century, long, low facades replaced this vertical emphasis, with the mansion of the Campbells of Blythswood built in 1660 by Colin Campbell, Provost of Glasgow, epitomising the style, eleven bays long and two storeys high, plus attics. The corporate wealth of the merchants' town was expressed in a series of fine structures in which the low, horizontal profiles were often relieved by a tower constructed behind the facade. A variation on this theme was the Town House, or Tolbooth, built in 1626, of which only the seven-storey tower, or steeple, originally completing the eastern end of a square-fronted block, five bays wide and five storeys high, survives today. Hutcheson's Hospital in the Trongate, built in 1641, and the merchants' Hall in Bridgegait, built in 1659, (Pl. 3.i) were good examples of the style, but the crowning architectural glory of the century in Glasgow, was the College, completed in 1656, (Pl. 3.ii) once probably the most distinguished collection of seventeenth-century architecture in Scotland[100]. Its two original courts with a tower placed asymmetrically over their central dividing range are echoed in the Victorian replacement on Gilmorehill in the West End.

Population estimates

Any attempt to progress from inanimate evidence of prosperity to actual population growth is fraught with difficulties. Figures advanced by

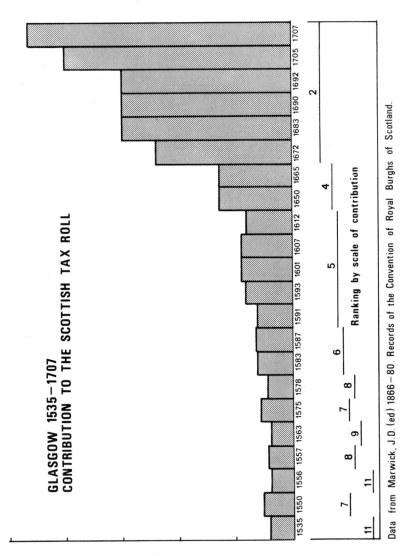

GLASGOW 1535–1707
CONTRIBUTION TO THE SCOTTISH TAX ROLL

Percentage Contribution

Ranking by scale of contribution

Data from Marwick, J.D. (ed) 1866–80. Records of the Convention of Royal Burghs of Scotland.

3.iii   *Glasgow 1535-1707; contribution to the Scottish Tax Roll* early historians tend to be repeated uncritically, and show a rise between 1560 and 1660 of over 10,000, to a total of 14,678, with a decrease and some fluctuation thereafter to a figure of 12,766 in 1707[101]. Certainly the great fire of 1652 and its successor of 1677 caused some people to remove themselves from the town, temporarily or permanently, and a combination of religious and political uncertainty together with opportunity overseas may have encouraged emigration. However, the same religious fractiousness may have been responsible for fluctuations in the figures for baptisms during the period. Between 1611 and 1617 the annual average was 294, rising to 564 between 1656 and 1659, and dropping to 473 between 1660 and 1663[102]. The restoration of episcopacy may have had an inhibiting effect on registration of births, but this does not necessarily imply a reduction either in actual population or in rates of growth. Certainly plague in the 1640s may have caused a reduction in population, but Smout is probably closest to the mark in his estimate of c.14-15,000 people based on hearth-tax returns of 1691[103]. Certainly if these domestic hearths burned coal, then there is evidence for rising demand, from its early mention in 1578 to the sinking of a series of shafts in Gorbals in 1655, 1666 and 1704, as well as in newly acquired lands in Carntyne in 1691 and Provand in 1704, when the town was said to be 'in great need' of coals, even if some went to meet the demands of industry[104].

By the beginning of the eighteenth century therefore, Glasgow had clearly emerged from the uncertainty of religious strife, and was steadily forging a mercantile and industrial base for booming prosperity. Her rising rank and increasing proportional contributions to the tax roll of Scottish burghs illustrate this clearly (Fig. 3.iii). From eleventh position in 1535, paying 2% of the total, she had climbed to second position by 1672, contributing 12%, and while she remained in this position until 1707, her contribution climbed steadily to almost 24% of the total[105]. In her report to the Convention of Royal Burghs in 1692, Glasgow pleaded that her trade was decayed, that there were nearly 500 houses standing waste in the town, and that property values had fallen greatly[106]. Decay may have been the keynote of the upper, ecclesiastical town, long deserted by its wealthy clergy and patrons, but pleading poverty in order to save taxes could not disguise the fact that on the eve of the eighteenth century a wealthy, confident and growing merchant town looked westward along the Clyde to new horizons and greater opportunities.

REFERENCES

1. Smout, T. C., (a) 1960. The development and enterprise of Glasgow, 1556-1707. *Scottish Journal of Political Economy*, vii, pp.194-212. (b) 1962. The early Scottish Sugar Houses, 1660-1720. *Economic History Review*, 2nd Series, No.14, pp.240-253. (c) 1968. The Glasgow Merchant Community in the Seventeenth Century. *S.H.R.*, 47, pp.53-71.

2. Brown, P. Hume., 1893. *Scotland before 1700 from Contemporary Documents*, pp.120-1.
3. Lythe, S. G. E., 1960. *The Economy of Scotland in its European Setting, 1550-1625*, p.243.
4. Brown, A., 1797. *History of Glasgow*, Vol. ii, p.312.
5. G.B.R., I, p.200.
6. G.B.R., I, p.187.
7. Lythe, S. G. E., 1960, *op.cit.*, p.131.
8. MacGeorge, A., 1880. *Old Glasgow: the Place and the People*, p.235.
9. Whyte, I. D., 1979. *Agriculture and Society in Seventeenth Century Scotland*, p.235.
10. Marwick, J. D., 1897. 'Charters' I, p.45.
11. Smout, T. C., 1960, *op.cit.*, p.200.
12. Lythe, S. G. E., 1960, *op.cit.*, p.228.
13. McUre, J., 1736, *op.cit.*, p.169.
14. G.B.R., I, p.262.
15. McUre, J., 1736, *op.cit.*, p.166.
16. G.B.R., I, pp.239, 265.
17. G.B.R., I, p.309.
18. Bain, J., 1895. The True Account of James Bell. *Scots Lore*, p.141.
19. McUre, J., 1736, *op.cit.*, p.166.
20. Smout, T. C., 1960, *op.cit.*, p.200.
21. Franck, R. 'Northern Memoirs' in Brown, P. Hume (ed.)., 1891. *Early Travellers in Scotland*, p.193.
22. G.B.R., II, p.154.
23. McUre, J., 1736, *op.cit.*, p.165.
24. Marwick, J. D. (ed.)., 1881. *Miscellany of the Scottish Burgh Records Society*, p.26.
25. G.B.R., II, p.283.
26. G.B.R., II, p.38.
27. G.B.R., II, p.94.
28. G.B.R., II, p.142.
29. G.B.R., II, p.229.
30. Marwick, J. D. (ed.), 1881, *op.cit.*, p.35.
31. Whyte, I. D., 1979, *op.cit.*, p.229.
32. McUre, J., 1736, *op.cit.*, pp.166, 167 and footnote p.167.
33. G.B.R., III, p.9.
34. G.B.R., IV, p.160.
35. McUre, J., 1736, *op.cit.*, p.169.
36. McUre, J., 1736, *op.cit.*, p.227.
37. McUre, J., 1736, *op.cit.*, p.170-171.
38. G.B.R., III, p.229; IV, p.7.
39. G.B.R., III, p.174.
40. G.B.R., III, p.159.
41. Bannatyne Miscellany, III, 1855, pp.383-384.
42. Bannatyne Miscellany, III, 1855, *op.cit.*, pp.385-388.
43. Bannatyne Miscellany, III, 1855, *op.cit.*, p.384.
44. Burton, J. (ed.), 1849. *The Darien Papers, 1695-1700*. Bannatyne Club, General subscription list; Appendix pp.371-409. Glasgow Subscription List; Appendix pp.410-417.
45. G.B.R., IV, p.194.
46. Pagan, J., 1847, *op.cit.*, pp.54-55.
47. Marwick, J. D. (ed.), 1881, *op.cit.*, p.27.
48. Marwick, J. D., 1897, *op.cit.*, p.459.
49. G.B.R., I, p.306.
50. Marwick, J. D., 1897, *op.cit.*, p.463.
51. G.B.R., I, pp.320, 328, 329 and 330.
52. G.B.R., II, pp.8 and 229.
53. *Report by Thomas Tucker upon the settlement of the Revenues of Excise and Customs in Scotland, 1656*, in Marwick, J. D. (ed.), 1881, *op.cit.*, p.26.
54. G.B.R., I, p.180.

55. G.B.R., I, pp.262 and 306; II, pp.272 and 383.
56. G.B.R., II, p.491; III, p.9.
57. G.B.R., II, pp.4 and 6.
58. G.B.R., II, pp.458, 465 and 480; III, p.96.
59. Marwick, J. D., 1897, *op.cit.*, pp.381-382, 384 and 406.
60. G.B.R., I, p.46.
61. G.B.R., II, p.417.
62. Marwick, J. D. (ed.), 1881, *op.cit.*, p.46.
63. G.B.R., III, pp.101, 103, 104, 108, 109 and 113.
64. G.B.R., III, pp.168, 180, 203 and 204.
65. G.B.R., III, pp.205, 219, 227, 228 and 231.
66. G.B.R., III, pp.284, 289, 336 and 337; IV, pp.29, 77 and 109.
67. G.B.R., III, p.133.
68. Smout, T. C., *op.cit.*, 1960, p.199.
69. G.B.R., II, pp.185, 186 and 187.
70. G.B.R., II, pp.200, 207, 215, 226 and 264.
71. G.B.R., II, p.435.
72. Scott, W. R., 1911. *The Constitution and Finance of English, Scottish and Irish Joint-Stock Companies to 1720*, Volume III, pp.187-188, 191-192, 195.
73. G.B.R., III, pp.134 and 309.
74. Smout, T. C., 1960, *op.cit.*, p.199.
75. McUre, J., 1736, *op.cit.*, p.227. Scott, W. R., 1911, *op.cit.*, p.131, repeats McUre's description, with additional material from a nineteenth century source.
76. G.B.R., III, p.112.
77. G.B.R., III, p.173.
78. Smout, T. C., 1961-62, *op.cit.*, pp.240-241.
79. Gibson, J., 1777. *The History of Glasgow*, pp.246-247.
80. G.B.R., IV, p.221.
81. Pryde, G. S., 1958. The City and Burgh of Glasgow; 1100-1750, in Miller, R. and Tivy, J. (eds.), *The Glasgow Region*, p.146.
82. Renwick, R. (ed.), 1894. *Abstracts of Protocols of the Town Clerks of Glasgow. A.D.1530-1600*, Vol. III, p.34.
83. Murray, D., 1924. *Early Burgh Organisation in Scotland*, Vol. I, Glasgow, p.119.
84. G.B.R., III, p.276.
85. G.B.R., III, p.276.
86. G.B.R., III, p.411.
87. G.B.R., III, p.422.
88. G.B.R., III, p.49.
89. Murray, D., 1924, *op.cit.*, p.106.
90. G.B.R., III, p.88.
91. G.B.R., III, p.102.
92. G.B.R., III, p.264.
93. G.B.R., IV, p.45.
94. G.B.R., III, p.194.
95. G.B.R., III, p.223.
96. G.B.R., III, p.280.
97. G.B.R., III, pp.30, 32, 62, 69, 95; IV, p.121.
98. Fraser, W. (ed.), 1875. *The Cartulary of Pollok-Maxwell*, 3rd division, p.151.
99. Gomme, A. and Walker, D., 1968. *Architecture of Glasgow*, p.42.
100. Gomme, A. and Walker, D., 1968, *op.cit.*, p.45.
101. Cleland, J., 1828. *Statistical and Population Tables relative to the City of Glasgow*, pp.1-2.
102. Sinclair, J. (ed.), 1793. *The Statistical Account of Scotland*, Vol. 5, p.507.
103. Smout, T. C., 1968, *op.cit.*, pp.54 and 71.
104. G.B.R., III, pp.68, 69; IV, pp.32, 372, 375.
105. Marwick. J. D. (ed.), 1866-80. *Records of the Convention of Royal Burghs of Scotland*. I, pp.48, 73, 74, 173, 174, 246, 365, 366, 451, 452, 518-523, 524-526, 530, 531; II, pp.562-564, 567; III, pp.356, 585, 622, 623; IV, pp.40, 121, 161, 371, 421.
106. Marwick, J. D., 1909. *The River Clyde and the Clyde Burghs*, p.135.

4. NEW HORIZONS

America and the Tobacco Trade: 1707-1775

Trade and the river

During the latter part of the seventeenth century development of trade and creation of industry had elevated Glasgow to the position of second city in Scotland. Exploitation of her advantageous geographical position as the focus of a large area of the western Lowlands which, though a poor hinterland in comparison with the agriculturally rich eastern Lowlands, still looked to Glasgow as its trading and commercial centre, had laid the foundations of commercial expertise. On a wider geographical scale the city lay at the head of navigation of a river which, however shallow and meandering its upper reaches may have been, widened into an estuary giving access to the western Highlands and Islands in one direction, and to Ireland and England in another. In addition to the trade of these regions, the extension of vision far out across the Atlantic to the new colonies of the American mainland and the West Indies, had ensured the aggregation of commercial expertise and capital. Some of the products of this merchant venturing, in the form of raw materials and finance became the foundation stones of a small but solid industrial base. The fact that a proportion of the trading product was acquired illegally, in defiance of the provisions of the English Navigation Acts of 1660-61, which ordained that English ports must be the first landing points for exports from English colonies, did not shake this foundation, although it undoubtedly restricted its growth.

In the first decade of the eighteenth century, political changes of great magnitude contained among their numerous provisions legitimising articles which removed this hampering brake from Glasgow's trade. The Crowns of England and Scotland had been united in 1603, and seemingly the next logical step within a United Kingdom was the merging of the English and Scottish Parliaments. In 1702, Scottish commissioners, one of whom was the Provost of Glasgow, travelled to London to discuss the complicated proposals for a Treaty of Union. They left behind them a Scotland in which the majority of the population was fiercely opposed to any such action, partly based upon suspicions of English interference with the young Presbyterian church, partly upon bitterness over the English role in the recent failure of the Darien scheme, and partly upon the prospect of a final loss of independence with the removal of the Scottish Parliament to London, and the re-organisation of Scottish Parliamentary representation. Nowhere did feelings run higher than in Glasgow, whose ancient independent representation in the Scottish Parliament, dating from 1546 at least, was to be replaced by a single member at Westminster for the combined burghs of Glasgow, Dumbarton, Renfrew and Rutherglen. Strong words and feelings erupted into rioting in the city in 1706, but this did nothing to alter the inexorable course of events, and Scotland was compelled to accept the Act of Union in 1707.

Whatever the fears of other sectors of the community, Glasgow's merchants were swift in realising certain implications of the Act and exploiting them to full advantage. Those same Navigation Acts which had acted against the interests of Glasgow now extended their protective and encouraging compulsion to the city. As a British port, Glasgow, using its outports, was entitled to the direct reception of American products, while its manufactured or purchased trade goods now ranked with those British goods which the American colonists were obliged to import. Seventy years after the Act, looking back along the lucrative path which Glasgow had travelled, Gibson was able to declaim that "we may from this aera (sic) date the prosperity of the city of Glasgow; whatever efforts the inhabitants had made, for the introduction and extension of commerce and manufactures, prior to this time, they were but trifling and unimportant"[1]. At first glance a sweeping, bombastic and dismissive statement by a man eager to extol the exploits of his own century, these words stand up well to a close examination of the progress of Glasgow between 1707 and 1775.

Since overseas trade provided a major stimulus to economic and structural development, charting of the course of Glasgow's progress in the eighteenth century should begin with an examination of that activity. The four principal theatres of trade were those of the previous century, namely Ireland, Europe, the colonies of the American mainland, and the islands and mainland possessions in the Caribbean. Each theatre of activity possessed distinctive characteristics of type and range of commodity, export and import, and the picture was made more complex by interchange between and among theatres. Customs Accounts record ships travelling from, for instance, Maryland to Port Glasgow, thence to Rotterdam and back to Maryland, or Jamaica to Greenock, then on to Cette in the Mediterranean. This triangular pattern of Atlantic sailing also operated with Irish trade, with vessels from Irish ports landing cargoes at Greenock or Port Glasgow, loading tobacco for France, Holland or Norway, then returning to Ireland[2]. Shipping activity increased dramatically throughout the century, from a position at the Union when Glasgow appeared to have no shipping of her own, to a registered tonnage of over 60,000 tons in 1777[3]. At first, Glasgow merchants chartered ships for the Atlantic trade, but in 1718, the first Glasgow-owned vessel, a Greenock-built ship of 60 tons, sailed to America[4]. By 1723 there were 20 to 30 ships and by 1727, nearly 50 every year, sailing to Virginia, New England and other colonies in America[5], besides an unknown number of vessels engaged in Irish and European trade. In 1735, 67 ships of 5,600 tons in total, were Clyde-registered, of which 18 sailed to mainland America, nine to the Caribbean, 14 to Europe, six to London, and the remaining 20 to Ireland, or in local trade in the Clyde[6]. The period after 1735 saw an even more significant increase in shipping, as revealed by Custom Port Books for 1742/4 and 1772, and shown in Table 4.i.

Table 4.i. Arrivals and Departures: Greenock and Port Glasgow:
(a) 1742/4 and (b) 1772.

	Greenock				Port Glasgow			
	In		*Out*		*In*		*Out*	
North America	(a) 36	(b) 49	(a) 34	(b) 46	(a) 43	(b) 87	(a) 24	(b) 57
West Indies	(a) 3	(b) 26	(a) 17	(b) 21	(a) 17	(b) 5	(a) 12	(b) 6
Europe	(a) 79	(b) 66	(a) 81	(b) 55	(a) 21	(b) 23	(a) 60	(b) 141
Ireland	(a) 19	(b) 167	(a) 22	(b) 84	(a) 36	(b) 62	(a) 18	(b) 79
Total	137	308	154	206	117	177	114	283

Sources. Customs Accounts of Port Glasgow and Greenock (S.R.O. Edinburgh), quoted in Gilfillan and Moisley, 1958, and Crispin, 1962.

Some degree of specialisation between ports is evident, with Greenock handling more Irish and European trade than Port Glasgow at both periods, and taking a lead in the sugar and rum trade from the West Indies by 1772, not just because of better harbour facilities, but because of the development of sugar processing in the town. Overall, however, although the numbers of ships handled by both ports at both dates show Greenock as numerically ahead, the smaller tonnage of vessels engaged in the Irish trade must be borne in mind, while the increased figures between 1742 and 1772 show Port Glasgow increasing handling by almost 100%, while Greenock managed only c.56%. By 1772, Clyde ports owned 56% of all Scottish shipping[7], a clear demonstration of the new geographical relationships operating in Scottish maritime commerce.

In his *History of Glasgow*, published in 1777, John Gibson gives a detailed account of the exports and imports of Glasgow, Greenock, and Port Glasgow for the period January 1771 to January 1772[8], from which it is possible to reconstruct the character of trade in each of the four principal areas. Seventeen ports in Ireland traded with the Clyde, exporting linen, flax, skins and foodstuffs, and importing a wide range of manufactured textiles, glass, herrings, coal, tobacco, rum, sugar and cotton wool, as evidence of Glasgow's entrepôt function. Trade with Europe was at once more complex in its spatial characteristics, and simpler in the range of products exchanged, as (Fig. 4.i.a) shows. Scandinavian ports, from Trondheim and Bergen round to Norrkoping on the Baltic, sent iron and forest products to the Clyde. Further south, from Rotterdam on the North Sea coast, by Bremen and Hamburg, round to Copenhagen, Danzig and Konigsberg on the Baltic, and as far as St. Petersburg, came

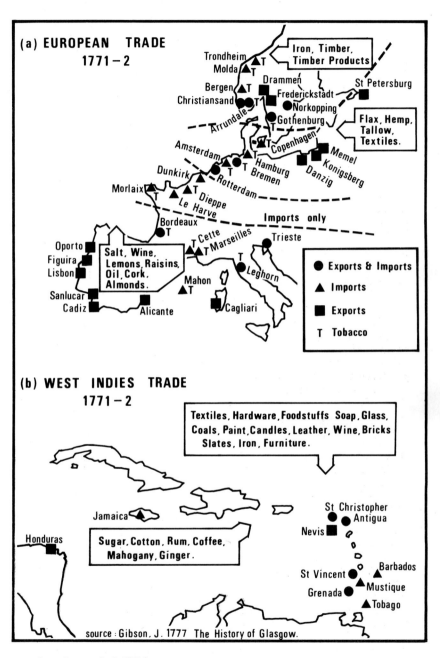

(a) EUROPEAN TRADE 1771 – 2

Trondheim
Molda
Bergen
Christiansand
Arrundale
Amsterdam
Dunkirk
Morlaix
Dieppe
Le Harve
Bordeaux
Oporto
Figuira
Lisbon
Sanlucar
Cadiz
Alicante
Cette
Marseilles
Mahon
Cagliari
Leghorn
Trieste

Drammen
Frederickstadt
Norkopping
Gothenburg
Copenhagen
Hamburg
Bremen
Rotterdam
Memel
Konigsberg
Danzig

St Petersburg

Iron, Timber, Timber Products

Flax, Hemp, Tallow, Textiles.

Imports only

Salt, Wine, Lemons, Raisins, Oil, Cork, Almonds.

● Exports & Imports
▲ Imports
■ Exports
T Tobacco

(b) WEST INDIES TRADE 1771 – 2

Textiles, Hardware, Foodstuffs Soap, Glass, Coals, Paint, Candles, Leather, Wine, Bricks Slates, Iron, Furniture.

Jamaica
Honduras

Sugar, Cotton, Rum, Coffee, Mahogany, Ginger.

St Christopher
Antigua
Nevis
St Vincent
Grenada
Barbados
Mustique
Tobago

source: Gibson. J. 1777 The History of Glasgow.

4.i.a   European Trade 1771-2
4.i.b   West Indies Trade 1771-2

flax, hemp, tallow and textiles. From southern Europe, from France, Spain, Portugal, the Balearics, Sardinia, Italy and the port of Trieste, came salt, wine, lemons, raisins, olive oil, cork, and almonds, drawn from as far away as Smyrna and the Levant. In return, the Clyde sent tobacco. Every one of the 21 importing ports in Europe took tobacco, and 16 of them took only tobacco, in enormous quantities.

Fig. 4.i.b indicates the character of commodity exchange with the islands and mainland of the Caribbean, which provided a small but reliable market for manufactured goods and European foodstuffs. While demand from this area, coupled with enormously greater demand from the North American colonists, acted as a stimulus to Scottish industrial production, Scotland alone simply could not meet their requirements. Irish and German linen supplemented Scottish exports, while London supplied a much wider range of manufactures for shipment. At the peak of trade, in 1771, Scottish industry could supply only 27% of the value of goods exported[9], thus confirming Glasgow's status as an entrepôt. In return, the West Indian trade ships brought sugar, rum, cotton and other exotics which provided crucial raw materials for Glasgow's early industry, and an alternative to the dominant tobacco upon the collapse of that trade. The role of cotton belongs to the last decades of the eighteenth and the early decades of the nineteenth centuries, but sugar had been important to Glasgow in the seventeenth century, and remained so throughout the eighteenth. The imposition by Irish revenue officers in 1780 of a rate of taxation on all goods imported from Scotland higher than that levied upon the same goods from England and Wales, brought vehement protests from Glasgow in which sugar was singled out for attention. The recent demise of tobacco may have conditioned the tone of urgency in the plea, but there is no equivocation in the statement that "the mercantile interest of Glasgow has relied on the purchases made by their neighbours and fellow-subjects in Ireland, who have hitherto usually taken off about one half of the quantity imported into Glasgow"[10].

However important sugar may have been to the merchants of Glasgow in 1780, only a few years before it had represented the merest fraction of the value of the most important commodity to which the Act of Union had given free access. In 1771, for every pound of sugar coming into the Clyde, 1,000 pounds of tobacco were shipped in, to the staggering total of 46 million pounds[11]. The trade had built up gradually through the century, and indeed, as outlined in the previous chapter, a taste for tobacco and the skills of processing it had been acquired during the previous century, but it was only in the post-Union period that the trade developed to any scale, and through a series of well-defined stages. After a slow start using chartered vessels, Glasgow's own ships, with those from other Clyde ports, steadily increased the volume of tobacco imports until the 1720s, when their success attracted the unwelcome attentions of English mercantile interests.

"The tobacco trade of Glasgow was now, however, in such a thriving condition, that it so much excited the jealousy of the merchants in

London, Bristol, Liverpool and Whitehaven, that they entered into a combination for the discouragement, if not the ruin of it."[12]

From 1717 to 1723 petitions were presented to Parliament claiming that Glasgow merchants were operating fraudulently, and the lengthy proceedings, culminating in the visit of inspectors and the appointment of new customs officers at Port Glasgow, had an inhibiting effect on the trade. Revival in the late 1720s brought a slow rise to a peak in 1735 (Fig. 4.ii.a), after which "the commerce of Glasgow advanced but slowly"[13] until 1750. The slump in customs receipts shown in Fig. 4.ii.a for the period between 1735 and 1750 possibly relates to unsettled political conditions. The illegal trading activities of British West India merchants provoked Spanish retaliation and the 'War of Jenkin's Ear' of 1739, and in 1742 Britain became embroiled in the War of the Austrian Succession. While the relatively sheltered waters of the Clyde and the much shorter sailing journey to America around the North of Ireland gave some protection to Scottish ships, the activities of French and Spanish naval vessels undoubtedly caused difficulties, especially to ships operating on the 'triangle' route between Scotland, North America and the Caribbean. Closer to home, the Jacobite rising of 1745-6 brought disruption in its wake, and although far from alone in her trials, Glasgow experienced costly interruptions to her affairs, prompting her to petition, and obtain, relief from Parliament[14].

After these doldrums, the tobacco trade entered a period of recovery, aided by new organisation, replacing the old barter system with a series of factors advancing credit, in the form of manufactured goods, against future crops. Guaranteed stocks of tobacco ensured a rapid turnaround of vessels, and Clyde ships could often sail in two or three weeks, while others could wait for three or four months[15]. Spatial relations and commercial expertise inspired a massive surge of rapid and sustained growth, with imports of tobacco reaching their peak on the eve of the American War of Independence (Fig. 4.ii.b), giving the Clyde an overwhelming dominance in the trade. In the period 1771-5, tobacco represented 38% of all Scottish imports, 56% of all exports, and 80% of all re-exports[16], a trade so lucrative that smuggling on a large scale was extremely profitable, if not always successful, since customs officers in the 60s and 70s regularly seized and burnt thousands of pounds of illicit tobacco at a time[17]. That the swift deflation of the trade with the onset of war did not ruin the Clyde completely is a phenomenon whose explanation must be sought within a range of mitigating factors, not least among which must be the diversification of the economy of Virginia and the Carolinas in the second half of the eighteenth century, with production and export of a wide range of commodities, and a consequent demand for European and other exotic imports. Table 4.ii shows the range of exports and imports to and from Virginia in 1771, many of which still managed to enter the trading stream during and after the war, by way of Newfoundland, Nova Scotia and Canada[18], while the removal of tobacco as a commodity encouraged growth in Caribbean imports.

Table 4.ii. Glasgow 1771: Exports and Imports, to and from Virginia

IMPORTS

Boards, pine	7350 feet
Copper still	one
Ginsang	86 libs
Handspikes	2 2 26 qdd
Heading, hogshead	2189 ps.
Hoops, wood	15,304 in no.
Indico	1524 libs
Iron, bar	227 tons
Iron, pig	508 tons
Lead, bar	31 1 6 libs
Logwood	1 ton
Mahogany	73,000 feet
Oars, boat	33 pairs
Rum	480 gallons
Skins, beaver	88 in number
Skins, deer, in the hair	11,848 in number
Skins, India half dressed	726 libs
Skins, elk	39 in number
Skins, otter	25 in number
Skins, wolf	3 in number
Shingles	5000 in number
Staves, barrel	9404 0 9 odd

EXPORTS

Ale, strong	290 3 firkins	Linen, checkered	108,548 yds.
Anvils	3 in number	Linen, printed	45,312 1/2 fq.yds.
Brimstone	41 0 21 libs	Leather, tanned, wrought	162,540 libs
Bushes, cart	24 in number	Leather, unwrought	30 3 6 libs
Buckskins, dressed	29 pieces	Leather, in hides	75 libs
Bandannoes	12 pieces	Lead, cast	105 2 1 libs
Cards, Cotton	51 dozens	Morees	2 pieces
Cards, wool	3 dozens	Nankeen	100 pieces
Coals	173.7/9 chalders	Oil, lintseed	1075 gallons
Candles, tallow	17,683 libs	Oil, lamp	54 gallons
Canvass, hessens	56 1 15 ells	Ovens, camp	70 in number
Canvass, spruce	1354 0 2 ells	Paper writing	21 reams
Cordage	1135 3 21 libs	Paint	5618 libs
Cordage, white	8 bolts	Pipes, tobacco	309 grofs
Coperas	22 1 27 libs	Pots, iron	244 in number
Corks	462 grofs	Rum	1015 gallons
Cutlary	9734 libs	Romal, cotton	one piece
Cheese	1800 libs	Sail Cloth	19,767½ ells
Diaper and sheeting	768 fq. yards	Sugar, refined	1573 3 9 libs
Drilling, Russa	8 3 16 ells	Stuffs of Silk	2094 10½ oz.
Faggots, steel	6 in number	Soap, hard	6189 libs
Frying pans	84 in number	Snuff, plain and rappee	817 libs.

Glass, green and manufactured	173,798 libs
Glass, flint	7 0 19 libs
Glass, crown	83 2 14 libs
Gun-powder	4850 libs
Ginger	4 3 0 libs
Grindstones	159 in number
Haberdashery	374,795 libs
Handkerchiefs, linen	1752 dozens
Hardware	17,420 libs
Hats, mens	2,971.9/12 dozens
Hats and bonnets, filk	44.9/12 dozens
Herrings, white	42.1/2 barrels
Horses	one
Iron, wrought	1,095,914 libs
Kettles, tea	18 in number
Linen, British	1,163,781 yds.
Linen, Irish	530,828 yds.
Linen, Russia	5 0 2 ells
Linen, Muscovia	2 1 27 ells
Linen, German narrow	2231 2 20 ells
Stones, hewn	14 in number
Saws	24 in number
Spades	2 dozens
Skins, sheep	0 1 0 libs
Stockings, thread	28 dozens
Skillets	37 in number
Sieves	36 dozens
Stationary	1656 libs
Taffaties	20 pieces
Thread	261 libs
Tobacco, roll	1075 libs
Twine	5549 libs
Tyking	161 fq. yards
Vices	3 in number
Ware, copper and tin	71,142 libs
Ware, delf	12,828 pieces
Ware, earthen	37,526 pieces
Ware, stone	25,078 pieces
Wine, Portugal	3958½ gall.
Woolens	405,257 libs

Source: Gibson, J., 1777. The History of Glasgow. pp.219, 227 & 228.

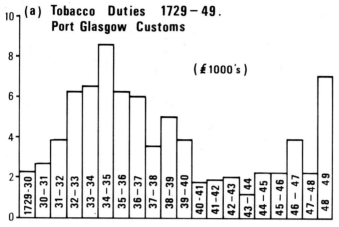

(a) Tobacco Duties 1729 – 49.
Port Glasgow Customs

(£1000's)

10
8
6
4
2
0

1729-30 | 30-31 | 31-32 | 32-33 | 33-34 | 34-35 | 35-36 | 36-37 | 37-38 | 38-39 | 39-40 | 40-41 | 41-42 | 42-43 | 43-44 | 44-45 | 45-46 | 46-47 | 47-48 | 48-49

source: Smith, J. 1836, The Cochrane Correspondence
regarding the Affairs of Glasgow 1745 – 46, p 106

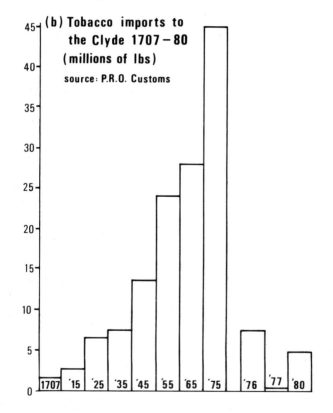

(b) Tobacco imports to
the Clyde 1707 – 80
(millions of lbs)

source: P.R.O. Customs

45
40
35
30
25
20
15
10
5
0

1707 | '15 | '25 | '35 | '45 | '55 | '65 | '75 | '76 | '77 | '80

4.ii.a   *Tobacco Duties 1729-49*
4.ii.b   *Tobacco Imports to the Clyde 1707-80*

Of equal importance as a buttress to the economy of the Clyde and especially Glasgow were the home-based activities of the tobacco merchants. Impressive though the enormous quantities of tobacco may have been, they simply passed through the west of Scotland, making no direct contribution to the stimulus of processing or manufacturing industry other than the setting up of a few, mainly suburban, snuff-mills. Equally, changes in the marketing pattern of the re-exported tobacco had no direct effects. In 1755, the Dutch were the principal purchasers, but with an uneven demand, and by the 1770s they had been supplanted by the French, whose Farmers-General of the customs operated a tobacco monopoly, entering into large-scale and reliable contracts and ensuring a steady flow of capital[19]. It was in the disposition of this massive capital accumulation that the tobacco trade had its most direct effects on the economy of the Glasgow region, and the continued prosperity of the tobacco merchants. Early intelligence of the impending colonial difficulties, and prudent preparations in the form of liquidation of colonial debts and stockpiling of tobacco undoubtedly cushioned the shock[20], but the colonial traders had already invested widely and wisely and were able to fall back upon a range of well-prepared positions. Never large in numbers, comprising only between nine and ten % of the Glasgow merchant burgess community in the decades between 1740 and 1780[21], the Tobacco Lords wielded a disproportionate influence in the region's affairs. In a speculative and often unprofitable trade, none of them relied solely upon tobacco, but diversified their interests as widely as possible, investing in land and industry, and by contributing considerable assets to the foundation of banking, provided loan capital for other entrepreneurs. In the land market, the 124 estates bought between 1770 and 1815 in Lanarkshire, Renfrewshire, Dunbartonshire and the Barony of Glasgow not only conferred landed status upon their purchasers but in many cases brought rich supplies of exploitable minerals, chiefly coal at first[22]. Merchant capital also found its way into tanning, boot and shoe manufacturing, rope and sailcloth making, ironworks, glassworks, coal mines, breweries, textile factories and dye works[23].

The Tobacco Lords were not alone in their promotion of industrial development. As early as 1726 the Convention of Royal Burghs had recognised the difficulties facing Scotland's most important industry, that of linen manufacture. Poorly organised and technologically deficient in organisation, integration, processing and marketing, the industry badly needed the attentions of the Board of Trustees for Improving Fisheries and Manufactures in Scotland, set up at the Convention's suggestion in 1727. Apart from stimulating the activities of yarn merchants in the towns, the Board assisted in setting up bleachfields, such as that at Gray's Green in Glasgow, and printfields at Pollokshaws in 1742 and Dalsholm on the Kelvin in 1750. By 1771, Glasgow was the principal town in Britain for linen manufacture, ranging in type from coarse osnaburgs and 'inkles' or tapes, to fine quality cloths, called 'Bengals' and 'Carolines', and handkerchiefs which constituted 75% of her production[24]. Linen was only one branch of manufacturing in the city, and the Old Statistical Account records euphorically that "It was ... in the period between 1725 and 1750 that the spirit for manufactures first became prevalent, and though it has ever since been increasing in energy, and diffusing its influence, its effects for a few years past have been wonderful. The variety of manufactures now carried on in Glasgow, which have extended in almost every branch, are very great"[25]. As Table 4.iii shows, in almost every decade from 1700, at least one new industry was started in the city, with some decades seeing as many as four or five foundations.

Table 4.iii   Industrial and Financial Enterprises in Glasgow: Creation by Decade, 1700-1777.

	Industries	Banks
1700-10	Checks	
1710-20	—	
1720-30	White linens; saddlery; green bottles:	
1730-40	Inkles; Printed linens and cottons; threads; Ironmongery for export:	
1740-50	Delft; lawns; stockings; copper- and tin-ware for export:	Glasgow Ship Bank
1750-60	Brushes; cambrics; carpets:	Glasgow Arms Bank; British Linen Co.*
1760-70	Cast iron; stoneware; gloves; grates; jewellery for export	Thistle Bank; Watson & Co. Bank; Merchant Bank
1770-77	Anchors; brass; cudbear (dye); crystal	

Source: Gibson, J., 1777. *The History of Glasgow*, pp.238-247.
Additional data: Pagan, J., 1847. *Sketches of the History of Glasgow*, pp.84-90; Slaven, A., 1975. *The Development of the west of Scotland, 1750-1960*, p.82.

*Issued notes from 1752, but only officially recognised as a bank in 1849.

Textiles constituted the largest proportion by value of all manufactures, totalling c.57% in 1771, while its closest rivals were leatherworking, with c.17.5%, and the metal industries with just over 8%[26]. Finance for the operation and expansion of industry and commerce was managed and provided by no less than six banks or note-issuing companies set up between 1740 and 1770.

However much the industry of Glasgow expanded, and however much her sea-borne commerce flourished, the condition of her major artery, the River Clyde, represented an insurmountable barrier to progress. Feeble attempts at improvement during the seventeenth century had done practically nothing to alter the character of the broad and shallow stream, braided and impeded by sandbanks and islands. John Watt's 1734 map of the river (Fig. 3.i.b) differs only in cartographic accuracy from that of Pont in the Blaeu atlas of 1662 (Fig. 3.i.a). In 1737, a council committee was appointed to find ways and means of deepening the river and its fords[27], but seems to have done nothing more than deliberate the problem. In the lower reaches of the Firth, navigational difficulties upstream of Ailsa Craig, in the passage between Little Cumbrae and Bute, were tackled by a coal-burning lighthouse, proposed in 1743, but only implemented by Act of Parliament in 1756[28]. Upstream, where shallows presented the principal problems, a survey in 1752 by James Stirling[29], with a view to deepening the Clyde by the use of locks, was followed by an invitation to John Smeaton in 1755. He sounded the river bed on 12 different shoals between Glasgow and Renfrew at low and high water, and at the former state of the tide found depths of only one foot six inches at the Hirst near the Broomielaw, one foot three inches at Pointhouse, and one foot six inches at Marlin Ford, while in the deeper parts the river appeared almost stagnant. From Pointhouse to Marlin Ford stretched almost one continuous sheet of light sand, and he therefore considered the latter place to be the best position for a lock and a dam, to give four and a half feet of water at all times at the Broomielaw[30]. Impatience with inaction probably prompted the Acts, published by the Merchants House and Trades House in 1757 proposing the construction of locks on the river, but in 1758 the necessary Act of Parliament was obtained. Alexander Wilson was paid for surveying the Clyde to decide the proper position for locks, and in 1759 a committee was constituted to provide materials for lock construction. Smeaton as engineer with Charles Freebairn as architect were duly contracted to lay a lock and dam across the Clyde at Marlin Ford[31].

It was probably as well for the future development of the river that these plans for blocking it came to nothing. The problem remained under consideration, and in 1764, a Doctor Wark, at the instigation of several Glasgow merchants, submitted a plan for building furze dykes to constrict the shallow parts of the stream, thus accelerating the flow of water, which in turn would scour a deeper channel[32]. Once again the plan bore no fruit, but may have left an echo to be transmitted to the next engineer invited to attempt a solution. In 1768, John Golborne surveyed the river and the harbour of Port Glasgow, made proposals for scouring the Port Glasgow basin and after deploring the state of nature in which he found the Clyde, proposed to "proceed on these principles of assisting nature when she cannot do her own work, by removing the stones and hard gravel from the bottom of the River where it is shallow; and, by contracting the channel where it is worn too wide. . . ." In 1769, James Watt followed Golborne's directions and aided by James Barrie, produced a plan as a basis for action[33]. By 1771, Golborne had caused 117 jetties to be erected, on both sides of the river, constricting its flow into a greatly narrowed channel and together with dredging operations using primitive rakes, had deepened the river to such an extent that vessels drawing six feet of water could reach the Broomielaw[34]. In 1772 Golborne was contracted to further improve the river from Longloch Point to Dumbuck Ford, a major obstacle which he managed to overcome, creating six feet of depth in this lower section of the channel[35].

Continued scour eroded the whole channel more and more deeply until by 1781, the depth at Dumbuck was 14 feet at low water, and as a bonus, infill between the jetties created new land, reported by Golborne in 1781 to be covered with grass[36]. Jetties and infill may be seen clearly in Ainslie's map of Renfrewshire, made in 1797, and their effect may be gauged by comparing the revenues of the river before and after their construction. Between 1752 and 1770 the revenue of river and harbour only amounted to £147, whereas by 1771 it had reached £1,044 and by 1780, £1,515[37]. This increased revenue was derived not just from improvements in downstream navigation, but from work on the Broomielaw itself. In 1722, a new quay had been built, extending wharfage from the Broomielaw to the Ducat Green, under a 1716 Act of Parliament, and in 1734, two timber wharfs extended the frontage further to the east[38]. Silting remained a problem, and £20 was allotted in 1736 for an experiment on clearing a sandbank as a model for future efforts in 1740 when the Port Glasgow dirt boat was ordered to be brought up for dredging the river and carrying away sandbanks at the Broomielaw[39]. The Act of Parliament obtained in 1770 for Golborne's scheme also authorised an enlargement of the Broomielaw Quay, which took the form of removal of the south side of Ducat Green and construction of a stone quay extending as far east as the Stockwell Street bridge, together with land reclamation and quay construction on the south bank of the river[40]. The growth of wharfage facilities attracted a coalyard and slateyard, a warehouse for imported Irish hides, whose salt could be washed off in the river, and the horse market[41].

Despite these developments, throughout the eighteenth century the bulk of Glasgow's river traffic was handled far downstream, at its outport of Port Glasgow, and at Greenock. The rapid expansion of trade early in the century created difficulties for the small and shallow Port Glasgow harbour which was enlarged by 1720 into a semi-circular basin enclosed by two stone jetties[42]. The partners in the Glasgow Ropework Manufactory were given leave to build a new quay in 1741[43], but dry dock facilities, though proposed, with an offer to finance them, by the feuars of Port Glasgow in 1725, were not undertaken until 1758, and under the direction of James Watt, were ready to receive ships by 1761, the first in Scotland to do so[44]. The graving dock was extended in 1772 and a central pier extended down the basin, while the perennial problem of silting was tackled by means of two reservoirs behind the town, giving a head of water sufficient to scour the basin, together with sluices on each side of the new pier to keep a constantly open channel[45]. In the late 1730s and 40s, new storage facilities were constructed, and the doors of existing warehouses enlarged to receive tobacco hogsheads, an inspector of herring curing and packing appointed, as well as a shoremaster to oversee mooring regulations[46]. Greenock's new harbour was completed in 1710, extended in 1734 and 1751, but never managed to attract as much shipping as Port Glasgow. However, by 1772, Greenock held a significant lead in tonnage registered, with 15,700 tons against Port Glasgow's 10,000. This may have developed as a manifestation of Greenock's growing interest in the whaling trade from 1752, and the larger vessels required for this purpose may have had some influence on Greenock's refitting and repairing activity, always greater than that of Port Glasgow[47]. The eighteenth century also witnessed the extension of water-borne trade to canals, but although their planning and constructional phases fall within the period under consideration, and are representative of the improving ethos of the time, their operational phases fall within the ambit of the next chapter.

Townscape and people

Development of the townscape of Glasgow in the eighteenth century took a variety of forms which varied according to location and period, and also according to whether the developer was the municipal authority or a private individual. In the first half of the century, activity was confined to internal change within the built-up area, sponsored by the town council, and thus continuing the process begun in the latter part of the seventeenth century. In the second half of the eighteenth century, beginning in the early 1750s, change took a new form, with extensive and rapid peripheral expansion, principally to the west, under the aegis of both the council, and on a greater scale, private individuals or associations. Between 1750 and 1775, 13 new streets or squares were planned, and with one exception, inaugurated, while a more grandiose project for the lands of Ramshorn and Meadowflats was under consideration. Growth in Glasgow's population during this period can be adduced as a motivating force for this expansion, since the majority of people continued to live in the crowded closes of the old town. This was precisely the time when massive fortunes were beginning to accumulate on the profits of Atlantic trade, and the aspirations of the merchant class, desirous of remaining close to their offices and exchanges yet no longer willing to endure the discomfort of living in close juxtaposition with the noisome warrens of medieval origin, may be seen as a crucial factor, with their new townhouses spearheading the movement to the west, and their business acumen recognising the speculative possibilities in the provision of more spacious and gracious modes of living for their fellows.

Street development in the immediate post-Union decades shows the strong controlling hand of the council, though action was often in response to requests from the citizenry. In 1711, a petition signed by 30 people, owners and tenants of houses and lands at the foot of Saltmarket, pointed out the fire danger from the numerous closely-packed thatched houses on the back lands. Apart from their flimsy and highly combustible construction, some were used for industry, one ground-floor bake-house having no chimney, and venting smoke and sparks through its doorway; while on some waste ground at the rear of one close, the bakers maintained large stockpiles of firewood for their ovens. The council responded to this plea by ordering the demolition of the offending premises and the creation of a causewayed street leading to the Molendinar Burn[48] (Fig. 4.iii). This type of tidying-up process, as in the widening of College Street in 1734[49], made no great demands on council or citizens, but in the 1720s there began the creation of new streets involving processes of compulsory purchase, demolition, street and plot regulation, building and land use controls, quite familiar in a modern context, though on a vastly different scale.

In April, 1722, a proposal was made to purchase lands for the construction of a new street to be named King Street, opening from the south side of Trongate and running south to Bridgegate (Fig. 4.iii). With admirable dispatch, the first lands were purchased within a month, and within a year, the timber, stones and growing trees of the houses and gardens in its path were sold at public auction, the ground cleared and the street causewayed along part of its length[50]. This was to be no medieval wynd or vennel, pursuing an angular course between burgage plots, but a proper street, nine metres broad with pavements 0.75m. in width; "such persons as shall have the privilege thereof and of building houses fronting there to be obligt to build these houses in a decent and uniform manner and after one and the same moddell". That model specified ashlar fronts on all buildings, which must be only two storeys high plus garretts, with each storey measuring 2.8 metres from floor to plaster, and each house having doors, windows, sills and lintels uniform in work and height, to be built within two years[51]. Purchase of additional land for King Street continued until 1724, and in the meantime, a further street was opened, running at right angles from King Street to Saltmarket, following and obliterating the line of Gibson's Wynd, renamed Princes Street[52] (Fig. 4.iii). Feuing of plots in the upper part of King Street and along Princes Street was relatively rapid, but the lower part of King Street was not so attractive, and in 1736 still contained a great deal of waste ground[53], an unheeded warning to speculators which was to echo frequently in the next hundred years. This phase of development concluded with the opening of two small sections of street, one along an existing lane, to provide access to the grand new church of St. Andrew rising on its proposed site to the east of the Molendinar, and giving its name to the two openings from Saltmarket and Gallowgate[54].

The second half of the century opened on to new vistas of peace and prosperity, with the defeat of the 1745 Jacobite rebellion ending political instability, fortunes accruing from trade, industry gradually expanding, and a reconciliation to the realities of Union all sponsoring a climate of experiment and expansion. In Glasgow, spatial expansion was long overdue, and the land for exploitation stretched away to the west, on either side of the Trongate – St. Thenew's gate – Westergate line, from the flood-plain of the Clyde up across the gentle slopes of the post-glacial raised beach and its arable croftlands. Within the croftlands, for instance in the Lang Croft, lying north of Trongate and stretching up to Back Cow Lone, later Ingram Street (Fig. 4.iii), the north-south alignment of the long strips or rigs of ground, a furlong in length, governed the layout of the new streets developed at right angles to the Trongate axis. Prominent

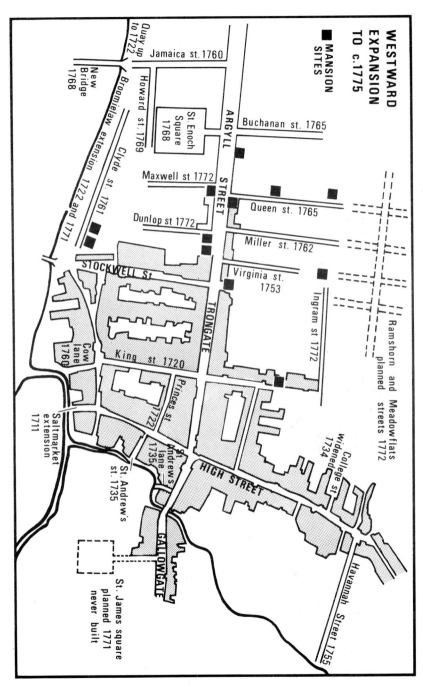

4.iii   *Westward expansion to c.1775*

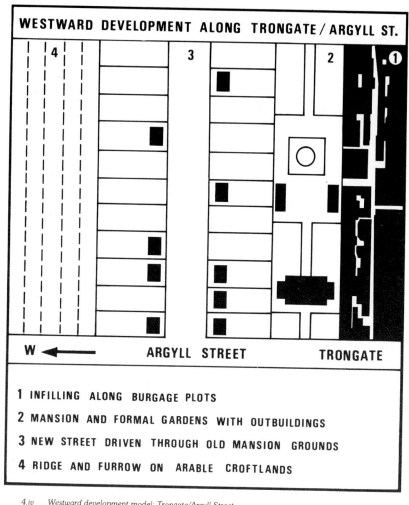

4.iv   *Westward development model: Trongate/Argyll Street*

merchants, moving westwards out of the town, often acquired title to groups of these rigs, building splendid mansions with ornamental approaches from the street, and long gardens and orchards stretching back along the plot. Realisation of the rising value of such land in many cases led to the demolition of the earlier mansion, and the laying out of a north-south street with smaller building plots set at right angles, upon which the aspiring merchant class were encouraged to build. The sequence is illustrated in Figure 4.iv, and the principal mansions shown in Figure 4.iii. Of the early streets, Virginia Street, Buchanan Street, Miller

Street, Dunlop Street, and Maxwell Street were opened along mansion gardens, in whole or in part, often involving demolition of all or part of the house[55]. In this process, as in so many others, the merchants of Glasgow led the way, not only as private proprietors, but as influential members of the town council.

Examination of the progress of new street development between 1750 and 1775 reveals both strong similarities and contrasts in the respective approaches and experiences of public and private developers. Both groups used the services of land surveyors to lay out the plots along their streets, and in fact the majority of plans were produced by one surveyor, James Barrie[56]. Both advertised the new steadings available through newspapers, in which their advertisements made clear the type of building which was preferred[57], and both endured very lengthy delays while their plots were taken up for building, since at this stage there was no question of speculative building ahead of potential purchasers. Perhaps the greatest contrast lay in the specification of building regulations and land use, in the enforcement of which the Council were notably more rigorous than the private developers. Certainly in the early advertisements for Buchanan Street in 1765, 1771 and 1777, the proprietor proposed to "enlarge his entry in Argyll Street opposite St. Enoch Square to 40 feet, free of every incumbrance such as stairs and other projections. This entry will lead into a street running to the northward opening equally on each side, so as to make it a streete of 70 feet in breadth"[58]. This was merely a statement of intention and entitlement, enforcing no regulations upon prospective builders. On the other hand, in the laying out of Jamaica Street, first proposed in 1751, and planned by Barrie 1761[59], explicit and stringent regulations were framed. A street 23 metres broad was to be laid out, at the sides of which proprietors would lay a flagstone pavement two metres broad. Each plot or steading, with a frontage of c.17 metres, and of varying lengths, had to be stobbed or staked out by its proprietor, who had then to lay out his building materials upon it, and not on the street. At the front of his land, he had to build within four years a stone tenement, with a ground and two upper storeys, garretts and a slated roof. No skin, tan, soap or candle works, or any similar nuisances were to be constructed[60], and it was probably for this reason that the petition of J. and G. Buegos, skinners, for a steading in Jamaica Street "with the privilege of the burn", was not taken up[61]. Whether because of the stringency of these regulations or whether simply through lack of demand, there was no immediate rush for the new plots, with only three of the 24 steadings being feued in 1762, a further four in 1763, and thereafter a trickle to 1772[62].

Even slower progress attended the development of Glasgow's first residential square, St. Enoch's Square, planned in 1768, but by 1775 having houses only at its Argyll Street entrance, and therefore having its projected layout distorted by the plans for Howard Street, along its southern side[63]. In the privately developed streets, plots stood empty for long periods. The narrow entry from Argyll Street to Buchanan Street may have inhibited prospective builders with only one house constructed by 1778[64], while Miller Street was considered to be too far out of town, and its first steading was not sold until 1771, nine years after its opening[65], demonstrating clearly that the level of demand for middle-class housing, or at least for plots upon which to build, was rather low. If western developments were slow to appreciate eastern projects were even less successful. Havannah Street, opened in 1755[66], never succeeded in attracting large numbers of merchants and its proximity to the swarming core of the city, and the industries developing along the Molendinar, doomed it to rapid decline, while ambitions for a development to be named St. James' Square, lying south of Gallowgate and east of the Molendinar, came to nothing. Houses built speculatively along the proposed line of the street were simply demolished and their materials sold[67]. The beginnings of spatial disaggregation of society can be seen in these late eighteenth century developments, and with the council purchase of large sections of the Hutcheson estates in Ramshorn and Meadowflats and the planned layout of a grid series of residential streets on a scale larger than anything hitherto attempted[68], the merchant drive to the west began to gather force, while behind it, the movement outward from the old core of mercantile business and small-scale industry, particularly textiles, brought further breaking down of the medieval lifestyle, to be pursued in the next chapter.

Quite apart from their ventures in town planning the council were extending their control over Glasgow's affairs in fields such as street maintenance, water supply, sanitation, and other public utilities. Spiritual welfare of the citizens was safeguarded by the construction of a series of churches, beginning with the Ramshorn church in 1718. The site was chosen to provide a fine architectural terminus for the north of Candleriggs and the records of land purchase from Hutcheson's Hospital incidentally shed light on the activities of the gardeners guild, since the yard acquired had been occupied by them, and cherry and apple trees, gooseberry and currant bushes, kale, leeks and other vegetables grown for the Glasgow market had to be cleared from the new church site[69]. A rising population encouraged the purchase of lands on the east bank of the Molendinar in 1734, and an ambitious project involved site clearance not only for a church, but for access roads, with tenements, brewhouses, stables and middensteads being demolished, two short streets paved, and two bridges built across the stream. All of this was done well in advance of the acceptance of Allan Dreghorn's plan for the beautiful St. Andrew's Church in 1740, and its commencement the following year[70]. Demolition of the Wynd Kirk in 1753 and its replacement in 1760[71] was followed by agreement to build a new church in Jamaica Street in 1767. Whether this was an attempt at amenity provision in order to tempt new settlers to the area is a matter open to conjecture, but no burial ground was to be permitted, so the town council were obviously keeping a canny eye on the worldly business of maintaining good building land as well as providing for the souls of their citizens[72].

They were also active in the central area of the town, pulling down and replacing derelict and decrepit structures, "warning away tennents to flitt", where necessary, and building fine new tenements on land long vacant after fire damage. On the 'burnt lands' of Gallowgate four-storey tenements with stone fronts were built, with shops occupying the ground floor, and 'peatches' or piazzas fronting the shops. In their desire to beautify the central area, the council insisted that private builders must respect existing piazzas when extending their buildings, and even went so far as to pay for pillars and piazzas in new buildings. That they were successful in their endeavours can be seen on a large-scale plan of the area around the Cross, where all four streets are lined with piazzas on both sides[73]. They also undertook the surfacing and lighting of streets, though they tried to encourage a more spacious layout by refusing to causeway any new streets unless they were at least 12 metres in breadth[74]. The problem of market provision for a growing population was tackled by regulations clearly delimiting those portions of the central streets within which stalls could be set up and goods sold[75], and on a larger scale by removal of the town's separate produce markets from their cramped juxtaposition, principally in the Trongate. Vacant land in King Street was used for the beef and mutton markets[76], "justly admired, as being the compleatest of their kind in Britain; the one upon the east . . . is entirely appropriated for butcher meat. Those upon the west side of the street are divided into three different courts, set apart for a fish-market, a mutton-market, and cheese-market"[77]. Land was purchased to ensure ready access from these markets to the new riverside location of the shambles, whose original position in the Trongate produced "disagreeable objects, presented by so nauseous a practice"[78]. These fine and costly buildings, with their pump wells for the washing away of filth and offal[79] went some way towards a more sanitary urban environment, but the scale of nuisance and pollution in the overcrowded town taxed the best efforts of the council.

Keeping the streets clean was virtually impossible, despite strictures on the removal of dunghills or middens from the streets within 48 hours. The contents of byres and stables were raked out on to the roadways, while feuing agreements involving the collection of night soil from closes involved the regular passage of noisome dung-carts. One of the reasons behind the removal of ornamental gates at the entry to Bell's Wynd was the practice of building dunghills and middens behind them, and the emptying of chamber pots from upstairs windows encouraged wariness in the pedestrian[80]. The attractiveness of the Molendinar and Gallowgate burns to industry ensured their rapid demise as clean water supplies. Tanworks, barkmills and dye-works proliferated along them[81], blocking the dams of one another's mill ponds, discharging dyes, bark and other effluents into the streams, and contaminating nearby wells[82]. New wells were dug throughout the period, while existing wells had pumps and covers fitted to them, to be locked and unlocked, night and morning, by an appointed keeper[83]. Water was conveyed in pipes from the Deanside Well to a public fountain, and in a few cases to individual houses[84], and the scale of the problem prompted the formation in 1769 of a committee to consider ways and means of bringing good water into the town. Getting sewage out of the town was also a problem, and any success in this venture

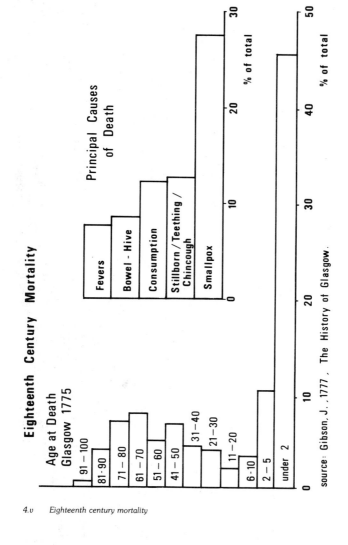

4.v   Eighteenth century mortality

4.i   John McArthur's map of Glasgow, 1778

was balanced by a contribution to the pollution level of local streams and the River Clyde. 'Syres' or sewers were constantly being blocked by middenheaps, straw from barns, and sundry materials piling up behind any obstruction, the sewer's contents thereafter obeying the dictates of gravity and flowing into cellars and ground-floor rooms. Unpalatable these open streams of filth may have been, but any covers tended only to increase the incidence of blockage and were forbidden under pain of severe penalties[86]. The attitude towards sewers was that of a public nuisance, and there was no connection made between foul water and the incidence of disease.

The same lack of awareness extended to the dwelling places of the bulk of the population, in the overcrowded closes of the old town. Contemporary plans[87] show clearly the congestion of ramshackle buildings along the burgage plots, accessible by narrow, overhung passages in which the free flow of open sewers was impeded by exterior stairs, dunghills, middens, byre sweepings and the cast-out by-products of a host of small industries. Into these odorous warrens crammed a rapidly increasing population, almost trebling itself in size between 1708 and 1785, from c.12,000 to c.18,000 by the time of Webster's calculations for the widows' fund in 1743, over 25,000 by the time of his national enumeration in 1755, and over 36,000 by 1785[88]. Overcrowding and poor sanitation may not have been entirely responsible for the appalling level of infant mortality, with over 45% of all deaths in 1775 occurring in the under-two age group, and a further 10% between the ages of two and five[89] (Fig. 4.v), but they certainly contributed to the contagion of the greatest killers, smallpox and consumption, while 'bowel-hive' and 'fevers' might have owed some of their origins to contaminated water[90] (Fig. 4.v). 1775 was not an 'unhealthy year' according to the authors of the Glasgow entry in the Old Statistical Account, and their lists of 1723, 1740, 1741, 1748, 1751 and 1772[91] might indicate the cyclical ravages of exotic diseases propagated under conditions and with effects to become horrifyingly familiar in the next century.

By the close of the Tobacco era, therefore, Glasgow seemed to have emerged fully from its medieval origins to become a thriving trading city and a centre of industry. The symbolic dismantling of the Barras Port, the West Port and the Gallowgate Port[92] and the creation of a series of fine new streets and squares mark the beginnings of a new townscape which would develop to fruition in the nineteenth century, but John McArthur's map of 1778 (Pl. 4.i) was still overwhelmingly dominated by the configurations of previous centuries, and the heavily repleted burgage plots of the old town were to remain a crucial focus of life until another hundred years had elapsed. However ready Glasgow was to leap into the Industrial Age, old patterns and old ways remained upon the palimpsest of the city.

REFERENCES

1. Gibson, J., 1777. *The History of Glasgow*, p.105.
2. Crispin, B., 1962. Clyde Shipping and the American War. *S.H.R.*, 41, pp.126/77.
3. Gibson, J., 1777, *op.cit.*, p.235.
4. Gibson, J., 1777, *op.cit.*, p.207.
5. Gilfillan, J. B. S. and Moisley, H. A., 1958. Industrial and Commercial Developments to 1914, in Miller, R. and Tivy, J. (eds.), 1958. *The Glasgow Region*, p.155.
6. Gibson, J., 1777, *op.cit.*, pp.210/211.
7. Gilfillan, J. B. S. and Moisley, H. A., 1958, *op.cit.*, p.156.
8. Gibson, J., 1777, *op.cit.*, pp.213-234.
9. Campbell, R. H., 1964. An Economic History of Scotland in the Eighteenth Century. *Scottish Journal of Political Economy*, 11.p.18.
10. 'Memorial of the Lord Provost, magistrates and merchants of the city of Glasgow, relating to the duties on Sugar'. Glasgow, 1780.
11. Gibson, J., 1777, *op.cit.*, p.222.
12. O.S.A., V, p.498.
13. Gibson, J., 1777, *op.cit.*, p.212.
14. 'An account of the late proceedings in Parliament relating to the money granted for the relief of the city of Glasgow'. Glasgow, 1749, see also; Smith, J. (ed.) 1836. *The Cochrane Correspondence regarding the Affairs of Glasgow, 1745-46*. Maitland Club.
15. Slaven, A., 1975. *The development of the West of Scotland: 1750-1960*, p.22.
16. Slaven, A., 1975, *op.cit.*, p.23.
17. Scott, A., 1859. Reminiscences of the Glasgow Custom-House. *T.G.A.S.*, I, p.56.
18. Slaven, A., 1975, *op.cit.*, p.24.
19. Stevenson, W. I., 1973. Some aspects of the geography of the Clyde tobacco trade in the eighteenth century. *S.G.M.*, 89, i, p.20 and figs. 1 and 2, pp.21 and 22.
20. Devine, T. M., 1973. Glasgow merchants and the Collapse of the Tobacco Trade, 1775-1783. *S.H.R.*, 52, pp.50-74.
21. Devine, T. M., 1975. *The Tobacco Lords*, p.4.
22. Devine, T. M., 1975, *op.cit.*, pp.22/23.
23. Devine, T. M., 1976. The Colonial Trades and Industrial Investment in Scotland, c.1700-1815. *The Economic History Review*. 2nd series, XXIX, No.1, pp.1-13.
24. Slaven, A., 1975, *op.cit.*, p.85.
25. O.S.A., p.501.
26. Gibson, J., 1777, *op.cit.*, p.248.
27. G.B.R., V, p.490.
28. G.B.R., VI, pp.132, 422, 456.
29. G.B.R., VI, p.355.
30. *Reports by Eminent Engineers on the Improvement of the Navigation on the River Clyde. From 1752 to 1834.* Trustees of the River Clyde and Harbour of Glasgow, 1834, p.1.
31. G.B.R., VI, pp.501, 502, 510, 521/2, 545; VII, pp.47, 48, 49.
32. G.B.R., VII, p.186.
33. *Reports by Eminent Engineers*, etc., 1834, *op.cit.*, p.3. G.B.R., VII, p.284.
34. Pagan, J., 1847, *op.cit.*, p.97. G.B.R. VII, p.285.
35. G.B.R., VII, p.389.
36. *Reports by Eminent Engineers*, etc., 1834, p.8.
37. Pagan, J., 1847, *op.cit.*, p.99.
38. G.B.R., IV, pp.678/9; V, pp.136, 414.
39. G.B.R., V, p.461/2; VI, pp.59, 70.
40. G.B.R., VII, pp.251/2, 348.
41. G.B.R., V, p.205; VI, pp.145; VII, 239.
42. G.B.R., IV, pp.429, 494. Stevenson, W. I., 1973, *op.cit.*, p.24.
43. G.B.R., VI, p.78.
44. G.B.R., V, p.208; VI, pp.524, 531; VII, p.72. McIntyre, D. M., 1921. The Port and its Development. *S.G.M.*, 37, i, p.43. Kinniburgh, I. A. G., 1960. John Ainslie's map of Port Glasgow in 1806. *S.G.M.*, 76, i, p.24.
45. Stevenson, W. I., 1973, *op.cit.*, p.24. *Reports by Eminent Engineers*, etc., 1834, *op.cit.*, p.3.

46. G.B.R., IV, pp.429, 526/7; VI, pp.13, 127, 145.
47. Kinniburgh, I. A. G., 1960. Greenock: Growth and change in the harbours of the town. *S.G.M.*, 76, 2, p.90. Stevenson, W. I., 1973, *op.cit.*, p.24.
48. G.B.R., IV, p.467.
49. G.B.R., V, p.419.
50. G.B.R., V, pp.81/2, 101, 106.
51. G.B.R., V, p.130.
52. G.B.R., V, pp.138/9, 168/9, 199.
53. McUre, J., 1736, *op.cit.*, p.131.
54. G.B.R., V, pp.419, 429, 450, 453, 475; VI, p.408.
55. Baird, A., 1899. House Nos.26-32. Buchanan Street. *Regality Club*, 3rd series, p.117. Brown, J. T. T., 1893. St. Enoch Square. *Regality Club*. 2nd series, p.134 (Miller Street). Donald, C. D., 1893. The Dunlop Mansion. *Regality Club*. 2nd series, pp.137-8 (Dunlop Street). Dunlop, C. D., 1883. Grahamston. *T.G.A.S.*, 2, p.144 (Miller Street). Mitchell, J. O., 1889. (a) The Dreghorn Mansion. *Regality Club*. 1st series, pp.54-73 (gives details of location of 15 mansions and processes of formation of various streets). Mitchell, J. O., 1889. (b) The Crawford Mansion. *Regality Club*. 1st series, p.113 (Queen Street). Muir, J., 1889. House No.71 Queen Street. *Regality Club*. 1st series, pp.87-96. Young, G. B., 1908. History of Buchanan Street and some of its proprietors. *Old Glasgow Club Transactions*, I, pp.210-212.
56. G.B.R., VII, p.77. Muir, J., 1889, *op.cit.*, p.90.
57. G.B.R., VII, p.77. Young, G. B., 1908, *op.cit.*, p.211.
58. Young, G. B., 1908, *op.cit.*, p.211.
59. MacGeorge, A., 1880. *Old Glasgow: the Place and the People*, p.157. G.B.R., VII, p.77.
60. G.B.R., VII, pp.20, 76/7, 98, 100, 102, 102/3.
61. G.B.R., VII, p.97.
62. G.B.R., VII, pp.98, 102/3, 111, 117/118, 129, 169, 210/211, 256, 263, 362.
63. G.B.R., VII, pp.277/278, 333/334, 401. Brown, J. T. T., 1893, *op.cit.*, p.133.
64. Young, G. B., 1908, *op.cit.*, p.211.
65. Dunlop, C. D., 1893, *op.cit.*, p.144.
66. G.B.R., VII, p.141.
67. Black, W. G., 1912. David Dale's House in Charlotte Street. *Regality Club*. 4th series, p.97.
68. G.B.R., VII, pp.378/379.
69. G.B.R., V, p.32.
70. G.B.R., V, pp.419, 429, 450; VI, pp.62, 72, 98.
71. G.B.R., VI, p.366; VII, p.14.
72. G.B.R., VII, pp.242/3, 245.
73. G.B.R., IV, p.497; V, pp.3/4, 6-9, 456, 459; VI, p.343/4. Barrie, J., 1776. Plan of junction of High Street, Saltmarket, Gallowgate and Trongate. Scottish Record Office (S.R.O.). R.H.P. 649.
74. G.B.R., VII, pp.24, 331, 345, 397, 398, 403.
75. G.B.R., V, p.235.
76. G.B.R., VI, pp.160, 362, 365/366.
77. Gibson, J., 1777, *op.cit.*, pp.149-150.
78. G.B.R., VI, p.366. Sinclair, J. (ed.), 1793. *The Statistical Account of Scotland*, (henceforth 'O.S.A.'), Vol.5, p.515.
79. Gibson, J., 1777, *op.cit.*, p.150. Brown, A. 1813. *Account of the Public Buildings in the City of Glasgow, barony and lordship of Gorbals, with the cost of each, 1756-1813.*
80. G.B.R., IV, pp.582, 628; VI, p.373.
81. Fleming, W., 1752. Plan of part of the City of Glasgow (shows the location and range of industrial establishments along the Molendinar).
82. G.B.R., V, pp.362, 372, 373, 388, 419; VI, pp.8, 31, 62.
83. G.B.R., IV, pp.543/4; V, pp.88, 323, 333.
84. G.B.R., V, p.419; VII, p.379. Marwick, J. D., 1910. *The Water Supply of Glasgow*, pp.45/46.
85. G.B.R., VII, p.308.
86. G.B.R., IV, pp.439, 484, 452; V, pp.12, 28; VI, pp.59, 81.
87. Plan of buildings on the North side of Trongate c.1770. S.R.O. R.H.P. 651. Plan of property adjacent to Jafrey's Close on the east side of Stockwell Street c.1770 S.R.O. R.H.P. 650/1.

88. O.S.A., 1793, *op.cit.*, pp.509-511.
89. Gibson, J., 1777, *op.cit.*, p.125.
90. Gibson, J., 1777, *op.cit.*, p.125.
91. O.S.A., 1793, *op.cit.*, p.511.
92. G.B.R., V, p.128; VI, pp.331, 386.

5. THE AGE OF COTTON: 1776~1841

The outbreak of the American War of Independence interrupted tobacco supplies to Scotland, and their disappearance with the continuation of hostilities dealt a blow to the economy of Glasgow. Prudent stockpiling of supplies in West of Scotland warehouses served to cushion the shortfall in imports at first, but the end of the trade was imminent, and it was never to recover its lost status. The result of this demise was apparent less in disruption of local industry, since tobacco processing was extremely limited in scale, than in change of emphasis in products, markets, and sources of supply. Re-exportation of goods continued to be a dominant feature of Glasgow's trade, and connections with existing outlets were intensified, with tobacco being replaced by linen and cotton textiles, sugar, coal, fish and chemicals in the European and Russian markets after the end of the American war in 1783. After 1800, West of Scotland merchants ventured farther afield, opening up markets in, and drawing raw materials from, South America, the Far East, and Australasia, following the example of James Finlay and Co. who sent a ship to Calcutta in 1816, being the first vessel cleared out of a Scottish port direct for the East Indies[1]. Thereafter names such as Pernambuco, Bahia, Valparaiso, Lima, Bombay, Madras, Batavia, and Singapore appeared regularly in consignment manifests[2], and the volume of raw and processed materials passing through the Clyde increased dramatically. In the early decades of the nineteenth century Customs duties collected at Glasgow increased from c.£3,000 in 1772, to over £40,000 by 1825, c.£270,000 by 1835, and over £630,000 by 1847[3]. Individual firms, specialising in exotic products, grew to huge enterprises, such as Pollock, Gilmour and Company, by the 1840s the largest timber importing business in the world, drawing a rich range of softwoods and hardwoods from temperate and tropical forests across the globe[4]. While the range of products increased, the pattern of the previous era re-asserted itself, with a single item attaining overwhelming dominance. The sugar, rum and logwoods of the West Indies still flowed through the Clyde, but cotton, amounting to only 503 bags in 1775, had risen to over 12 million lbs. imported by 1807[5], and its processing and manufacture were to dominate the economy of the West of Scotland until the 1860s. Cotton ushered in the textile phase of the Industrial Revolution and transformed the urban and peri-urban landscape with its mills, factories, bleachfields, printworks and workers' tenements, while raw materials and finished products were transported along arterial links of river, canal and railway, giving articulation to the industrial economy.

River, canals and railways

By the end of the eighteenth century, the Clyde had been the focus of numerous attempts at improvement, some more successful than others, and from c.1800 onwards the twin spurs of mercantile opportunity and industrial demand goaded the Clyde Navigation Trustees to greater efforts. Golborne's system of jetties had contained the flow and increased the scour of the river, but complaints from landowners and others about damage to their property and livelihood illustrated a major defect. While the lands of Whiteinch and Elderslie were diminished by scour induced by jetties on the opposite bank, a newly built-up sandbank at the mouth of Inchinnan Water made passage to Paisley very difficult[6]. Thus material eroded at one point, successfully clearing the channel, was simply being deposited at another, causing obstruction. This consideration may have prompted John Rennie to suggest parallel dykes linking the jetty ends[7], providing a streamlined flow endorsed by Thomas Telford in his 1806 report[8] in which he emphasised the need for bringing a greater volume of tide-water upstream. Gradual widening of the river downstream from the Broomielaw, together with the use of piles, and blocks of whinstone rubble to secure the banks aided the swifter flow of tidal waters up to Glasgow, thus not only scouring the channel, but permitting the more rapid passage of deep-draught vessels[9]. A series of plans by Thomas Kyle shows the changing course of the Clyde, as it was eased into a series of gentle curves between walled banks, and as its upstream width was progressively reduced[10]. Even with deeper water in a greatly improved channel, the narrow 'canal' form of the river, together with wind obstruction caused by shelter belts of trees and houses, made it difficult for ships to sail the upper reaches, and horse tracking paths, or towpaths, advocated in Telford's 1806 and subsequent reports, can be seen clearly on later maps[11]. This adoption of canal technique, in an era of feverish canal activity, together with the slow rate of progress of river improvement, may have stimulated the project of a canal from Bowling Bay to the Broomielaw, designed to permit heavy vessels engaged in foreign trade to bypass the difficult stretch of the river and reach a set of docks above the Broomielaw, connected to it by locks. Opposition to the scheme was based on the fact that major efforts of civil engineering, such as building an aqueduct over the River Kelvin, would have made the canal too costly, while in an era of increasing steamboat activity, the canal could only take sailing vessels[12].

Downstream of the Broomielaw, therefore, activity remained concentrated on the river, while within the city itself, the creation of dock and wharfage facilities received attention. Although Telford and Rennie disagreed on its position, both were adamant on the subject of a proper wet-dock for vessels, rather than a simple extension of quay frontage[13]. However, despite these and further recommendations, cost dictated quay extension, to the west along the Anderston frontage by 1814, then further downstream by 1831, adding c.600 metres to the Broomielaw[14]. Significant improvement though this was, the greatly increased traffic on the river swamped it. In 1834, c.27,000 vessels passed Renfrew Ferry, and at some periods in the year between 20 and 30 passed in one hour[15]. It was not uncommon for vessels to wait five or six days before obtaining an inside quay berth for unloading, and although some cargoes could be discharged from outside berths, there was always a considerable extra expense involved, while vessels in the coal trade had always to wait for an inside berth. In winter and spring, the harbour became so crowded that vessels had to lie alongside each other in tiers of five or six, or even seven and eight, constantly shifting and re-mooring at tide-times, while coal wagons, grain carts and other vehicles piled up along the quays[16]. Obviously improved facilities were urgently needed, and calculating eyes were turned on all possible open spaces, including Glasgow Green. In 1834 it was proposed to reduce cartage costs and congestion by the creation of new wharfage at the Green, reached by a canal 30 metres wide, running parallel to, and just above, a narrowed River Clyde. Behind the wharves, docks of any shape or size could be built, while warehouses would parallel the canal[17]. These imaginative proposals, creating a new harbour complex close to areas of industrial production in the east end of the city, met with the approval of industrialists and merchants, but received no official support. By 1840, despite numerous proposals for the cutting of wet docks at Anderston, Lancefield and Windmillcroft, the harbour consisted of c.1000 metres of quay on the north side, and c.400 metres on the south[18]. Opinion had hardened on Windmillcroft as the best site for a wet-dock, but although the 1840 Navigation Act empowered its construction, and contemporary maps showed the outline of a 'Proposed Dock', or 'Contemplated Wet-Dock'[19], part of the site was used to widen the river to match its upstream breadth, and a new length of quay was built along its frontage[20]. Navigation upstream of the Broomielaw was also a contentious issue, and from the 1820s interested groups, with support from Telford, stressed the need to deepen the shallows at Dalmarnock ford and provide a navigable channel as far east as Clyde Ironworks. The quantities of coal shipped at the Broomielaw were considerable, with 40,000 tons per annum required as fuel for steamboats alone, without considering exports for domestic and industrial use. Since the Monkland fields were just opening up, and the greatest number of existing collieries lay to the south and east of the city, navigation on this upper stretch would obviate the necessity of convoys of coal carts negotiating their slow way through congested streets, and would have a beneficial effect on the price and regular supply of coal[21]. As with other seemingly logical projects, nothing was done, not only because developing canal and railway transport with their vested interests negated support, but because of other complicating factors, including negotiations over property rights, and varying perceptions of the potential market. However, the effects of channel and harbour improvements can be seen in the changing scale and composition of shipping in Glasgow. In 1810, only four foreign vessels, averaging less than 100 tons, reached the Broomielaw, whereas in 1834, 89 foreign vessels of which 49 were over 100 tons, unloaded in the harbour[22]. Inclusive of foreign ships, the total number and aggregate tonnage of vessels arriving at Glasgow increased dramatically in the early decades of the nineteenth century (Table 5.i), while the number of steamboats rose to 59 in 1820, and 71 in 1841. These vessels made regular sailings with goods and passengers within the Firth of Clyde and up the west coast of Scotland, across to Ireland, and south to Liverpool, which run engaged the largest vessels, some of over 400 tons[23]. Table 5.ii shows the rise in number and tonnage of Glasgow-registered ships.

Table 5.i.   **Arrivals at Glasgow, 1796-1823. Numbers and tonnage**

Tons	1796	1806	1810	1816	1821	1823
Under 60	1,209	1,228	1,279	1,994	2,969	2,608
60-80	117	394	633	672	1,016	873
80-100	—	49	99	176	264	204
Over 100	—	7	10	19	103	252
Total tonnage	55,980	80,683	101,316	115,008	199,482	190,507

Source: Letter to Thomas Telford, 1824. *Clyde Reports*, p.15.

Table 5.ii. Ships registered at Glasgow 1810-1840. Number and tonnage

	Number	Tons	Average tonnage
1810	24	1,956	81.5
1815	59	4,829	81.8
1820	77	6,131	79.6
1825	111	14,084	126.8
1830	217	39,432	181.7
1835	297	54,335	182.9
1840	403	185,707	460.8

Source: after Marwick, J. D., 1909. *The River Clyde and the Clyde Burghs*. Appendix II, p.237.

The steady industrialisation of Glasgow and the West of Scotland brought demands for the transport of raw materials and finished products which overwhelmed the capabilities of a poor road system and the slow process of river improvement. As elsewhere in Britain, the construction of a series of navigable cuts or canals was seen as a potential solution, though as in the case of river improvements, schemes attracted both supporters and detractors, principally mercantile-industrial interests against landowners. In 1763, the Board of Trustees for Encouragement of Fisheries, Manufactures and Improvements in Scotland, a body dominated by landowners, requested John Smeaton to survey two possible routes to link the Forth and Clyde rivers. Landowners in the Lothians and Stirlingshire preferred the longer route by Stirling, the upper Forth, the River Endrick to Loch Lomond, and the River Leven to the Clyde, while the 'Glasgow' group of merchants and manufacturers supported a more direct cut through Dullatur Bog, although they asked James Watt to survey an amended route, terminating at Glasgow rather than Dalmuir[24]. Within the landowning group, attitudes ranged from those who foresaw loss in income through national equalisation of grain prices, with the north-eastern counties gaining access to the growing south-western market[25], to the powerful Dundas family who would gain financially from having the eastern terminal on their estates[26]. Within the latter group also, were individuals like Robert Dreghorn, a prominent Glasgow merchant, who stood to gain considerably both through his mercantile interests, and through the disposition of portions of his Ruchill and Dalmuir estates to the canal company[27]. This division of interest acted in favour of the Glasgow group, and the Act of Parliament of 1768 authorised and initiated excavation of the canal along the more direct route, though terminating at Dalmuir Burn rather than Glasgow. By 1777 navigation was possible from the Forth to Stockingfield, near Maryhill, and instead of proceeding to the Clyde, a branch had been dug to Hamiltonhill, where a large basin was excavated, and granaries and other buildings erected. Lack of money halted work until the mid-1780s, when a loan from the Forfeited Estates Commissioners financed extension to a new western terminus at Bowling, rather than Dalmuir, and the Hamiltonhill basin having been found inadequate, eight acres of ground were purchased, c.800 metres north of the city of Glasgow at Hundred Acre Hill, where a barge basin and a timber basin were excavated, and more granaries built, precursors of a new village, to be called Port Dundas[28]. In 1790, an Act of Parliament authorised a junction between the Forth and Clyde, and Monkland canals, and its strategic location at this junction, as well as in close proximity to a rapidly growing city made Port Dundas exceptional among canal junction settlements in the scale and range of industries attracted to it[29]. Traffic on the Forth and Clyde developed rapidly, chiefly in grain and timber at first, with carriers' carts simply being loaded on to the boats, then in commodities such as coke, of which over 2,000 tons per year were being sent to the Glasgow market by 1839, and semi-finished iron, sent from the Carron Works near Falkirk to the Phoenix works at Port Dundas. Passenger numbers also rose swiftly, with an estimated 23,000 per year embarking at Kirkintilloch alone by the 1830s[30]. From the beginning, there was a conjunction of interest between the canal and the city, with a committee of council set up in 1789 to co-operate in "laying off proper and commodious streets and communications between the city and the intended canal basin at Hundred Acre Hill", initiating urban development to the north of the westward-expanding Georgian suburbs[31], and creating a linear zone of iron foundries, breweries, distilleries, chemical and dye works as an important segment of the city's growing industrial base (Fig. 5.i).

The Act of Parliament which authorised and initiated work on the Monkland canal stipulated among its provisions that the canal would reduce the price of pit coal and provide relief for the poor[32]. The list of subscribers appended to the Act demonstrates the high level of interest in Glasgow with 24 Glasgow merchants subscribing as individuals, together with later subscriptions from the Town Council, the University, the Trades House, and the Guilds of Maltmen, Fleshers, Bakers, Wrights and Masons. The Town Council at first wanted a guaranteed supply of coal to be written into the agreement, then settled for a £5,000 subscription by every landowner along the line of canal, including Robert Dreghorn of Ruchill, already involved in the Forth and Clyde scheme[33]. Financial difficulties made the canal less successful than had been hoped, and its shares were sold off by public auction in 1781. Glasgow bought some of them, but during the decade, the total issue was acquired by the Stirling brothers, merchants in Glasgow, who transformed the venture into a great success, especially after persuading the Forth and Clyde company to form a junction with their canal[34]. Between 1822 and 1827, 18 Lanarkshire collieries sent c.174,000 tons of coal to Glasgow each year[35], while by 1831, the figure had risen to over 200,000 tons, together with 9,000 tons of iron for Glasgow's foundries, and 25,000 passengers, and although the canal had reduced its rates by one-third, in the face of railway competition, its revenues were thriving[36]. However, 1840 was a turning-point, with a peak in disposable surplus of £5,070, which dropped to a deficit of £2,767 in 1842, and thereafter remained in deficit until the company was sold to the Forth and Clyde company in 1846[37]. The role of the canal in creating the eastern portion of the linear zone of industry previously mentioned is clearly demonstrated by a plan of 1836, showing the St. Rollox Chemical Works and St. Rollox Foundry Company buildings aligned to the canal and its branch through the chemical works[38], while in open country to the east, its docks, basins and graving dock at Blochairn were beginning to act as a nucleus of industrial attraction in 1829[39].

Less successful than either of its fore-runners was the Glasgow, Paisley and Ardrossan canal, first proposed in 1791, but not surveyed by Telford until 1805, when he proposed a route commencing in a brickfield on the south side of Glasgow, suitable for laying out basins and wharves, and ideally suited to direct communication with the city[40]. The western terminal would be a new harbour with wet and graving docks, to be built at Ardrossan. According to the Subscription Paper, "A well-grounded hope may be entertained that Ardrossan will become to Glasgow what Liverpool has long been to Manchester", giving some indication of the contemporary perception of the low potential of the Clyde. Telford proposed branches to Hurlet Alum Works, Kilmarnock and central Ayrshire, and an extension up the south bank of the Clyde past Rutherglen to Clyde Iron Works, to tap the coal and iron resources of Lanarkshire, and the authorising Act of Parliament of 1806[41] outlined the benefits of using the canal to supply Ireland with coal in return for grain. Glasgow was not slow to perceive the potential benefits of the scheme, advancing 20 guineas for the initial survey, supporting the Earl of Eglinton's Bill, and subscribing £1,000 to the venture[42]. Excavation was begun in 1807, but undersubscription and rising costs meant that the canal was only finished between Glasgow and Johnstone. However, the line with Paisley provided regular passenger demand, with light iron boats carrying 307,275 passengers in 1834, and 423,186 in 1836[43]. An early feuing plan of 1834 shows the canal running south of the proposed villas and gardens of Dumbreck, and advertises a Light Passage Boat every hour[44]. The Glasgow terminus, Port Eglinton, became the nucleus of an industrial zone, on a smaller scale than that of Port Dundas, but containing its own important specialised functions, such as William Dixon's coal depot, supplied by his local collieries, shipping coals to Paisley as well as supplying numerous steamboats, foundries, bottle-works, gas companies and bakeries, many of which had depots or operated in the area[45].

The latest of the canal schemes affecting Glasgow was the Edinburgh-Glasgow, or Union canal, designed to effect a junction with the Forth and Clyde canal at Lock 16, near Falkirk. The attractions of an increased supply of coal, a reduction in Glasgow's high grain prices brought about by cheaper transport of Lothian grain, and a market in Edinburgh for Glasgow's sugar, together with a promised increase in Glasgow's Forth and Clyde stock value, prompted the council to subscribe £500 to the plan[46], while 51 Glasgow individuals, merchants and writers being most numerous, became proprietors[47]. This was a successful venture, not least because of the awareness of the committee of management of the need to actively encourage industrial location along the line of canal by permitting the use of water for processing, and to co-operate rather than compete with the new railways[48]. A special sub-committee was set up to review communications between the line of canal and other public undertakings, such as the Glasgow and Garnkirk Railway and the Ballochney Railway[49], and successful co-operation ensured the swift movement of passengers between Glasgow and Edinburgh. The joint efforts of the Forth and Clyde, Paisley, and Monkland Canals brought 655,000 passengers in and out of Glasgow in 1836, together with the bulk of the c.500,000 tons of coal, and a broad range of vital supplies needed by the fast-growing city[50].

By the 1830s, however, the shadow of railway competition was beginning to fall over the canals. Horsedrawn mineral lines operating along plateways rather than proper railways had been known from the 1750s at Knightswood and Govan, taking coal to the Clyde, and the earliest transitional and proper railways of the nineteenth century were simply conceived as mineral lines at first, with some subsidiary passenger carriage later. Perhaps because of a commitment to canal transport, Glasgow town council averred to "have no interest or concern" in a proposal from Greenock magistrates in 1802 about a Glasgow-Paisley-Greenock railway, yet seven years later, felt able to subscribe 30 guineas to survey a route from the Monkland Canal to Berwick-on-Tweed[51]. Such ambivalence may have reflected the changing relative influence of landowners, many of whom opposed railway intrusion to their estates, preferring especially where in close proximity to the city, to see them developed as middle-class villa suburbs, and industrialists, who quickly perceived the advantages of mineral link lines, connecting with river and canals. These linkages were epitomised by the 1824 Monkland and Kirkintilloch, and 1831 Glasgow and Garnkirk Railways, forming junctions with the Monkland, and Forth and Clyde canals, and the mineral lines of Lanarkshire such as the Ballochney, and Wishaw and Coltness lines[52]. The horse-drawn Monkland-Kirkintilloch line was a canal feeder, delivering 49,000 tons of coal and 3,325 tons of pig-iron to the Forth and Clyde in 1835 for the fuel-hungry city of Glasgow[53], where proprietors of cotton mills and factories, and owners of steam boats clamoured support for any scheme which would reduce the price of coals[54]. An Act of Parliament of 1830 permitted a line from collieries in Pollok and Govan to run to the Broomielaw, with a branch to the Glasgow-Ardrossan canal, affording not only exporting facilities for coal and other minerals, but a junction between canal and river[55]. The Glasgow-Garnkirk line, from St. Rollox to Gartsherrie, was opened in 1831 in competition with the Monkland canal, inaugurating a new set of transport relationships which were to end with triumphant railways absorbing moribund canals. The low freight rates on this line greatly reduced the price of coal in Glasgow, as well as taking valuable passenger traffic from the Monkland canal. To compete with a twice-daily canal boat, the railway ran four passenger-carrying trains per day from Glasgow to Airdrie, carrying 118,882 passengers in 1834, and 146,296 in 1836[56].

This emphasis on passengers characterised the two other railway lines whose opening occurred within the period under consideration, but a much more ambitious scale of operations was their dominant feature. The Glasgow, Paisley, Kilmarnock and Ayr Railway (Glasgow and Ayrshire Railway, 1841), was first proposed in 1830, and the Greenock Railway Company having applied for an authorising Act at the same time, the companies agreed to share the expense of a joint line from Glasgow to Paisley. Operations commenced in May 1838 on a large scale, with 1,400 men employed on one half-mile stretch of the Elderslie cut, and the Glasgow-Paisley section opening in July 1840. From August to December of that year, 165,689 passengers travelled on the Ayr line, with 247,849 on the joint line, greatly exceeding predicted demand[57]. Goods traffic was slow to develop because of slow completion of the main freight-handling facilities, but the small station in Bridge Street, Tradeston had a goods station under its arches, to which waggons were lowered on a platform operated by a small steam engine to waiting carts for trans-shipment[58]. The Edinburgh-Glasgow line was a response to the growing demand for swifter passenger transport between the two cities, obviating the time-consuming Union, and Forth and Clyde canal journeys and changes of vehicle, which even using link railway lines, could take seven hours. The intrusion of this line directly into the heart of the city, with the acquisiton of mansion property on the north side of George Square, can be seen clearly on Martin's 1842 map[59], and signifies the beginning of another phase of railway development, to be examined in the next chapter, when the railways became active agents in the transformation of the townscape.

Industry and the townscape

Scotland's share in the proceeds of colonial expansion included the export markets upon which her growth industries came to depend as much as they relied upon these same areas for cheap and plentiful raw materials, especially cotton, and cheap food to make up for the deficiencies of local agricultural production, lagging far behind population increase. Less money spent on food meant a surplus purchasing power, creating internal demand which further stimulated the production of industrial goods. At the same time, the production of cotton textiles, chemicals, and latterly iron products, went through a series of technological changes which brought about concentration, and especially in the case of textiles, a reliance on the production of coarse, mass-produced fabrics. This move away from specialist, quality production into more competitive, general fields had ominous undertones from which many hard lessons were to be learnt[60]. In the first phase of textile production, "cotton mills, bleachfields, and printfields ... (were) ... erected on almost all the streams in the neighbourhood"[61], but production remained low until the application of steam power transformed the mechanics of the industry and permitted city locations, such as that of Houldsworth's cotton mill, built in Cheapside Street in Anderston in 1804-5, using steam not only to drive the machines, but conveying it upwards through the hollow iron structural columns of the multi-storey factory to provide central heating[62]. By 1831, there were 41 mills, employing over 1,000 spinners, in Glasgow and its immediate suburbs[63], and a nineteenth-century historian could claim that "Glasgow has all along been the centre of the trade, and nearly the whole of the cotton goods manufactured in Scotland are made by or for firms having their headquarters in that city"[64].

Production of dyestuffs and chemicals for cloth processing was intimately connected with the textile industry, and the beginnings of cudbear production in 1777, and Turkey Red dye in 1785, led to a range of specialisms, such as the patent bleaching liquor of Charles Tennant, whose St. Rollox chemical works were the largest in Europe by the 1840s[65]. Also ancillary to textile manufacture was the fabrication of the necessary machinery, including steam-engines. By 1825, there were 310 steam-engines in and around the city, mainly in textile works, but also in coalmines, quarries, ironworks, and boats[66], and by 1840 there were 14 firms making steam-engines or mill machinery, three of them employing over 1,000 people[67]. Henry Bell's successful 'Comet' introduced the steam engine to water-borne transport in 1812, and although by 1830, only c.5,000 tons of steam shipping had been built on the Clyde, thereafter tonnage increased rapidly, with early orders coming from lines such as the East India Company[67]. Pioneering marine engineers such as Tod and McGregor and the Napier brothers, linked the demand for shipping with the new technology of iron-founding, whereby the 'hot blast' of J. B. Neilson, erstwhile engineer of the Glasgow Gas Works, enabled the splint coal of Lanarkshire to be used uncoked to reduce the rich local blackband iron ores in massive quantities[69]. With availability of plate iron in quantity, Tod and McGregor built the first sea-going iron steamers, the 'Royal Sovereign' and the 'Royal George' in 1838, followed by Robert Napier's first iron vessel, built at Govan in 1842, sowing the first seeds of a growth whose rise to fruition must be followed in subsequent chapters.

A comparison of the location and range of industry within the city between 1807 and 1842 (Fig. 5.i) shows not only its rapid growth, but its effect in extending and transforming the townscape, in which four principal concentrations of industry may be discerned. In the east end of Glasgow, the development of suburban weaving villages at Calton and Bridgeton encouraged the aggregation of a work-force skilled in textile production, and the rapid growth of the cotton industry saw the establishment of a large number of spinning and weaving factories, rising from c.12 in 1807, to c.46 in 1842. The location of these works on greenfield sites indicates the way in which industry led the outward growth of the built-up area, with the laying-out of streets and erection of workers' dwellings quickly following the establishment of factories. Chemical and dye-works, producing processing agents for the textile industry, with some foundries, potteries, breweries and distilleries contributed to a landscape of mixed uses, dominated by industry and its infrastructure. On the northern edge of the city, the loops of the Forth and Clyde/Monkland canal, with the possibilities of bulk transport and water for processing, attracted a nucleus of industrial establishments to Port Dundas, where iron foundries and glassworks vied with chemicals for location, the latter group being dominated by Tennant's enormous works a little further to the east along the canal. As in the east end, rapid development of streets and housing followed industrial creation. A third concentration of industry developed on the north bank of the Clyde, west of the Broomielaw, where the weaving village of Anderston acted as the focus for a range of textile works and potteries, but where iron foundries and engineering establishments rapidly became dominant. On the south side of the river, in Hutchesontown and Tradeston a zone of mixed industrial enterprises developed, once again leading the wave-front of urban growth by setting up on open sites. Lying just beyond the continuously built-up area, though destined to be incorporated by its spread, lay Port Eglinton, with Glasgow's largest carpet factory, employing 600 hands in 1837, and the huge ironworks of William Dixon, still building. Brick and tile works and neighbouring collieries used the canal, and eventually the network of railways, for transport[70]. Further to the west

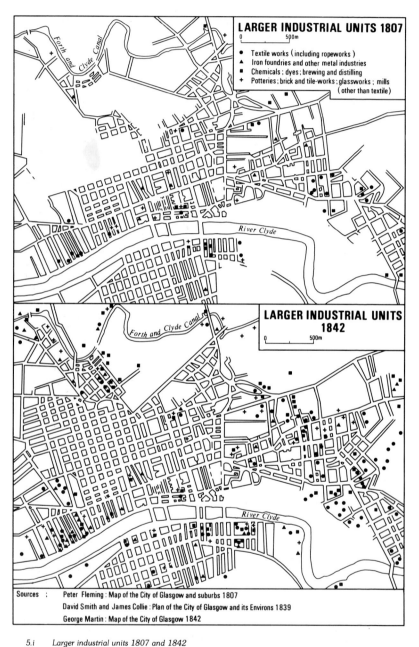

LARGER INDUSTRIAL UNITS 1807

0   500m

- ● Textile works (including ropeworks)
- ▲ Iron foundries and other metal industries
- ■ Chemicals; dyes; brewing and distilling
- + Potteries; brick and tile-works; glassworks; mills
      (other than textile)

Forth and Clyde Canal

River Clyde

LARGER INDUSTRIAL UNITS 1842

0   500m

Forth and Clyde Canal

River Clyde

Sources :   Peter Fleming : Map of the City of Glasgow and suburbs 1807
              David Smith and James Collie : Plan of the City of Glasgow and its Environs 1839
              George Martin : Map of the City of Glasgow 1842

5.i   *Larger industrial units 1807 and 1842*

around the riverside village of Govan, textile processing, dye-making and the beginnings of marine engineering were creating another industrial nexus destined to contribute heavily to Glasgow's future[71].

While rapid industrialisation led the outward growth of the city's margins, industry was also involved in a process of internal colonisation in the built-up area. Residual industrial units, such as the tanneries and dye-works located by the Molendinar Burn, and the ropeworks and small breweries of the city centre continued to function, but in addition to these, the growth of the textile industry, and its cotton sector in particular, brought a proliferation of small industrial units to the central area. Textile growth did not simply take the form of numerical expansion of manufacturing, finishing and dealing firms, but, as contemporary trade directories show, involved a growing sophistication at all levels. The first Glasgow directory, published in 1783[72], lists c.19 categories of occupation connected with the textile industry, from comb- and shuttle-makers, through thread manufacturers, lawn and cambric manufacturers, linen printers and dyers, to cotton dealers and yarn merchants, while individual concerns often operate in more than one category, such as 'thread manufacturers and bleachers', or 'manufacturers and drapers'. By 1820, the number of categories had increased to 29, with less occupational overlap, and greater specialisation appearing in such occupations as print block cutters, shuttle, loom and warping mill makers, and cotton yarn twisters[73], while by 1840, 53 categories included weavers' utensil makers, embroiderers, starchers, cotton waste dealers, and wadding manufacturers[74], indicating the growth of interlocking functions. Growth in the number of firms brought increasing demand for central locations which the crowded tenements and backlands of the old city core could no longer supply, and at the same time, the laying out of new streets and squares to house the middle classes accelerated their westward migration, making available for colonisation premises in the eighteenth century streets contiguous with the medieval town. Fig. 5.ii demonstrates clearly the way in which all sectors of the textile industry, but especially the manufacturing sector, took advantage of this opportunity. By 1820, over 270 concerns, of which 218, or over 80%, were involved in the manufacture of threads, yarns, and a wide range of textiles, had invaded streets opened as select residential enclaves only a few decades before. Internal subdivision of properties brought as many as eight manufacturers to one building, while in others, manufacturers, finishers and dealers virtually eliminated transport costs by the propinquity of their location, laying the foundations of a garment and warehousing district persisting to the present day. The links between manufacturing and wholesaling of textiles on the one hand, and retailing on the other, were established by firms such as J. & W. Campbell and Company, who built premises for themselves in Candleriggs Street in 1823, selling both wholesale and retail their own and other manufactured textiles, building a turnover of £156,000 in 1824 to £423,000 in 1834[75], and thereby encouraging the growth of numerous similar establishments in the area.

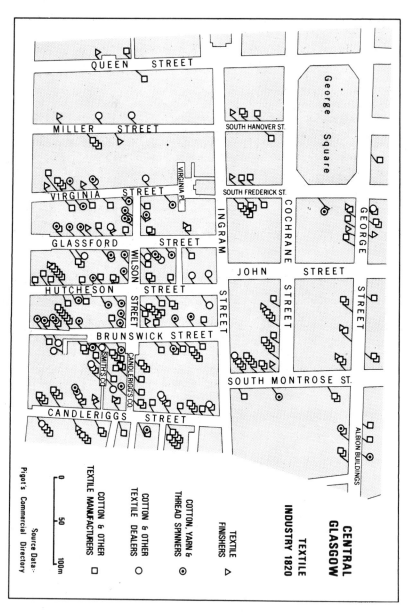

5.ii   Central Glasgow: textile industry 1820

Georgian and Regency residential developments

While industry spearheaded the outward growth of the built-up area in some sectors, the combined efforts of landowners and building speculators, the latter operating as individuals or as members of joint-stock companies, brought about residential expansion to the west and south, on a much larger scale than anything previously attempted. Between 1779 and 1815, no fewer than 48 new streets were opened on the north side of the Clyde[76], even before the main phase of feuing of the Blythswood estates, between 1823 and 1837, and that of Laurieston on the south side, where the principal period of activity was from 1818-21[77], though neighbouring Tradeston and Hutchesontown had been slowly developing from the 1790s. The key to this rapid and extensive expansion was the release on to the land market of large acreages previously held in trust, or as private estates, but whose position contiguous, or close to an expanding town offered the possibility of considerably increased revenue from house building.

Hutcheson's Hospital held the lands of Ramshorn and Meadowflats, which lay mainly on the Post-Glacial Marine Terrace to the west of the medieval town (Fig. 5.iii), while further west again lay the estate of Campbell of Blythswood. South of the river, the Town Council, the Trades House, and Hutcheson's Hospital jointly owned a broad swathe of land stretching from Windmill Croft in the west to St. Ninian's Croft in the east, and it was the disposal of all of these units which initiated large-scale expansion. In 1772, the Ramshorn and Meadowflat lands were bought by the Town Council (*ibid.* p.74) who immediately advertised them for resale. Smaller portions, including the grounds of the Hospital itself, were sold during the 1700s, while from the 1790s, the lands on the south side of the river were feued by their respective owners, and after tentative disposal of a small area in 1804, large sections of the Blythswood Estates were opened up for feuing.

While lack of capital reserves inhibited Scottish landowners from emulating the speculative adventures of their wealthier English counterparts, they benefitted by the provisions of Scottish law, under which the sale of land gave them an initial sum, plus a fixed payment, or feu, usually in perpetuity, thereby providing an inducement to permit entrepreneurial development. At the same time the speculator was faced with a stiff initial outlay together with an annual payment high enough to take account of future inflation, before he had even begun to build. Demand, expressed in the ability to pay for housing, lay principally with the middle classes, often conforming to the decisions of landholders to permit only good quality residential development on their estates, and involving speculators in massive capital outlay leading often to bankruptcy before any return of profits. Surfacing and paving streets, laying in water and sewerage, and even the provision of churches, halls, markets and other amenities[78], were necessary inducements to middle-class settlement whose financial burden the speculator had to bear. On the other hand, a high and rapid yield of income could be obtained by building flatted tenements of three or four storeys, thereby crowding a large number of paying customers on to any given area of ground, and it was in this direction that many speculators were turning by the 1820s and 30s, providing both middle-class, and the beginnings of new working-class housing. Local planning experience was extremely limited, and based solely upon the simple regulations laid down by the Town Council on building and plot size, frontage features, and street width. In consequence, early developments owed more to the model of London's disassociated series of squares, developed from the 1630s, than to Wood's less informal grouping of features in Bath from the 1730s, or Craig's 1767 plan for the first new town of Edinburgh, based on more integrated Continental models. Even in later stages of Glasgow's new town development, when integrated schemes of square and streets were introduced, uncertainty of demand mitigated against speculative large-scale terrace construction, denying Glasgow the handsome unitary architectural conceptions of Bath or later Edinburgh. David Laurie's Carlton Place was a notable early exception, as can be seen by the piecemeal plot development evident on contemporary maps[79], and John Brash's small 1823 terraces comprising Blythswood Square compare badly with Edinburgh's second new town, nearing completion at that date, or the bold conception of its Moray Estate, just beginning. It was only by the late 1830s, when the middle-class drive to the west was beginning to spread residential growth beyond the Blythswood estates, that elegant and grand curving facades of terraces appeared in the townscape[80].

The availability of large blocks of land, as in Ramshorn and Meadowflats, did not end the process of opening single streets characteristic of the later eighteenth century. Although the northward extensions of Queen Street and Buchanan Street might justifiably be regarded in their later phases as part of a more widely integrated plan, the purchase of the grounds of Hutcheson's Hospital and the Glassford mansion and its gardens preceded the cutting of Hutcheson and Glassford Streets running north-south between Trongate and Ingram Street[81]. However, in 1781, James Barry produced a plan for a series of streets on the Ramshorn Lands, centred on a small square, and although the complete feuing of these streets took several decades, and in fact the final street pattern did not conform to Barry's layout, some idea of the conception and its relationship to the existing town plan may be gained from his 1782 map of Glasgow[82]. In 1782, a council committee decided to lay out five streets, from 13 metres to 18 metres wide, with ground reserved for George Square, (Pl. 5.i) and in 1784, steadings were advertised for sale[83]. The bulk of the lots were sold between 1786 and 1788, some to individuals, but many to the proprietors of the Glasgow Building Company, who were largely responsible for the relatively rapid development of the streets immediately north, east and south of George Square[84]. Further to the west, growth was slower, despite the Company's strenuous efforts, and although Craig, the planner of Edinburgh's first new town, was called upon in 1792 to plan a layout for Meadowflats in keeping with his ideas for the adjacent Blythswood lands, ten years later the

5.i   George Square, c.1870

5.ii   *Blythswood Place, St. Vincent Street, 1828*

Incorporation of Gardeners were requesting the use of unsold portions of the ground, a clear indication of low demand[85]. By the early 1820s, while most plots had been built upon, functional change had brought industrial and commercial invasion of Ramshorn and Meadowflats (Fig. 5.ii), together with inns, warehouses and wood yards[86], and while the grid of streets centred upon George Square is sometimes referred to as Glasgow's first 'New Town', its lifespan as a residential suburb was as limited as its integrated conception, and it scarcely deserves this appellation.

West of Buchanan Street, the steep-sided drumlin of Blythswood Hill was developed in the early decades of the nineteenth century on a rigid gridiron plan, not particularly well-suited to the topography. In 1800, the Glasgow Building Company purchased a portion of the northern flank of the hill, opening the street later known as Bath Street, but little building took place until William Harley, the principal speculator on the Blythswood Lands, opened baths in 1804, and encouraged rapid early feuing. The development of this new town illustrates the perils facing the speculator, with its history of 'bankruptcies, sequestrations, trusts, reversions, and sudden flight'[87]. By 1814, Harley was in financial difficulties, and the trustees who took over his affairs in 1816 themselves went bankrupt. Many of his feus were taken over by the Garden family, whose affairs in turn were put into the hands of trustees in 1826, while even speculators operating on a small scale suffered a similar fate. Contemporary maps, however, record the gradual progress of building on the hill. By 1821, a few small terraces and single buildings had appeared on its eastern and northern flanks, and by 1828, the terraces around Blythswood Square were laid out, and limited colonisation of the western face of the drumlin was beginning. Plans of 1830-42 show some infilling of gaps in the central area, but little extension on to the steeper western and southern slopes[88]. Despite the presence of byres, woodyards and marble works on its eastern edge, the development was almost exclusively domestic until the 1840s, providing an elegant middle-class residential enclave in the west (Pl. 5.ii).

On the south side of the river, residential development began east and west of the ancient village of Gorbals. Discussions on feuing proposals were held by the Town Council, Trades House, and Hutcheson's Hospital in 1787, and the first houses sold in Tradeston in 1791, Hutchesontown in 1794, and Laurieston in 1802[89] (Fig. 5.iii). The most ambitious plan was that for the 47 acres acquired by David Laurie in 1801/1803, and named after himself. Heavy expenditure on riverside reclamation preceded the construction of two elegant, very long terraces begun in 1802, named Carlton Place. The gap between the terraces formed the riverside terminus of South Portland Street, the pivot of a residential development conceived on a grand scale, but never completed. Three hundred and seventy four properties were planned[90], but from 1803 to 1818, there was virtually no building along the pretentiously-named Oxford, Portland, Cumberland, Norfolk and other streets. From 1818 to 1821, building activity became intense, and the development was complete by 1826, but too long a period of inactivity had permitted the intrusion of industrial activities such as brick and tile-making and the Clyde railway of the Govan Coal Company[91], and the fine middle-class tenements of streets such as Abbotsford Place soon lost their original tenants. Despairing of the lack of social amenities, seeing their property values diminish in the face of ineffective regulations against industry, and tired of paying tolls on their daily trips to places of business in the city, the middle-class residents moved out during the second half of the century. Laurie, however, was an energetic proponent of the virtues of his suburb, issuing a stream of pamphlets aimed at its protection either directly by the exclusion of industry, or indirectly, as by the improvement of its socially deteriorating neighbour, Gorbals, by various schemes such as the building of extensive new markets[92], and there is no doubt that his efforts were attended with some success. Analysis of city directories shows a rapid increase in Laurieston entries between 1822-3 and 1842-3, from c.100 to c.600, with over 40% of the North Laurieston entries being of the two-addresses type, with the second address located in the Exchange district of Glasgow, the contemporary C.B.D. Streets such as Carlton Place and South Portland Street contained high concentrations of the homes of professionals and merchants in the 1840s[93]. Tradeston and Hutchesontown, though initiated before Laurieston, never managed to attract the same level of high-status tenants, and because of poorly defined and enforced building and land use regulations, and the influence of prominent shareholders such as William Dixon, the colliery owner and ironmaster, quickly lost any early status. A Tradeston feuing plan shows clearly the dominance of canal, railways and large-scale industry in its southern sector, while the railway line running north through the development is paralleled by plots occupied by engineering and cotton works, engine and carriage sheds and workshops[94]. Similar industrial intrusion in Hutchesontown (Fig. 5.i) brought rapid deterioration.

If middle-class residential plans for the south side met with varying fortunes, those for the east side seemed doomed to failure from a very early stage. There was no integrated plan of development, and each street or square flourished or decayed in isolation. Charlotte Street, opened in 1779 after an earlier false start (infra Ch. 4, p.74), at first attracted professionals and manufacturers, such as David Dale, and managed to maintain a relatively high status for a few decades, (Pl. 5.iii) while St. Andrew's Square, closer to the old town, deteriorated much more quickly. Planned in 1786, steadings were being sold in 1791, but in 1797 a dispute over the location of the egg, butter and fowl market in the square revealed a picture far removed from the serene residential elegance of contemporary George Square. A principal complaint by the proprietors was that dust and rubbish from the markets was blown into their warehouses, thereby damaging their goods[95], while city directories for 1801 and 1823 show increasing numbers of manufacturers, artisans and warehousemen operating in the square. Graham Square, planned as an eastern residential enclave sufficiently distant from the city to be free of its pollutants, completely failed to attract residents. Tait's Directory of 1783

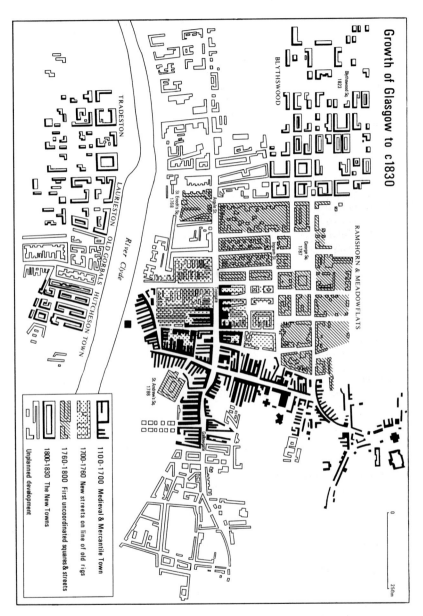

5.iii   *Growth of Glasgow to c.1830*

5.iii   *Charlotte Street, 1839*

lists one gentleman resident, while Fleming's map of 1807 shows only two houses on the approach street, with otherwise derelict steadings and in 1817 the council took over the vacant ground for a live cattle market[96]. Too close or too distant, these failures provided unheeded lessons to the effect that speculative venturing in the east end was a risky business, and the opening of Monteith Row in 1819, after decades of plans for feuing portions of Calton Green[97], merely provided another short-lived middle-class terrace whose huge apartments had to be subdivided in the second half of the century. Even astute industrialists, businessmen and politicians such as Kirkman Finlay and Henry Monteith misjudged the speculative value of east end property. An 1821 Act of Parliament permitted them to form a joint-stock company, in which the town council took shares to the value of £1,000 in 1823, to form a street from Glasgow Cross to Monteith Row, but in 1837, 57 unsold lots of houses, shops, steadings and vacant ground were put up for auction at upset prices "so low as to render this a most desirable investment"[98].

The middle classes of Glasgow had set their faces solidly towards the west, and the 1836 Act of Parliament which authorised the making and maintenance of a road from Anniesland Toll to St. George's Cross began Great Western Road, whose development belongs to the next chapter. Even the new north-eastern approaches planned for the city focussed on Bath Street and the Blythswood Estate, rather than the older portion of the city[99]. However, the built-up area was gradually extending in a number of directions, connecting with once-distinct units, like Anderston, Bridgeton and Cowcaddens, and prompting extensions of legal jurisdiction. In 1800, 96 acres of Ramshorn, Meadowflats and parts of the eastern Green were added, but despite petitions for extension by the inhabitants of Tradeston, Anderston, Finnieston, Laurieston and Hutchesontown in 1807, and the feuars of Blythswood in 1828/9[100], only the 296 acres of Blythswood and some adjacent lands were added at the next extension in 1830, with a further 213 acres of Milton and Port Dundas added in 1843. Thus even the main trend of boundary extension was resolutely west by north-west.

Internally, townscape change was limited largely to building replacement, not just in the erection of new public buildings, but in the construction of terraces of combined houses and warehouses with ground floor shops, as a response to new requirements[101]. Some limited infilling of small new streets took place in the central area, but plans for others were abandoned as space for expansion became available on the perimeter[102]. The needs of a growing population overwhelmed existing market accommodation, and new specialised buildings were erected, partly in an effort to ease congestion from street stalls. At the same time, the number of shops multiplied rapidly, especially along the four ancient streets of the city centre. Where there had been 202 shops in the city in 1712, by 1832 there were 2,141, with a further 1,043 in Gorbals and Barony parishes[103], and although more than half of these sold provisions, many specialist shops catered for the growing middle-class demand for furnishings, clothing and jewellery. Pressure for shopping space was such as to prompt the extension of shop-fronts to the edges of the piazzas of which the city had been so proud, and despite the pleas of shop-keepers, two decades of wrangling elapsed before the first extensions were permitted[104]. Much more acceptable to the council was the introduction of gas lighting, proposed in 1816, adopted in 1817, and on the basis of proven success, extended by the Glasgow Gas Light Company to the suburbs in 1822, -25 and -26. "Streets, Squares, Market Place, private Houses, Shops, Counting-Houses, Warehouses and Public Works and Manufactories and other Buildings"[105], exchanged the fitful glow of oil lamps for the bright, steady gleam of gas, while its by-products, coke, tar, pitch and asphalt, were also pressed into useful service.

If the supply of gas was a relatively painless procedure, that of water was another matter entirely. Rapid growth of industrial pollutants and human effluent overwhelmed the crude sewerage system, and the few public wells which remained untainted could not meet the rising demand. From the 1780s, a constant stream of petitions demanded the excavation of new wells in the extending suburbs as well as the repair of old wells in the increasingly congested core[106]. Council committees failed to act on expert advice on tapping the Monkland Canal, or using steam engines to raise water from the Clyde[107], and it was left to private enterprise to provide a supply. In 1804, William Harley, the Blythswood Estate developer, led water from springs on his lands of Willow Bank to a reservoir in what is now West Nile Street, successfully selling large quantities at ½d per stoup[108], and the formation of limited companies followed swiftly. In 1806 the Glasgow Water Works Company received Parliamentary assent, and from their reservoirs at Dalmarnock on the Clyde, began pumping supplies in 1807. By 1810 they were applying to construct extra reservoirs at Duke Street and Rottenrow, and by 1814 had laid over 50,000 metres of pipe to houses and factories[109]. The Cranstonhill Water Works Company, incorporated in 1808, was less successful, and its use of the Clyde at Anderston Quay as a source was dubious from the start, forcing it to move to Dalmarnock in 1819, and in 1838, to sell out to its rival company, a monopolistic move bitterly contested by council and public[110]. The Companies were under no obligation to lay pipes into areas where it would not pay them to do so, and the poorer districts, whose inhabitants could not afford the high water rates anyway, were left without a fresh supply. Clamour for opening of wells in 1834 revealed that of the town's 30 wells, for a population of over 200,000, only 14 were in good order[111], rendering the most densely populated area of the city ripe for epidemics of typhus and cholera when they struck.

Population and society

Any discussion of population changes affecting the city of Glasgow in the eighteenth and nineteenth centuries is made complex by varying definitions of the area comprising the city and suburbs, and for this reason, actual numbers are perhaps less interesting than rate of increase. Table

5.iii attempts to achieve some consistency by using figures for pre-Census years quoted by James Cleland, who was also responsible for the preparation of a number of the census returns. The 55% increase between 1780 and 1791 is anomalous, and probably stems from an under-estimate of the 1780 population, but the most remarkable feature is the steady and consistent increase from 1801, always over 30% and latterly over 35%, bringing the population total to over 274,000 by 1841. While growth of this magnitude could have been sustained by natural increase, the high mortality levels of the period point clearly to net migration as the major source of new population, and several migrant streams can be identified. In the 1780s and 1790s, the processes of agricultural improvement in the west central Lowlands, resulting in dissolution of multiple tenancy farms, enclosure of arable land and the changing status of thousands of rural families provided many of them with the choice of remaining on the land as hired labourers, perhaps on a temporary basis while the constructive work of improvement was carried out, or migrating to seek the security of a job in the developing textile centres. Factory production of yarn supported large communities of hand-loom weavers in Calton, Bridgeton and Anderston, and by 1819 they constituted over 40% of the employed population of these areas[112]. Thousands of other families found work for men, women, and children in the spinning mills, situated on semi-rural water-power sites at first, but rapidly moving to more central locations on the edge of the growing city. In the Highlands, the collapse of the traditional mainstays of kelp-gathering, fishing, and black cattle rearing, revealed a dangerous level of over-population on a meagre resource base. A steady trickle of migrants was swelled to a greater stream by the pressure of an unforgiving environment, reinforced by agricultural changes in subsequent decades, and a new ethnic group, of which a large proportion was Gaelic-speaking, was added to the city.

Table 5.iii.	Population of Glasgow: 1780-1841 (including suburbs)	
Year	Number	% increase on previous base
1780	42,832	—
1791	66,578	55.4
1801	83,767	25.8
1811	110,460	31.8
1821	147,043	33.1
1831	202,426	37.6
1841	274,324	35.5

Source: Cleland, J., 1828. *Statistical and Population Tables relative to the City of Glasgow*. Census of Great Britain, 1831 and 1841.

The third major element in the migrant stream derived from Ireland, whose seasonal migrants had laboured to bring in the Scottish harvest from early in the eighteenth century. Ironically, the agricultural improvements which forced so many Scots to move away from the land provided, in their initial constructive stages of enclosure, drainage, marling and tree-planting, a more permanent source of employment for Irish migrants, and many of those who swelled the early movement to the towns derived from this source[113]. After 1790, a combination of political unrest and industrial decline forced even more Irish to emigrate, and the rapidly growing cotton industry of the west of Scotland attracted large numbers, while the Irish-born proportion of Glasgow's population swelled from c.10% in 1819 to c.25% in 1845, taking into account offspring born in Scotland[114]. While many found employment in building houses, factories, canals, docks and railways, a high proportion entered branches of the cotton industry. In 1833, Houldsworth's Anderston mills employed 300 Irish, and the situation was similar in Woodside, Partick, Springfield, Bridgeton and Barrowfield. One manufacturer employed 400 Irish hand-loom weavers, and even in its declining years, with the advent of mechanisation, many Irish continued to enter, and bring up their children to, the trade[115].

In an 1841 police report on over 1,000 destitute persons in the city, c.30% are Irish, a proportion comparable to that within the total population, and over 63% of those listed had been under 35 years of age on arrival in Glasgow, thus contributing strongly to the potential fertility of the city's population[116]. The spatial characteristics of their settlement were such that high fertility levels combined with rising density to produce conditions of severe overcrowding in central parts of the city.

Table 5.iv. **Migrants in City and adjacent parishes. 1819 + 1841**

		1819			1841
	Parishes	% non-Scots	% Irish	% Lodgers	% non-Lanarkshire
Inner City	St. Mary Tron	17.05	15.8	13.43	59.87
	St. John	15.81	14.54	10.21	41.28
	St. James	14.73	13.3	11.77	39.2
	St. Andrew	11.79	9.88	10.88	50.1
	College	11.06	9.76	12.33	43.64
Outer City	St. Enoch	7.7	6.14	12.55	51.0
	Outer High	5.72	4.09	11.78	39.92
	St. George	5.67	3.6	9.12	50.76
	St. Mungo	4.65	4.44	5.8	44.2
	St. David	4.37	1.79	12.76	47.12
Barony	Calton	21.73	20.5	11.42	54.84
	Anderston	13.96	12.7	11.44	53.52
	Bridgeton	12.1	11.29	11.46	40.59
	St. Vincent St.	8.26	5.86	9.24	59.04 (Maryhill)
	Port Dundas	6.44	5.6	8.29	52.46 (Gorbals)

Source: Cleland, J., 1828. *Statistical and Population Tables relative to the City of Glasgow.* Census of Great Britain, 1841.

As Table 5.iv indicates, the inner city parishes attracted large concentrations of all migrants, not just Irish. St. Mary Tron, immediately south-west of the Cross contained the highest proportion in 1841, but high percentages are apparent in those other central parishes stretching to the east of the Cross, and lying contiguous with Calton, whose developing textile industry had attracted the largest number of migrants in 1819. Anderston, and to a lesser extent Bridgeton, also exerted an industrial pull, in strong contrast to the outer city parishes, embracing the westward-expanding new town and the old cathedral area, where migrant densities were extremely low. Within this group, however, there may have been variations in density which the 1819 enumeration does not indicate. Scots born outside Glasgow are not enumerated, but the high percentages of lodgers in St. Enoch, St. David, and Outer High parishes may indicate the presence of this group. Certainly by 1841, migrants had come to constitute between c.40% and 60% of the population of all city and suburban parishes, with St. Mary Tron appearing clearly as the principal reception area in the city.

Housebuilding had not managed to keep pace with this deluge of incomers, and the inevitable effect was overcrowding of existing dwellings. A ratio of 4.4 persons per inhabited house in 1819 rose to 4.6 in 1821, 4.8 in 1831, and 5.2 in 1841[117], but the increase was spatially selective, both between and within parishes. While Outer High parish registered a ratio of 4.9, in 1841 that of St. Mary Tron registered 5.5, and in St. John's parish in 1819, densities varied between 3.5 and 5.9 persons per house[118]. The greater proportion of houses being built consisted of spacious and sanitary middle-class dwellings, while the working classes occupied increasingly congested, small and unhealthy warrens of apartments along the backlands of central burgage plots, or tiny 'made-down' cells in once-large apartments where middle-class demand had failed to materialise. At the lowest end of the scale thousands of incomers found the only available shelter to be rat-infested lodging houses, some 6-700 of which existed in the city, 240 of them between Saltmarket and Stockwell Street, contributing their quota of misery to the already overcrowded St. Mary's Parish[119].

Contemporary descriptions of living conditions beggar the imagination.

"I have seen human degradation in some of its worst phases, both in England and abroad, but I can advisedly say, that I did not believe until I visited the wynds of Glasgow, that so large an amount of filth, crime, misery and disease existed on one spot in any civilised country.

The wynds consist of long lanes, so narrow that a cart could with difficulty pass along them; out of these open the 'closes', which are courts about 15 to 20 feet square; round which the houses, mostly of 3 stories high, are built; the centre of the court is the dung-hill, which is probably the most lucrative part of the estate to the laird in most instances, and which it would consequently be deemed an invasion of the rights of property to remove. The houses are for the most part let in flats, either to the lowest class of labourers or prostitutes, or to lodging keepers; these latter places are the general resort and favourite abodes of all those to whom a local habitation and a name are professionally inconvenient. They are likewise the resting places of outcasts of every grade of wretchedness and destitution. In the more costly of these abodes, where separate beds are furnished at the price of 3d per night, the thieves and prostitutes chiefly congregate. . . .

In the lower lodging-houses, then, twelve and sometimes twenty persons of both sexes and all ages sleep promiscuously on the floor in different degrees of nakedness. These places are, generally as regards dirt, damp and decay, such as no person of common humanity to animals would stable his horse in. . . . It is my firm belief that penury, dirt, misery, drunkenness, disease and crime culminate in Glasgow to a pitch unparalleled in Great Britain."[120]

The 1841 Police report on destitute persons in Glasgow speaks of "poor helpless children almost starving . . . five children in fever — no work — no bed . . . beds only straw on floor . . . house damp and very unhealthy . . . five feet six inches only from floor to ceiling . . . a poor, starving and helpless being"[121] and so on through an endless catalogue of misery, more sympathetic in its tone than some of the pronouncements of municipal bodies on the topic of vagrants. As early as 1782, Glasgow appointed an officer to prevent "stranger poor from settling in the city for such time as to entitle them to charity", but a massive influx of migrants overwhelmed his efforts, and by 1818, the directors of the town's hospital were protesting against an impossible task, while increasing numbers of Irish beggars and vagrants prompted stern police measures, including the erection of stocks as a deterrent in Calton[122]. By the 1830s, in the face of a total of 18,500 persons on relief, subscribers were demanding a change in the method of levying the poor rate[123], but such measures did nothing to reduce the burgeoning numbers of the destitute, condemned to penury by forces beyond their management or understanding.

From the end of the eighteenth century, poor harvests brought sharp rises in the price of grain, and corresponding hardship to those unable to pay higher bread prices. In 1783 and 1799 subscriptions were raised to buy up stocks of grain to provide food for the poor, and distillation from grain was suspended, though neither measure had great success, since grain shortages continued to cause distress and unrest through the early decades of the nineteenth century[124]. From 1810 onwards, trading and manufacturing recession, felt most keenly in the textile industry, brought widespread unemployment to both male and female workers. Mechanisation of many tasks in factories particularly affected handloom weavers, although many female operatives were also thrown out of work. Schemes to assist weavers in particular by employing them on harbour schemes or on improvements to Glasgow Green only provided relief for a limited number of families, while the wives and families of many men who had abandoned the struggle for employment only to die on Napoleonic battlefields, were left destitute[125]. Desperation bred militancy, and rioting in the suburbs and in Tureen Street was followed by more peaceful demonstrations in which thousands of workers marched through the city. Alarmed civic authorities applied for military assistance in holding down potential insurrection, and for three months cavalry and infantry had to be stationed in the city[126]. The level of municipal fear, if not the actual scale of threat, may be gauged by the town council's votes of thanks in 1820 to Major General Thomas Bradford, commanding forces in North Britain for his "energetic suppression of late insurrectionary movements in the manufacturing districts of Scotland", and to the Rifle Brigade, 7th and 10th Hussars, 13th Regiment, Royal Artillery, Corps of Glasgow Sharpshooters, Corps of Glasgow Volunteer Light Horse, and the East and Midlothian, Ayrshire, and Dumbartonshire Yeomanry Cavalry Regiments[127].

Of far greater immediate consequence than epidemics of social disturbance were epidemics of contagious disease, breeding and proliferating through the airless, stinking warrens of the poorer districts, then erupting to claim victims throughout the city and suburbs. The combination of pools and streams of stagnant sewage and a contaminated, inadequate water supply rendered water-borne diseases endemic, with frequent epidemic outbreaks. The "contagious fever" of 1818 was typhus, which raged unchecked for a year, providing a death rate for the city 42% higher than the previous five-year average. The Royal Infirmary, opened in 1794, treated 1,371 patients, and another temporary fever hospital had to be opened. During subsequent outbreaks in the 1820s and 1830s, these and further hospitals proved hopelessly inadequate to cope with the flood of fever victims, and many remained at home to spread the disease. Even at the height of the 1832 cholera epidemic, typhus accounted for over 30% of all patients admitted to the Royal Infirmary, twice as many as cholera victims[128]. Cholera first appeared in the city on February 9th, 1832, and in its first eruption, claimed its victims largely from the ranks of the poor, spreading in a second wave of infection to all classes and all neighbourhoods of the city[129]. The virulence of the disease terrified people. In the Albion Street cholera hospital, 79% of all victims died, and 3,000 died in the city between February and November[130]. In the whole of the city south of the river there was one doctor, as was the case in the village of Anderston, while in Calton and Bridgeton there was none. Attempts at quarantine were crude and ineffective, and centres of contagion such as public houses could not be closed[131]. Small wonder, therefore, that further outbreaks took their toll in the 1830s and 1840s.

Severely congested living conditions accelerated the contagion of diseases affecting children. Outbreaks of measles, and particularly smallpox, gave enhanced levels of child mortality among those under five, rising to 70 per 1,000 in 1821, and an appalling 112 per 1,000 in 1841[132], and the benefits of inoculation were offset by population growth, dirt, ignorance and hunger. The rate of mortality for the whole population rose from one in 41 in 1822, to one in 30 in 1828, and one in 24 by 1837 as fevers and pulmonary diseases, always under-registered and grossly accentuated by overcrowding, took a terrible and growing toll of the young and healthy migrant stream[133]. The industrial city was on the verge of choking in its own effluent, and a depleted countryside was becoming gradually less able to replace workers consumed by the industrial machine. By the time of the 1841 Census, Glasgow was a city in crisis, industrially and socially, requiring the *deus ex machina* of public health awareness and change in industrial emphasis to sweep to its rescue. Adam Smith's 1776 prophecy of workers brutalised by urban living had been borne out by Sir John Sinclair's 1825 description of, "a servile, pallid, and sickly race, brought up in the confined air of cotton mills"[134], and yet Glasgow's Industrial Revolution was barely under way.

REFERENCES

1. Pagan, J., 1847. *Sketch of the History of Glasgow*, p.82.
2. James Finlay & Co., Textile Manufacturers and Merchants, Glasgow. Manuscript Book of overseas consignments, 1818-54. Glasgow University Archives, Colquhoun Business Collection, UGD/91/6 (henceforth, G.U.A., C.B.C.).
3. Pagan, J., 1847, *op.cit.*, p.83.
4. Pollock, Gilmour & Co., Timber Merchants, Glasgow, 1800-1873. Minute Books, G.U.A., C.B.C., UGD/36.
5. Wilson, J., 1812. *General View of the Agriculture of Renfrewshire*, p.230.
6. G.B.R., VIII, pp.124/5, 311; IX, p.385.
7. Riddell, J. F., 1979. *Clyde Navigation*, p.58.
8. Mr. Telford's report respecting the Clyde, 1806, p.19, in *Reports on the Improvement and Management of the River Clyde and Harbour of Glasgow from 1755 to 1853*. Clyde Navigation Trustees, 1854 (henceforth, '*Clyde Reports*').
9. (a) Logan, D., 1835. Report on the improvements of the River Clyde and Harbour of Glasgow ordered by the Parliamentary Trustees, with tables of soundings and borings. *Clyde Reports*, pp.10/11.
    (b) Report by Mr. J. S. Russell, January 1838, to the Chairman and Committee of Trustees of the River Clyde. *Clyde Reports*, p.75.
10. (a) Kyle, T., 1839. Map of the River Clyde as in 1839, with the water lines thereof as in 1800, S.R.O., R.H.P. 2862. This plan in ten sections shows the river downstream to Dumbarton, with proposed lines of improvement.
    (b) Kyle, T., 1840. Plan of Springfield Quay. S.R.O., R.H.P. 1326/1-2. Shows on a large scale areas reclaimed from 1799 to 1840, and land uses thereon.
    (c) Kyle, T., 1833. Plan of division of waterside land at Govan. Glasgow University Archives, (G.U.A.). Plan 20838. Shows straightening of bank from waterline of 1800.
11. Kyle, W., 1837. The lands of Springfield. S.R.O., R.H.P. 492/1.
12. Walker, J., 1836. Report by James Walker to the Parliamentary Trustees for Improving the Navigation of the River Clyde and enlarging the Harbour of Glasgow. *Clyde Reports*, pp.1-4.
13. Telford, T., 1806, *op.cit.*, p.20. Rennie, J., 1807. Report and Plans by Mr. Rennie, of a wet-dock in the channel of the River; also of one in the Windmill Croft. *Clyde Reports*, pp.24-25, 28, 39-40, 43.
14. Cleland, J., 1828. *Statistical and Population Tables relative to the City of Glasgow*, Appendix, pp.196/7. Cleland, J., 1832. *Enumeration of the Inhabitants of the City of Glasgow and County of Lanark for the Government Census of 1831*. Appendix, p.198.
15. N.S.A., Vol.VI, 1836. City of Glasgow, p.198.

16. Letter and Tabular Details by Captain William Johnstone and Mr. Russell relative to the accommodation offered to vessels at the Harbour of the Broomielaw, 1835. Strathclyde Regional Archives. (S.R.A.). T-CNI (Clyde Navigation).
17. Mr. J. Hartley's Report, April 1834, to the Dean of Guild and the Committee of Management of the River Clyde. *Clyde Reports*, pp.59/60.
18. N.S.A., Vol.VI, 1836. City of Glasgow, p.198.
19. Kyle, T., 1839, *op.cit.* Martin, G., 1842. Map of Glasgow.
20. Riddell, J. F., 1979, *op.cit.*, p.178.
21. (a) 'D.B.', 1820. Hints for extending the navigation of the River Clyde above Glasgow etc. S.R.A., T-CNI.
    (b) Account of the rise and progress of the plan for improving the navigation of the River Clyde, from Dumbarton Castle to the City of Glasgow; with the present state of the trade in the harbour at this city; together with hints for farther improvements on this river; for the consideration of Thomas Telford. 1824. *Clyde Reports*, pp.28/29.
22. (a) Letter to Thomas Telford, 1824, *op.cit. Clyde Reports*, p.15.
    (b) Johnstone and Russell, 1835, *op.cit.* Appendix "Abstract of Shipping; Foreign Arrivals at the Broomielaw".
23. Cleland, J., 1820. *Enumeration of the Inhabitants of the City of Glasgow and its Connected Suburbs, together with the population and Statistical tables relative to Scotland and England*, p.33. G.P.O., *Directory of Glasgow*, 1840-41, p.46.
24. Smout, T. C., 1964. Scottish Landowners and Economic Growth, 1650-1850. *Scottish Journal of Political Economy*, II, p.222. Martin, D., 1977. *The Forth and Clyde Canal: A Kirkintilloch View*, p.3.
25. O.S.A., Vol.II, 1790. Parish of Kirkintilloch, pp.279-280.
26. Smout, T. C., 1964, *op.cit.*, p.22.
27. Registered Disposition: Robert Dreghorn to the Company of Proprietors of the Forth and Clyde Navigation, 8th March 1793. Murray, D. Collections for the history of Dunbartonshire, Vol.5, No.137. Dunbartonshire Public Library, Watchmeal Collection.
28. O.S.A., Vol.V, 1790. Appendix. Account of the Forth and Clyde Navigation, p.588. O.S.A., Vol.V, 1790. Parish of Barony of Glasgow, p.125.
29. Porteous, J. D., 1977. *Canal Ports: The Urban Achievement of the Canal Age*, p.42.
30. N.S.A., Vol.VI, 1836. Lanarkshire, Parish of Cadder, p.411. N.S.A., Vol.VIII, 1839. Dunbartonshire: Parish of Kirkintilloch, pp.178 & 204.
31. G.B.R., VIII, p.135., Fleming, P. 1807. Map of the City of Glasgow and Suburbs.
32. 10 Geo., III, c.105, p.1.
33. G.B.R., VII, pp.315, 316, 317.
34. G.B.R., VIII, p.11. Thomson, G., 1950, *op.cit.*, p.132.
35. Cleland, J., 1832, *op.cit.*, p.33.
36. N.S.A., VI, 1840. Parish of Old Monkland, p.665.
37. Monkland Navigation: Condensed view of Traffic Receipts, 1837-1845. Letter to stockholders proposing Forth and Clyde merger, and detailing negotiations with the Edinburgh/Glasgow Railway Company. Both items from G.U.A., C.B.C.; UGD/8/111.
38. Thomson, A., 1836. Plan of branch canal at St. Rollox and adjoining properties. S.R.O., R.H.P., 125.
39. Scouller, J., 1829. Plan of the estate of Blochairn, the property of the heirs portioners of the late Robert Dreghorn, Esq. of Ruchill. S.R.O., R.H.P., 3520.
40. Telford, T., 1805. *Report relative to the proposed Canal from the City of Glasgow to the Harbour of Ardrossan, on the West Coast of the County of Ayr, in Scotland.*
41. 46, Geo., III, Cap. 75.
42. G.B.R., IX, pp.350/1, 517, 528.
43. Cleland, J., 1837. *An Account of the Former and Present State of Glasgow*, p.14.
44. Smith, D., 1834. Plan for laying out part of the lands of Dumbreck into Villas. G.U.A. Plan 10357.
45. William Dixon and Sons; Coal and Iron Masters, Glasgow. Manuscript Sales Book, Canal Basin Depot. 1825-26. G.U.A., C.B.C., UGD/1, 55/1.
46. G.B.R., X, pp.201, 207/8, 355.
47. Manuscript list of proprietors of the Union canal resident in or near Glasgow, 1834. G.U.A., C.B.C., UGD.8/42.
48. Edinburgh and Glasgow Union Canal Company. Annual General Assembly, 1836. Report.
49. Report of a Sub-Committee of the Directors of the Union Canal Company, on Communications betwixt the line of Canal and other public undertakings, 1835.

50. Cleland, J., 1837, *op.cit.*, pp.14, 16.
51. G.B.R., IX, p.301; X, p.19.
52. Sketch of the Lanarkshire Railways Shewing the Public Works in connexion therewith, 1832. Mitchell Library, Glasgow.
53. N.S.A., Vol. VIII, 1839. Dunbartonshire, Parish of Kirkintilloch, p.203.
54. G.B.R., XI, p.255.
55. 2 George IV, Cap. lxii, p.1941. Stevenson, A., 1849. Railway plan of south side of Glasgow. S.R.O., R.H.P. 214. (Shows build-up of network from 1780.) Menzies, J., 1843, Plan of West Street in Tradeston of Glasgow showing the Pollok and Govan Railway. (Shows coal depot, wharves and intended wet dock, and foundries, gasworks and other coal-using industry.) S.R.O., R.H.P., 158.
56. N.S.A., Vol. VI, 1840. Lanarkshire, Parish of Old Monkland, p.665. Cleland, J., 1837, *op.cit.*, p.14.
57. Report of the Directors to the Shareholders of the G.P.K. & A. Railway Co. at their eighth half-yearly General Meeting. February, 1841.
58. Guide to the Glasgow and Ayrshire Railway, 1841.
59. Martin, G., 1842. Map of the City of Glasgow.
60. Campbell, R. H., 1980. *The rise and fall of Scottish industry.* 1707-1939, pp.II, 14, 15, 57.
61. O.S.A., Vol.5, 1793. Parish of Glasgow, p.502.
62. Hay, G. D., 1974. Houldsworth's Cotton Mill, Glasgow. *Post-Medieval Archaeology*, pp.8, 92, 98.
63. Cleland, J., 1832, *op.cit.*, p.151.
64. Bremner, D., 1869. *The Industries of Scotland: their Rise, Progress and Present Condition*, p.279.
65. O.S.A., Vol.12, 1793. Parish of Barony of Glasgow, pp.113, 114; G.B.R., IX, p.213; N.S.A., V, 1840. Parish of Glasgow, p.163.
66. Hamilton, H., 1966. *The Industrial Revolution in Scotland*, p.210.
67. N.S.A., Vol. VI, 1840, *op.cit.*, p.140.
68. Bremner, D., 1869, *op.cit.*, p.66.
69. Bremner, D., 1869, *op.cit.*, p.39.
70. Guide to the Glasgow and Ayrshire Railway, 1841, pp.15/16.
71. N.S.A., Vol. VI, *op.cit.*, 1840. Parish of Govan, pp.696/7.
72. Tait, J., 1783. *Directory for the City of Glasgow, Villages of Anderston, Calton, and Gorbals, etc.*
73. Pigot, J. & Co., 1823. *Commercial Directory of Ireland, Scotland, and the Four most Northern Counties of England, from 1821-22 and 23.*
74. Post Office Directory for Glasgow, 1840-41.
75. N.S.A., Vol. VI, 1840, *op.cit.*, pp.169-170.
76. Cleland, J., 1816. Annals of Glasgow, Vol. II, pp.479-480.
77. Kellett, J. R., 1961. Property Speculators and the Building of Glasgow, 1780-1830. *Scottish Journal of Political Economy, VIII*, p.22.
78. Kellett, J. R., 1961, *op.cit.*, pp.223-4.
79. Fleming, P., 1807. Map of the City of Glasgow and Suburbs. Fleming, P. and Smith, D., 1821. Map of the City of Glasgow and Suburbs. Smith, D. and Collie, J., 1839. Plan of the City of Glasgow and its Environs.
80. Taylor, A., 1839. Feuing Plan of the Lands of Kelvingrove. G.U.A. Plans, 20839.
81. G.B.R., VII, pp.560, 561, 594; VIII, p.38.
82. Barry, J., 1782. Plan of the City of Glasgow, Gorbells, Caltoun and environs.
83. G.B.R., VIII, pp.61, 153, 154, 155.
84. Kellett, J. R., 1961, *op.cit.*, pp.217-219.
85. G.B.R., VIII, pp.420, 475; IX, 298.
86. Smith, D., 1823. The ancient and extended royalty of the city of Glasgow. S.R.O., R.H.P., 308 & 309.
87. Gomme, A. and Walker, D., 1968. *Architecture of Glasgow*, p.74.
88. Fleming, P. and Smith, D., 1821. Map of the City of Glasgow and Suburbs. Smith, D., 1828. Plan of the City of Glasgow and its environs. Lumsden, J., 1830. City of Glasgow and Suburbs. Smith, D. and Collie, J., 1839. Plan of the City of Glasgow and its environs. Martin, G., 1842. Map of the City of Glasgow.
89. G.B.R., VIII, p.229. Kellett, J. R., 1969. *Glasgow*, p.12 in Lobel, M.D. (ed.) *Historic Towns* (contains invaluable reconstruction maps of Glasgow, c.1800, together with extensive and useful commentary).

90. Kyle, W., 1803. Plan of Ground in Laurieston Feued off by James Laurie Esquire etc., S.R.O., R.H.P., 250/1, see also Laurieston Feuing Book with complete Kyle plan. Mitchell Library No.548595.
91. Kellett, J. R., op.cit., 1961, p.225.
92. Laurie, D., 1810. A project for erecting Public Markets, and a Grand Academy, on improved principles, in the Gorbals.
93. Robb, J. G., 1978. Suburb and Slum in nineteenth-century Gorbals. Discussion Paper, I.B.G. Urban Studies Group; Glasgow, September 1978, pp.9, 10, 11 and figs. 2 & 3.
94. MacLure and Macdonald (No date, prob. c.1840/50). Plan of that part of the Six Pound Land of Gorbals and Bridgend belonging to the Trades House and Incorporations of Glasgow. Feued by them and now called Tradeston. S.R.A. Historical Plans. Guide to the Glasgow and Ayrshire Railway, 1841, p.14.
95. G.B.R., VIII, pp.212/5, 444; IX, 71, 73, 96/7, 110, 122-5.
96. G.B.R., X, pp.392/3.
97. Kyle, W., 1813. Plan of the Green of Glasgow exhibiting a design by James Cleland. G.B.R., VIII, p.462; X, pp.120, 135-7, 634; XI, pp.15, 39, 115, 142, 144, 333-4.
98. G.B.R., XI, pp.37/8, 39. Black, R., 1837. Plan of London Street property divided into lots for sale, S.R.O., R.H.P., 93.
99. Smith, D., Kyle, W., McQuisten, P. and Cleland, J., 1829/30. Proposed routes for new approaches to city from north, in Edinburgh to Glasgow Railway Report, 1830 etc. Mitchell Library, G.313841, 313844, 313845.
100. G.B.R., IX, pp.545, 548; XI, pp.302/3, 344, 348/9.
101. Jaffrey, J., 1792. Elevation of terrace of houses and shops on the west side of High Street. Plan of part of College Street (Elevation) G.U.A. Plans Nos.833, 834 & 835.
102. G.U.A. Plans Nos.885 (proposed new street from Blackfriars Wynd to Hunter Street, 1815) and 20881 (proposed road from Duke Street to Blackfriars Street, 1836). G.B.R., XI, pp.104/5 (King Street/Saltmarket, 1824). IX, pp.472/3 (Queen Street/Clyde Street, 1805).
103. Cleland, J., 1832, op.cit., p.215.
104. G.B.R., VIII, pp.430, 526; IX, pp.140, 202, 207, 232, 249/50, 286; X, p.60.
105. Geo., III, Cap. xli. June, 1817, p.1013.
106. G.B.R., VIII, pp.203, 326/7, 376; IX, pp.3, 409, 444.
107. G.B.R., VIII, pp.266, 482/3; IX, pp.161, 190.
108. Cleland, J., 1817. Abridgement of the Annals of Glasgow, p.394.
109. Abstract of the Balance of the Books of the Glasgow Water Works, 1809/10; Report of the Committee of Management on the Glasgow Water Works to the Proprietors, 1814, p.2.
110. G.B.R., IV, p.625; XI, pp.589/90, 598. Marwick, J., 1910. The Water Supply of Glasgow, pp.97, 105.
111. Marwick, J., 1910, op.cit., p.99.
112. Cleland, J., 1828, op.cit., p.8.
113. Handley, J., 1947. The Irish in Scotland, p.43.
114. Handley, J., 1947, op.cit., p.55.
115. Handley, J., 1947, op.cit., p.56.
116. Miller, H. (City Marshal and Superintendent of Police), 1841. Return showing . . . particulars of . . . destitute persons within the City of Glasgow.
117. Cleland, J., 1828. Statistical and Population Tables relative to the City of Glasgow, p.9. Census of Great Britain; Enumeration Abstract . . . Scotland; 1821, 1831, 1841.
118. Census of Great Britain; Enumeration Abstract . . . Scotland; 1841. Cage, R. A. and Checkland, E. O. A., 1976. Thomas Chalmers and Urban Poverty; The St. John's Parish Experiment in Glasgow, 1819-1837. Philosophical Journal, 13.1 p.42.
119. Laidlaw, S., 1956. Glasgow Common Lodging — Houses and the People Living in Them, p.18.
120. Symons, J. C., 1839. Reports from Assistant Hand-Loom Weavers Commissioners.
121. Miller, H., 1841, op.cit., pp.2-10.
122. G.B.R., VIII, p.62; X, pp.346, 426, 443. Ord. J., 1912. The Story of the Burgh of Calton, p.11.
123. Statement on behalf of the Committee of Subscribers for promoting a change in the Mode of Assessment for the Poor of the City of Glasgow, 1831.
124. G.B.R., VIII, pp.80/81, 85, 105; IX, pp.168-171, 264, 265, 646.
125. G.B.R., X, pp.83/4, 337, 349, 499, 519, 529; XI, pp.10, 205, 208.
126. G.B.R., X, pp.354, 443, 523, 532. N.S.A., Vol. VI, 1836, op.cit., pp.121/122.

127. G.B.R., X, pp.551, 552, 553.

128. G.B.R., X, p.426; XI, p.10. N.S.A., Vol. VI, 1836, *op.cit.*, p.121. Cowan, R., 1837. *Vital Statistics of Glasgow. 1. Statistics of Fever and Small Pox prior to 1837*, p.7. Easton, J. A., 1832. Report of Diseases among the Poor of Glasgow. *Glasgow Medical Journal* V, No.18, pp.97, 232, 441-2.

129. Watt, G., 1832. On the Origins and Spread of Malignant Cholera in Glasgow and its Neighbourhood. *Glasgow Medical Journal*, V, No.19, pp.298-308; No.20, pp.384-394.

130. Lawrie, J. A., 1832. Report of the Albion Street Cholera Hospital. *Glasgow Medical Journal*, V, No.19, pp.309-331; No.20, pp.416-429.

131. Remarks on the Proceedings of the Glasgow Board of Health. *Glasgow Medical Examiner*, Nos. X + XI, Jan/Feb., 1832.

132. Flinn, M. (ed.) 1977. *Scottish Population History from the 17th century to the 1930s*. Table 5.5.2., p.378.

133. Cowan, R., 1832. On the Mortality of Children in Glasgow. *Glasgow Medical Journal*, V, No.19, pp.353-361. Watt, A., 1844, The Glasgow Bills of Mortality for 1841 and 1842.

134. Sinclair, J., 1825. *Analysis of the Statistical Account of Scotland*, Vol.1, p.170.

6. IRON IN THE SOUL: 1841~1914

In just over seven decades, between the Census of 1841 and the outbreak of the First World War, Glasgow quadrupled its population, spread its urban tentacles outwards to absorb the surrounding ring of industrial and residential burghs, transformed its industrial base and its supporting infrastructure, and led the growth of the Scottish economy into the modern age. At the end of a period of growth of such rapidity and complexity, the transition to stability was remarkably abrupt, and just as Glasgow had led Scotland, and the world, in the development of shipbuilding and heavy engineering, so it became one of the first of the great industrial cities to stop growing. The artificial stimulus of war, with its insatiable demands for munitions and machines, masked the incipient decline indicated by large-scale emigration from the city from c.1905 onwards. It may be that "great cities contain in their very greatness the seeds of premature and rapid decay"[1], and the brevity and brilliance of Glasgow's flourishing may have exhausted the nutritive capacity of people and hinterland alike, leaving little with which to resist the bleak decades of depression. However, Glasgow's Victorian summer is a phenomenon sufficiently outstanding to merit close scrutiny, both in its own right, and as a signpost to the future.

Industrial change

After 1840, the surging growth of the textile industry, which had provided the economic basis for Glasgow's expansion for fifty years, slowed then faltered, in the face of European and American competition, and the disruption of raw cotton supplies caused by the American Civil War brought severe contraction during the 1860s throughout West Central Scotland. However, while prominent textile manufacturers such as Finlay and Houldsworth either sold off mills or abandoned the trade entirely[2], thread-making, textile-finishing, and carpet-weaving employed thousands of workers in the city until the end of the century. As late as

1861, the 48,500 textile workers vastly outnumbered c.4,500 shipbuilding and metal trade workers in Glasgow and Govan, but by 1891 the relative roles had changed. Textile workers had contracted to c.29,000, while ship and metal trades had increased to c.33,000, of whom 7,500 worked in Govan. By 1911, shipbuilding, engineering, and their allied trades employed 47,000 workers in Glasgow and 13,000 in Govan, while textiles could only muster c.24,500[3]. One of the roots of industrial change lay in the large-scale expansion of production of cheap iron, which acted as a stimulus to coal production, and railway construction, and provided raw material for shipbuilding. By the mid-nineteenth century, 90% of Britain's exports of pig iron came from Scotland, largely shipped out from the Clyde, while control of the industry was centred in Glasgow[4]. However, ready access to plentiful raw material was much less important than the climate of innovation and experimentation wherein Clydeside shipbuilders experimented with new materials of construction and modes of propulsion, thereby leading development and capturing markets far ahead of any rivals. In national terms, the Clyde was relatively insignificant in the era of wooden ships, launching only 5% of British tonnage in 1835, but with the change to iron hulls, the proportion rose dramatically to over 70% between 1851 and 1870[5]. From the late 1870s the use of mild steel to provide a lighter hull, together with concentration on screw propulsion from compound steam engines brought further increases in production. The 1858 figure of 40,000 tons launched had soared to over 400,000 tons by 1883, and an incredible peak of 757,000 tons in 1913[6]. Naval orders played a significant part in increasing tonnages, but specialisation and variety were evident from an early date. A description of Clyde shipbuilding in the late 1860s lists ironclads, frigates, gun-boats, steamers, launches, lighters, dredgers, and floating graving docks destined for Saigon and Callao[7].

Experimentation and expansion in production of steam engines was not confined to marine engineering. The strong local tradition of manufacture of textile machinery expanded to include railway locomotives, pumps, boilers, sugar machinery and numerous other branches of engineering with their ancillaries. Locomotive engineering in particular became concentrated in and around Glasgow, until by 1914, Glasgow was the foremost centre of manufacture in Europe, with c.two-thirds of locomotive production going for export[8]. Synchronous with the large-scale growth of the heavy engineering sector of industry, the relative decline of the heavy chemicals sector echoed that of its parent, textiles. Changing technology favoured English chemical works, and amalgamations left Scottish works vulnerable to closure. The great St. Rollox chemical works lost its prime position, just as the whole of Glasgow's chemical industry lost its lucrative contracts with bleachers and dyers, metal refiners, and farmers, in home and export markets[9].

These ominous indications of growing over-dependence upon heavy engineering were ignored by industrialists, as were the signs of vulnerability within the marine sector, the lynchpin of the whole structure. The long slumps of 1874-81 and 1884-88 should have rung warning bells on overproduction of ships and engines, and the dangers of dependence upon foreign orders, but every upturn in the fortunes of the shipyards encouraged further massive capital investment in new plant and workshops[10], drawing inexorably into the shipbuilding web those engineering firms specialising in cranes, dockyard construction, and electrical apparatus. From the turn of the century, large government contracts for warships disguised the lack of foreign orders, and drew into the mesh gunnery-systems, munitions, and instrument firms. Viewed in hindsight, the processes by which a single group of industries, locked in close and complex integration, and vulnerable to the fluctuations of overseas demand, came to dominate the industrial economy of Glasgow, may seem to have been mortgaging the future against an uncertain present. However, this would be to deny the overwhelming contemporary logic of specialisation, and the conviction of the entrepreneurs in the rightness of their decisions. Their burgeoning confidence, echoed by their fellows in business and commerce, found vigorous expression in the expanding physique of the city.

River and port

Matching the tempo and meeting the requirements of industrial change, large-scale improvements to the River Clyde and Glasgow harbour were undertaken. The fifth Clyde Navigation Act of 1840, embodying widening schemes for the river, initiated a downstream migration of industrial concerns, including shipyards, whose previous locations had inhibited river improvement close to the city. The confluence of the River Kelvin with the Clyde came to roughly delimit the commercial sector of the river, upstream to the central city, from the shipyard sector, downstream to Clydebank. Between 1848 and 1882, Mavisbank and Plantation Quays on the south bank, and Finnieston and Stobcross Quays on the north bank, together with improvements upstream of the Broomielaw, greatly increased wharfage space, but the limitations to downstream expansion created by shipyards at Govan and the Kelvin mouth outlined the need for off-river facilities. Dry-docks for ship repair were constructed just upstream of Govan in 1875, 1886 and 1898, while tidal basins opened on the north bank at Queen's Dock in 1877, and on the south bank at Kingston Dock in 1867 and Princes Dock in 1897, provided badly needed quay space.

As Table 6.i indicates, not only the gross tonnage, but the unit tonnage of ships using Glasgow harbour increased greatly, rising to meet and overwhelm new harbour space at all periods. Glasgow's huge mineral trade, with exported coal representing one-third of the total trade of the harbour, and massive imports of iron ore replacing exhausted local supplies, encouraged the opening of a separate mineral dock, Rothesay Dock at Clydebank, with a rail link to Glasgow. In the same way, cattle lairages and timber storage facilities were gradually transferred downstream[11]. Also to be seen in Table 6.i is the relatively high unit tonnage of Glasgow-registered ships, partly a reflection of the distant overseas trading and passenger-carrying interests of Glasgow shipping companies, and partly evidence of the capacity of Clyde yards to meet growing demand for larger vessels. The removal of a rock bar at Elderslie between 1903 and 1907, and large-scale widening and straightening of bends opposite and downstream from Clydebank, permitted the construction of giant vessels such as the Lusitania and Aquitania, the latter completed a few months before the outbreak of the Great War.

Table 6.i. Gross and unit tonnages: (a) ships using Glasgow Harbour; (b) Glasgow-registered ships

	(a)		(b)		
	Gross tonnage	Unit tonnage	Gross tonnage	Unit tonnage	Number of ships
1841	1.14 million	75.1	95,062	220.5	431
1861	1.5 million	93.5	218,804	332.2	679
1881	3.05 million	172.1	827,435	657.7	1,258
1891	3.37 million	209.1	1,316,809	835.5	1,576
1908	6.0 million	368.8	1,957,391	1,151.4	1,700

Source: Marwick, J. D., 1909. *The River Clyde and the Clyde Burghs*. Appendix Tables II and III.

A truly massive investment of capital, both public and private, transformed the River Clyde between 1840 and the outbreak of the Great War (see Fig. 7.i, p.152). The river became a long ship-canal, wide and deep enough to permit the passage of ocean-going vessels to the port of Glasgow, where the most modern cranes and other dockside facilities provided rapid turnaround for the ships which brought the products of the world to Glasgow's long rows of warehouses and waiting railways. From the complex of shipyards and engineering works which lined its banks, ships of every shape, size and function sailed out to the oceans, rivers, lakes and seas of the world. The Clyde was at last a great river, and Glasgow one of the world's great ports.

Outward growth and inward change

Development of the townscape involved the two major processes of outward, additive and absorptive growth, and internal transformative change. Development of a transportation infrastructure accelerated both processes, together with the complex social and functional disaggregation which accompanied them. By 1850, a broad division was apparent, into an eastern area of factories and workers' residences, and a western area of business premises and middle class dwellings. By the late 1870s, greater complexity in spatial patterning had appeared, with strong differentiation between working class districts in the core and at the periphery.

The old medieval core area of Glasgow passed through a cycle of change involving concentration, up to c.1870, of unskilled and disadvantaged working class groups, creating overcrowded and insanitary slums which were partially cleared by the joint action of the City Improvement Trust and certain railway companies, during the 1870s. Thereafter, rapid falls in population left an area characterised by storage premises, and the least socially mobile working class, living in lodging houses and the poorest quality accommodation[12]. Immediately to the west of this area, the middle class residential streets on Ramshorn and Meadowflats had been invaded by business and administrative functions, following the tide of middle class colonisation as it flowed west across the Blythswood estate. The neat, two-storey Georgian residences were replaced by the headquarters of shipping companies, insurance brokers, and merchant bankers, as the central grid of streets became dominated by four- and five-storey office blocks whose elegant facades symbolised the confidence and prosperity of Glasgow's businessmen (Pl.6.i). The luxuriantly Italianate Stock Exchange, built in 1875 at the corner of Buchanan Street and St. George's Place, provided vital evidence of Glasgow's role in international commerce, while the ebullient mixture of styles in the fabric of the Municipal Chambers, begun on the eastern edge of George Square in 1883, is a flaunting both of the prestige of the city, and the power of its Council. Blythswood itself underwent similar functional change as the growth of banking and commerce in the 1870s and 1890s raised central land values, bringing competition for central city location and forcing smaller business and professional concerns into its eastern edge. The intrusion of railway termini and the growth of a centralised retail sector intensified the development of a central business district, whose characteristics will be examined in the next chapter.

Industry led the outward growth of working class areas. The line of the Forth and Clyde canal, at first forming a northern boundary, was by-passed as locomotive engineering was developed in Springburn, and as large industrial units such as the Saracen Foundry sought expansionist sites beyond the crowded city, and complexes of factories and tenement squares spread beyond Port Dundas into Possil and Maryhill. Westward, along both banks of the Clyde, shipbuilding and engineering brought concentrations of working class housing to Partick and Whiteinch, Kingston and Govan. In the east, foundries, chemical works, potteries and brick-works led a wave-front of rapid urbanisation[13]. Then, east and west, industry was overtaken by the outward urban growth of tenement dwellings, and its nodes remained embedded as islands in a great proletarian sea. The tenements disposed their rigid squares and rectangles in gridiron street patterns, aligned to older routeways which became the focal core streets of the new tenement districts, and which gave them their names. Shettleston, Dumbarton, Cathcart, Maryhill and

6.i   *St. Vincent Street, looking east to George Square, 1894. The City Chambers (centre distance) have replaced the Georgian houses seen in Plate 5.i.*

Garscube Roads became tenement canyons, with ground-floor lines of small shops, public houses, and other services, while in their tenement hinterlands, churches, schools and halls reinforced the growth of community identities.

West of Blythswood, the middle class residential drive continued across the estates of Kelvinhaugh and Sandyford to Hillhead and Kelvinside, wedged between industrial suburbs to north and south. In the 1870s and 1880s the wealthier middle classes used commuter railways to continue their outward drive to Lenzie, Kirkintilloch, Bearsden, Milngavie and even Helensburgh on the north shore of the Firth of Clyde, while fast steamer services carried city businessmen from Gourock and Wemyss Bay to and from their homes in Rothesay, Dunoon, and other small select communities on the Firth. The gaps in West End villa development left by this departing group were quickly colonised by the terraces and grander tenements of the lower middle classes[14], creating a distinctive urban landscape dominated by an admixture of middle-class residences (see Fig. 7.iii & Pls. 6.iii and iv). The drumlin summits were crowned by the mansions of the wealthy, or by institutional buildings such as the new University, transferred in 1870 from its ancient location in the medieval core to a new site and new premises on Gilmorehill, more in keeping with the middle-class backgrounds of its students. Below the drumlin crests, elegant terraced houses and spacious tenement flats covered the slopes, while roads and commuter railway lines snaked out along the sinuous valley bottoms between the drumlins. However, expansion was not sustained until the end of the century, and on the western periphery, the owners of the estate of Knightswood, advertising it for sale in 1885, miscalculated in listing among its attractions the fact that Great Western Road reached its western terminus only half a mile distant, and that as "Glasgow is extending rapidly. . . . Building sites may soon be taken up"[15]. The era of contiguous westward expansion was over, and Knightswood remained as farmland until the advent of the municipal building schemes of the late 1920s and 1930s.

South of the river, the villa suburb of Pollokshields provided the only rival to the West End, until commuter railway and tramway lines encouraged villa, terrace and tenement building for the middle classes in Crosshill, Langside, Mount Florida and Cathcart. Developing their own central service cores, numbers of these small communities became Police Burghs, and bitterly contested their subsequent absorption into an expanding city, extending its rating base and rationalising its services by annexing peripheral communities. This absorptive growth was part of a phenomenon seen by some as the single most distinguishing characteristic of the Scottish city, the extension of civic control over many aspects of urban life[16]. Glasgow municipalised its water supply in 1855, gas in 1869, electricity in 1891, tramways in 1894, and telephones in 1900. While the latter were sold to the Post Office in 1907, the others endured, as did housing of the working classes, begun in 1871[17]. As more and more aspects of their city's life came under their control, the councils saw themselves in the forefront of constructive change. "So it

6.ii   *Dumbarton Road, c.1955*

6.iii   *Victorian mansion, Dowanhill*

6.iv.   *Park Circus*

comes that in many — almost all — the important modifications of social legislation the towns and cities have been pioneers; . . . So also it comes that municipal rule is now being recognised as coming closer to the everyday interests of the people than the enactments of the Imperial Senate. . . ."[18] The bitter experience of half a century of war against squalor may have justified the former sentiment, but a certain lack of humility in the latter was to have unfortunate consequences for the future.

Population and public health — the demographic transition

During the period 1841-1914 Glasgow went through a demographic transition from a situation of dangerous imbalance, with high birth rates eclipsed by even higher death rates, and a population growth maintained only by the injection of fresh migrant blood, to a stage, just before the First World War, where population growth was sustained on a lowered birth rate by the survival of a much higher proportion of births, together with a greatly reduced net migration. The crucial processes during these decades were the beginnings of public health awareness, the framing of the necessary legislation, and the acceptance by municipal authority of the daunting challenge to improve the health of its people.

Table 6.ii. **Population growth: Glasgow and West Central Scotland: 1841-1912**

Census Year	West Central Scotland	% of total Scottish pop.	Glasgow	% of total Scottish pop.	% of W. Cen. Scottish pop.
1841	790,696	30.2	255,650	9.75	32.33
1851	926,221	32.1	329,097	11.39	35.53
1861	1,060,132	34.6	395,503	12.91	37.3
1871	1,241,952	37.	477,732	14.21	38.46
1881	1,460,638	39.1	511,415	13.69	35.
1891	1,657,616	41.2	565,839	14.05	34.13
1901	1,976,640	44.2	761,709	17.03	38.53
1911	2,169,754	45.6	784,496	16.47	36.15
1912	Glasgow Boundaries Act Annexation		1,008,487	21.17	46.47

Sources: Census of Scotland: Enumeration Abstracts 1851, 1861, 1871, 1881, 1891, 1901, 1911, and appendix to 1911 Abstract, "Population of Area affected by Glasgow Boundaries Act, 1912".

Glasgow's growth during the latter half of the nineteenth century and the early decades of the twentieth must be seen in the context of broad spatial processes of population change within Scotland, principally Highland-Lowland, and rural-urban transfers. In general terms, the Lowland share of Scotland's population, and within that category, that of the West Central Lowlands, rose steadily. Similarly, urban population gained at the expense of rural population, with the largest urban units, and especially Glasgow, gaining most (Table 6.ii). By 1861, while the urban/rural balance in percentages was 58 to 42 for Scotland as a whole, that of the West Central Lowlands was 80 to 20, demonstrating clearly the trend towards overwhelming urban dominance which was to develop during the next 50 years[19].

Description of the relative roles of natural increase and net migration as components of Glasgow's population growth is rendered complex by the operation of a third process, that of absorption of peripheral population groups. Major additions to the city's territory and population began with the annexation of the Barony of Gorbals in 1846, but were concentrated in the latter part of the period, with extensions into Maryhill, Hillhead, Crosshill, Govanhill and Pollokshields adding over 53,000 in 1891, Kinning Park adding 14,000 in 1905, and the huge acquisition of 1912 including the populous industrial burghs of Govan, Partick and Pollokshaws among its c.224,000 new citizens. Despite these distortions, a pattern of growth radically different from that of the period 1790-1840 can be discerned. While the rate of natural increase of population maintained a steady level, that of migration varied greatly, producing considerable irregularities in growth rate as a whole. From 1841 to 1871, there was a large net inflow, while in the 70s and 80s, especially the former, the flow was reversed. A resurgence of in-migration in the 1890s was followed by an even steeper level of outflow lasting to the end of the period, and corresponding to a wider change in migration flows out of the British Isles altogether, instead of to the cities[20]. The low immigration flows to Glasgow in the 1870s and 1880s, are not representative of the area as a whole, since suburban communities, especially those such as Govan or Partick, where shipbuilding and engineering were booming, experienced sharp population rises. Between 1871 and 1891 the population of Partick rose from 17,707 to 36,538 people, that of Govan went from 19,200 to 61,589, while even a residential suburb such as Pollokshields went from 3,314 to 9,709[21]. Thus within the greater area which was to constitute the new Glasgow after boundary change, the rates of immigration and population growth fluctuated less than within the pre-1891, or pre-1912, city.

It was not solely the employment opportunities presented by peripheral industrial growth which brought about this dichotomy of population development between core and periphery, but the activities of the City Improvement Trust, operating after 1866 to demolish large sectors of the central slums of Glasgow, thereby dispossessing scores of thousands of people and creating a similar pattern of central population loss and peripheral population gain within the boundary of the city itself. Of the city's 24 Sanitary Districts, 14, representing a contiguous central core, lost population at rates varying from four to 56% between 1871 and 1881, while the remaining peripheral districts gained population at rates of between three and 66% (Fig. 6.i). Blythswood, St. Enoch and Exchange lost population through encroachment by the public buildings and offices of the growing central business district, and the intrusion of railway lines

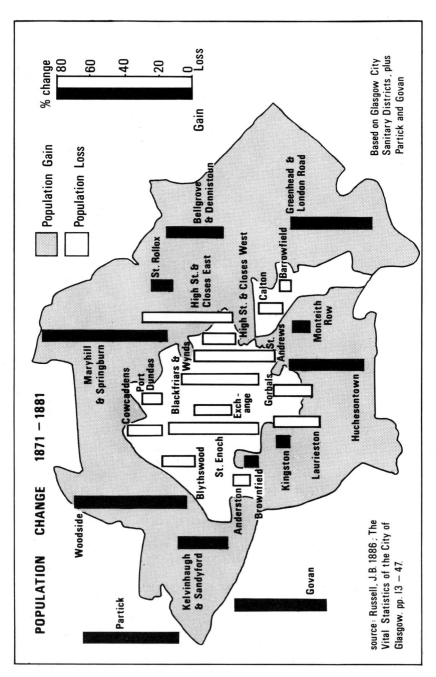

6.i   Population change 1871-1881

and termini, while the remaining losses were due mainly to Improvement Trust demolition. Of the ten districts which gained population, Springburn and Maryhill, St. Rollox, Bellgrove and Dennistoun, Greenhead and London Road, Kingston, Hutcheson Square, Kelvinhaugh and Sandyford, and Woodside, contained the mass of recently erected tenements in the city, and comprised the 'New Glasgow'[22], of mixed industrial-residential character in the north, east (Pls. 6.v + vi) and south, and principally residential in the west (Pls. 6.vii + viii) which attracted not only displaced central city residents, but immigrants. While population losses in the city core numbered 54,603 between 1871 and 1881, gains in peripheral city districts numbered 79,246, indicating a migrant preference for the newer tenement areas.

However, migrant residential preference was as varied as the composition of the migrant stream, which changed proportionally over time. The decade 1841-51 continued the trend of extremely high rates of immigration established during the previous 30 years, but from the 1851 peak, when almost 56% of the population was not city-born, the level fell steadily throughout the later nineteenth and early twentieth centuries. Scots constituted the largest component, with the greatest contribution from short-distance migrants from the western, and to a lesser extent, the eastern lowlands. The failure of successive potato crops in Ireland and the resultant famines brought a further tide of migrants in the 1840s and 1850s, though numbers dropped rapidly thereafter. A small, but steady trickle of English migrants grew in absolute numbers throughout the period, while in the decades around the turn of the century, Italians, and Russian and Polish Jews arrived in small numbers, the latter concentrating mainly in Gorbals (Table 6.iii). The densely-packed warrens of cheap housing in the central districts exerted a magnetic influence on all migrants, but especially on the Irish. Even after the large-scale demolitions of the 1860s and 1870s had reduced the quantity of poor quality houses available, and selective out-migration had reduced the population of central Glasgow to an ageing group, with large numbers of residual single-parent families with Glasgow-born heads, sure signs of social decay[23], Irish migrants continued to inhabit the area. The district around St. Mary's or Tron parish, with a population 45% Irish-born in 1851, still had 32%

Table 6.iii.   **Birthplace of migrants to Glasgow, 1851-1911** (% of city's population)

Birthplace	1851	1861	1871	1881	1891	1901	1911
Scotland (ex. Glasgow)	34.68	30.04	34.52	31.56	29.89	*27	26.18
Ireland	18.17	15.69	14.32	13.12	10.57	8.87	6.73
England & Wales	2.51	2.63	3.06	3.16	3.36	3.72	3.81
Other	0.53	0.86	0.67	0.85	0.96	1.67	1.74
Total	55.89	49.22	52.57	48.69	44.78	*41.26	38.46

Source: Census of Scotland: Enumeration Abstracts; 1851-1911. (*Lanarkshire-born residents have been estimated at c.20,000 to give the Scottish total for 1901.)

6.v   *Tenements and mill, James Street, Bridgeton*

6.vi   *Tenement industry, Calton*

6.vii   Middle-class tenements, Woodlands

6.viii   Working-class tenements, Yorkhill

Irish in 1881, after the considerable clearances in Tron, Bridgegate and the Wynds, while outer areas such as Kingston, and Kelvinhaugh and Sandyford, had only 8% and 6% respectively in 1881[24], and the 1904 report on housing in the city noted the Irish preference for cheap housing in the inner city[25]. While displacement of large numbers of Irish did take place, with Bridgegate, and High Street (West) losing respectively 46% and 36% of their Irish-born population between 1881 and 1891, movement was mainly to adjacent inner-city areas, and the new lodging-houses erected by the Improvement Trust in cleared areas attracted large numbers of young single men, many of them Irish[26]. The process of 'filtering-up' through the housing market was not one in which Irish migrants figured greatly. The higher rents charged for newer and better tenement flats were out of the reach of the mainly unskilled labouring Irish, and these properties attracted mainly Scots-born artisans, moving either within or from outside the city. At the lowest artisan income levels, supplementary finance to pay higher rents was obtained by taking in lodgers, usually single males, but sometimes whole families, and in this way the conditions of severe overcrowding of the core, excised by the surgery of demolition, to some extent replicated themselves in the newer tenement areas.

Table 6.iv. **Blackfriars and West End Districts, 1860. Vital Statistics**

	Blackfriars	West End
Population	10577	2972
Density per acre	328	34
% pop. under 5	13.6	9.11
Birth rate (per 1000)	44	17
Death rate under 5 (per 1000)	213	34
Death rate over 5 (per 1000)	95	5.3

Source: Strang, J., 1861. *Report on the Vital, Social and Economic Statistics of Glasgow for 1860.*

The combined effects of natural increase and net migration brought about population increases which, despite boundary extensions, created increased densities of population throughout the city. The crude rise in density reached its peak in 1881, but the general city rate hid wide internal variations. In 1860 the extremes were represented by St. Mary Tron, with 715 persons per acre, and Springburn, still mainly rural, with 15 persons per acre. Closer to the mean for core and periphery were Blackfriars and West End districts, whose characteristics, summarised in Table 6.iv, show considerable disparity not only in density, but in all social characteristics. Figures for 1871 and 1881 (Table 6.v columns 1 + 2) show that while density range began to narrow, largely as a result of central area clearances, pockets of extremely high density persisted in the core, while at the same time, population transfers and new migrant choice brought rising densities to outer sanitary districts. Ground within the city became overcrowded with houses, tenements and factories, the tenements were

Table 6.v. City Sanitary Districts: Comparative Density & Mortality, 1871-1881: 1 & 2-room houses 1881 (%)

No.	Name	Density per acre		Total death rate (per 1000)		Death-rate under 5 yrs.		1 apt.	2 apts.
		1871	1881	1871	1881	1871	1881	1881	1881
0.	Blythswood	126	101	20.6	16.1	75.5	52.9	9	26
17.	Kelvinhaugh & Sandyford	37	43	20.4	17.2	69	54	7.5	37
15.	Woodside	81	134	25.5	20.9	90	64.2	20	43
9.	Monteith Row	39	42	23.5	21	81.1	70.1	15.5	33
1.	Exchange	123	96	22	21.7	78.8	67.4	18	38
19.	Kingston	100	97	25.6	21.8	86.3	73.4	18	36
4.	St. Rollox	289	316	30.8	21.8	102.5	69	27	56
23 + 24	Springburn & Maryhill	17	26	28.4	22.4	84.7	68.6	31	59
5.	Bellgrove & Dennistoun	37	47	29.4	23.1	94.5	72.3	32	44
12.	St. Enoch Square	93	44	31.3	24.4	109.6	87.7	24	34
21.	Hutcheson Square	99	121	26.4	24.9	87.6	79.3	31	52
7.	Greenhead & London Rd.	36	52	31.1	26.7	106.4	87.5	43.5	47
20.	Laurieston	251	186	29.8	27.2	102.7	88.5	30	50
2.	Port Dundas	73	64	33.9	27.3	126.1	83.5	28.5	63
18.	Anderston	249	229	32.5	28.4	116.3	101.7	33	47
10.	St. Andrews Square	365	189	38.3	28.7	144	93.1	29	33
22.	Gorbals	350	274	38.5	29	138.2	103.8	29	45
3.	High St. & Closes West	301	239	45.7	29.9	165.8	95.6	46.5	38
8.	Barrowfield	245	233	31.2	30.3	108.2	103.3	47.5	46
13.	Brownfield	337	348	38.3	30.7	138.9	99.3	24	56
11.	Calton	388	335	36.7	30.9	124.5	108.4	43	46
16.	Cowcaddens	316	249	33.9	32	116.1	116.6	45	47
6.	High St. & Closes East	351	155	40.7	37.8	148.9	128.5	53	33
14.	Bridgegate & Wynds	408	223	42.3	38.3	166.1	138.7	49	35

Source: Russell, J. B., 1886. *The Vital Statistics of the City of Glasgow.* Pt.1, pp.13-47.

N.B. this table should be read in conjunction with the map of population change, Fig. 6.i.

Table 6.vi.a.   **House and room occupancy: Glasgow 1911**

Rooms (apartments)	% of housing stock	% of population	Persons per house	Persons per room
1	23.1	13.7	3.1	3.1
2	46.3	48.3	4.8	2.4
3	18.6	21	5.2	1.7
4	6.6	7.1	5	1.2
5	8	9.6	5.5	0.7

Table 6.vi.b.   **Death rate (per 1000) by age group and house size: Glasgow 1912**

Rooms	under 1 year	1-5 years	10-15 years
1	187	39	4.5
2	143.5	28.5	3
3	114.5	16.5	2
4+	88	10	1.5
City	151	28.5	3

Sources: (a) adapted from Chalmers, A. K., 1916. *Health and Housing*, p.7

       (b) adapted from Chalmers, A. K., 1914. Public Health-Vital Statistics in *Municipal Glasgow: its evolution and enterprises.*

overcrowded with rooms, and the rooms in turn with people[27]. From an overall city density of 50 persons per acre in 1841, the swift rise to a peak of 97 per acre in 1881, and a slower decline thereafter to 60 per acre in 1911, was paralleled in the surging death rates fuelled by contagion, followed by decline as public health measures began to take effect.

Table 6.vi charts the progress of national and municipal response to the public health problems of the Victorian city. In Glasgow the large population increases of the early decades of the nineteenth century had overwhelmed housing and water supply alike, creating ideal conditions for the spread of disease.

"Though typhus did not arrest attention by any epidemic prevalence until 1818, it was in the city from the beginning of the century. Its subsequent history was that of an active volcano, periods of deceptive repose alternating with violent eruptions. For short intervals it smouldered in the wynds. When the steady influx of immigrants attracted by the prospect of work had reproduced a susceptible population, it burst out into an epidemic. Smallpox . . . was scarcely ever entirely absent . . . three severe epidemics of cholera . . . 1832 : . . 1848/9 . . . 1853/4. An outbreak of relapsing fever in 1843 attacked more than a quarter of the inhabitants of the poorer districts. Underneath these periodic eruptions flowed a continuous condition of ill-health, which represented the chronic, as the former represented the periodic, results of precisely the same physical circumstances in the environment of the population."[28]

Public authority response to the conditions described above by James Burn Russell can be grouped into three broad approaches, operating at different scales. In the period 1855-75, the scale was city-wide, with the provision of fresh water supplies from Loch Katrine attacking one of the principal breeding-grounds of disease, in the polluted waters of public wells and the River Clyde. The 1862 Glasgow Police Act authorised the creation of a sanitary department, and in 1863 Dr. W. T. Gairdner was installed as the first of a series of energetic, innovative and committed Medical Officers of Health for the city. The provision of fever hospitals, albeit of temporary construction, and the erection of washing-houses for infected bedding and clothing, began to have effects upon the death-rates from water-borne diseases. By the mid 1870s, epidemics were spatially limited within the city, arising mainly from infected milk sources rather than polluted water, and affecting substantially fewer individuals. Cholera shrank in the face of fresh water. Smallpox, though remaining endemic and occasionally, as in 1900, erupting epidemically, responded to stricter vaccination controls from 1871 onwards. The completion of Belvidere hospital in 1878 provided the crucial isolation of smallpox victims needed to contain its virulence[29]. Typhus, spread rapidly by body lice in overcrowded conditions, was tackled by attempts to eradicate substandard housing. The first of a series of Improvements Acts empowering municipal authorities to demolish congested slum property followed hard on the heels of Glasgow's worst typhus outbreak in 1864/65, during which districts such as Tron and Garngad suffered respectively 33 and 27 cases per 1,000 of their population[30]. Together with the provision of washing, disinfecting, and isolation facilities, these measures largely brought typhus under control by the 1880s.

It had been recognised from the earliest stages of sanitary and housing reform that vile living conditions, poverty and its attendant malnutrition, and prevalent disease were intimately linked, and the next stage of municipal intervention addressed itself mainly to provision of sanitary facilities at district level.

"In the experience of epidemics, great and small, and in chronic prevalence of fevers kept in vigorous activity by dirt, overcrowding and want, Glasgow in no way differed from other large British centres of population. Our sins were greater, it may be, and in proportion was our punishment."[31]

Expiation for sins took the form of intensifying the provision of facilities such as district baths and wash-houses, removal and destruction of domestic refuse, and cleaning of streets and courts. The benefits of refuse destruction may be imagined from the fact that in the heat of mid-summer, 1874, almost 29,000 tons of refuse were stored in city depots[32].

The introduction of free treatment for fever patients, and more stringent vaccination regulations combined with other measures to greatly reduce the incidence of typhus, and to keep smallpox at a minimal level. A gradually increasing proportion of the highly susceptible infant population was thereby enabled to survive the depredations of these diseases, only to succumb in great numbers to children's ailments. While a chance decline in the virulence of the scarlet fever streptococcus reduced its level of fatality[33], diseases such as measles and whooping cough took a growing toll of young lives. Deaths of children under five as a proportion of total deaths within the city had dropped from over 50% in the period 1855-9, to c.45% between 1860 and 1864, but from 1865 to 1869, the proportion rose to 47.5%, and until 1890, the average for each five-year period never fell below 43.5%[34] (Fig. 6.ii). Just as five-year averages disguised extremes such as a 54% death rate in 1861[35], so city-wide generalisations hid concentrations of wretchedness in the poorer districts reflecting themselves in infant death rates. In 1858, infant mortality was nearly double among illegitimate as opposed to legitimate children, while one in 13 illegitimate children were stillborn, compared to one in 26 legitimate[36].

The third great phase of assault on misery focused at the scale of the individual house. The Shaftesbury, Torren and Cross Acts, culminating in the Housing of the Working Classes Act of 1890 sought to eradicate unhealthy houses, and their accumulation in unhealthy areas[37]. (The application of the latter Act to Glasgow, together with preceding and subsequent legislation aimed specifically at the city, will be discussed in a later section on housing.) Statutes on water closet provision maintained the battle for sanitation, while those on cubic air space inside and clean air outside tenements were aimed at the most efficient group of contagious killers of the nineteenth century, the respiratory diseases, principally tuberculosis, bronchitis, and pneumonia. Declining mortality from other infectious diseases permitted more children to survive into adulthood, only to succumb to wasting of their lungs through living in overcrowded homes, and going outdoors to breathe polluted industrial air. Once again, average rates disguised spatial concentration. Cities suffered more than rural areas, and the level of mortality increased with city size to the peak of Glasgow. Within Glasgow, the poor congested districts produced the largest number of victims. The separate categories of disease were not always distinguished in reports, but tuberculosis, or pthisis, maintained the highest incidence until the 1870s, when bronchitis took over as the principal killer. A combination of housing legislation and restrictions on pollution began to reduce the dreadful effects from c.1900, but into the 1920s and 1930s, respiratory diseases took a heavy toll of Glasgow's people.

By the turn of the century, therefore, there had been two decades of slow decline of mortality rate, paralleled by a slowly declining birth rate. The next two decades saw a much more rapid reduction in both rates, so that by 1920, Glasgow had passed through its demographic transition. In achieving this change, the two-pronged attack on general sanitation and

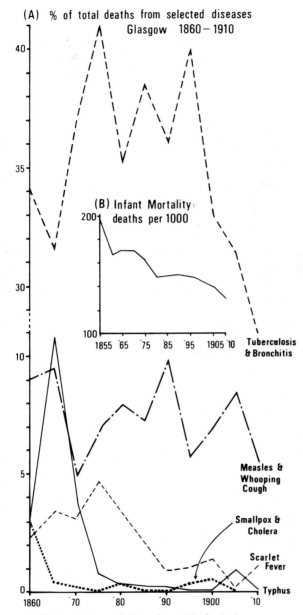

(A) % of total deaths from selected diseases
Glasgow 1860 – 1910

(B) Infant Mortality:
deaths per 1000

Tuberculosis & Bronchitis

Measles & Whooping Cough

Smallpox & Cholera

Scarlet Fever

Typhus

sources : (A) Annual Reports, Registrar General for Scotland.
(B) Chalmers, A.K., 1914, Municipal Glasgow ; its Evolution and Enterprises . adapted from p. 212 'Public Health – Vital Statistics'.

6.ii.a   Percentage of total deaths from selected diseases: Glasgow 1860-1910
6.ii.b   Infant mortality: deaths per 1000: 1855-1910

health on the one hand, and upon unhealthy houses on the other, had differed in effect, with the former exhibiting markedly greater success than the latter, for reasons to be examined in the next section.

Housing

In the minds of many of those active in the field of public health improvement in Glasgow there was no doubt about the importance of the house in the environmental equation.

"Glasgow stands alone with the highest death-rate, the highest number of persons per room, the highest proportion of her population occupying one-apartment houses, and the lowest occupying houses of five apartments and upwards. . . . These facts prove beyond a doubt that the predominant factor in the health of cities is the proportion of house-space to inhabitant[38]. It is those small houses which give . . . the striking characteristics of an enormous proportion of deaths in childhood, and of deaths from diseases of the lungs at all ages. Their exhausted air and poor and perverse feeding fill our streets with bandy-legged children."[39]

These condemnations were written by James Burn Russell almost 20 years after his predecessor, W. T. Gairdner, Glasgow's first Medical Officer of Health had identified overcrowding as the greatest cause of disease in towns, producing a horrific liability to epidemic disease, especially consumption and diseases of the lungs, and an enormous rate of mortality in young children in particular[40]. Thirty years after Russell, A. K. Chalmers could still ask "Why has local administration succeeded . . . in improving the conditions of external environment, and met with such indifferent success that it may be said to have failed to find any adequate solution to the problem of housing"[41]. While municipal control had been extended over a wide range of public services, the scale of intervention in housing had been limited. Enforcement of the provisions of a growing array of national and local statutes, many of them vague in content and intention, had enhanced the effects of general sanitary reform, but physical intervention in the field of housing provision proceeded only very slowly. The main emphasis was on eradication of blight, with c.11,000 houses demolished between 1866 and 1901[42], and only a limited number built or acquired by the local authority. By 1914, only 1.4% of households lived in municipally-owned accommodation, and apart from the equally limited operations of the Glasgow Workmen's Dwelling Company, commenced in 1892, the management of existing housing and the provision of new accommodation, was left entirely to the private sector, in which the type and level of house provision reflected too accurately the play of market forces. Fig. 6.iii.a reflects what one writer called the "extraordinary violence of fluctuations in the Glasgow building trade"[43]. Severe depression initiated by events such as the failure of the City of Glasgow Bank in 1878 brought a large-scale and long-term downturn in house building, but slumps in the capital goods industries, especially shipbuilding, drastically reduced short-term demand. The combination of demolition of unhealthy property, conversion of larger houses to single apartments, multiple-household sharing and taking in of lodgers, exacerbated low levels of house building and encouraged severe overcrowding. Even in boom periods there was little alleviation of overcrowded conditions, since the majority of houses built were of only one or two rooms (Fig. 6.iii.b). Between 1862 and 1901, c.77% of all new houses were of these types, reflecting the demand from a growing working-class sector which could afford only the lower rent levels which such properties could command. A clear relationship existed between these small houses and the high death rates characteristic of the city, and their continued construction up to World War I was an important factor in the retardation of death rate reduction. Table 6.vi.a shows the level of overcrowding in these houses, while Table 6.vi.b demonstrates the strong relationship between house size and death rates within the city. Spatial concentrations of one and two-apartment houses correlated closely with locally high death rates. In 1881, a district such as Kelvinhaugh and Sandyford with only 44.5% of its housing stock consisting of small houses, exhibited low death rates for its whole population, as well as for children, while at the other end of the spectrum, rates of 108.4 per 1,000 for children under five, and 30.9 per 1,000 overall, occurred in Calton, with 89% small houses in its stock. In Bellgrove and Dennistoun, death rates and small houses occupied the middle of the range in 1881 (Table 6.v), but even by 1901, when the area's overall death rate had dropped to 19 per 1,000, its one-apartment houses produced a rate of 36 per 1,000[44].

High population densities in Scottish cities were a reflection not just of overcrowded rooms in overcrowded houses, but of masses of these houses packed together in the typical structure, the tenement. Deriving its name from the medieval burgage plot, via the house built at the head of the plot, rising to several storeys to maximise plot use, the tenement was only abandoned as a mode of housing the working class for one decade between the World Wars. The physical model of the tenement, with its possibilities of producing multiple rents from a single plot of ground, recommended itself to the nineteenth century building speculator, required under Scots Law to lay out substantial sums of money prior to house-letting, and therefore looking for as large a financial return as quickly as possible. Enlargement of industrial nuclei, and relocation of expanding core-located industries on peripheral sites, with subsequent migrant demand for housing, provided the impetus for the phases of tenement building shown in Fig. 6.iii.a. In nineteenth-century Glasgow, working-class tenement housing accommodation was of three basic types; inner-city dwellings packed along the medieval burgage plots; small units 'made-down' from unsuccessful middle-class development, and the regular hollow squares and rectangles of the industrial tenement proper.

The character of housing in the first category has already been described (ibid. p.144) and by 1870, densities of 600-1,000 persons per acre had developed over considerable areas, often with a single tap in the close, or common entry, the only water supply for a six-storey tenement,

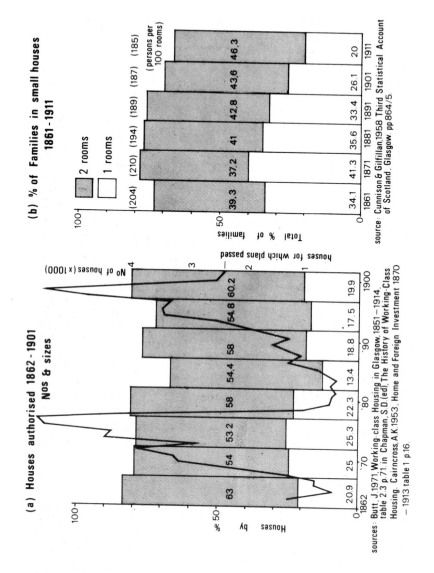

(b) % of Families in small houses 1861-1911

2 rooms

1 rooms

(persons per 100 rooms)

	(204)	(210)	(194)	(189)	(187)	(185)
2 rooms	39.3	37.2	41	42.8	43.6	46.3
1 rooms	34.1	41.3	35.6	33.4	26.1	20
	1861	1871	1881	1891	1901	1911

Total % of families

source: Cunnison & Gilfillan.1958 Third Statistical Account of Scotland. Glasgow. pp 864/5

(a) Houses authorised 1862-1901 Nos & sizes

Nº of houses (x 1000)

houses for which plans passed

	63	54	53.2	58	54.4	58	54.8	60.2
	20.9	25	25.3	22.3	13.4	18.8	17.5	19.9
	1862	'70		'80		'90		1900

Houses by %

sources: Butt, J 1971. Working-class Housing in Glasgow, 1851-1914. table 2.3 p.71 in Chapman. S.D.(ed) The History of Working-Class Housing. Cairncross. A.K.1953. Home and Foreign Investment 1870 - 1913 table 1 p.16.

6.iii.a   *Houses authorised 1862-1901: numbers and sizes*
6.iii.b   *Percentage of families in small houses: 1861-1911*

6.ix   *Close, 75 High Street; note the open drain, the sink on the exterior stair, and the well at the close-mouth on the left.*

Table 6.vii. Epidemic disease and Public Health response

Epidemic disease		Public Health response	
1843	Relapsing Fever	1843	Police Act: Inspector of Cleaning (streets & public places) appointed.
1847	Typhus		
1848/9	Cholera		
1851	Fever		
1853/5	Cholera	1853	Compulsory infant vaccination (smallpox). Not enforced.
		1855	Loch Katrine Act: Scottish Registration Act (compulsory registration of diseases).
		1856	Nuisances Removal Act.
		1857	Committee on Nuisances.
		1859/60	Loch Katrine Scheme — fresh water to city.
		1861	Police Act: Sanitary Dept. set up & M.O.H. appointed.
1864/5	Typhus	1864	First municipal disinfecting & washing-house: High Street.
		1865	First municipal fever hospital: Parliamentary Road.
1866	Cholera	1866	Police Act (sanitary clauses): City Improvements Act (housing).
1869	Typhus	1867	Public Health (Scotland) Act
1870	Relapsing Fever	1870	Sanitary Dept. extended. Temporary fever hospital, Belvidere.
		1872	First reception house for families of Typhus victims.
1873	Relapsing Fever (M)	1873	City Improvements Amendment Act; Vaccination station opened.
1875	Typhoid & Enteric Fever (M) Camphill		
1877/8	Enteric Fever (M) West End	1878	Permanent small-pox hospital, Belvidere. First proper isolation.
		1878/84	Opening of district baths & wash-houses.
		1879	Dairies & milkshops order.
1880	Enteric Fever (M) North & Central	1880	City Improvements Amendment Act.
		1881	Free treatment for fever patients. Returns of vaccination defaulters First refuse destructor (others 1884, 1890, 1894, 1897, 1902).
		1883	Washing & disinfection station, Belvidere.

1884	Enteric Fever (M) Hospitals	1889	Infectious Disease (Notification) Act.
1888	Scarlet Fever (M) Garnethill	1890	Housing of the Working Classes Act. (Part V. Scotland.)
			Glasgow Police Amendment Act (water closet provision).
1892	Scarlet Fever (M) Paisley Road	1892	Glasgow Building Regulations Act: Ruchill Rever hospital started.
			Further Powers Act — Smoke penalties.
1893/4	Scarlet Fever (M) Kelvinside	1894	First sewage purification unit, Dalmarnock; disinfection station, Ruchill.
		1897	Public Health (Scotland) Act: Glasgow Corp. (Improvements etc.) Act.
1900	Smallpox	1904	Sewage purification works, Dalmuir & Partick.
		1907	Notification of Births Act: Glasgow Infant Health Visitors Association.
		1908	Children Act.
		1910	Kinning Park & Shieldhall sewage purification works.

(M) = infected milk source

containing 60-70 families[45] (Pl. 6.ix). Sanitary facilities were equally rudimentary, with a report as late as 1891 stating that:

> "The provision made for the disposal of the excrement of the inhabitants of these tenements demands immediate attention. Several places are noted where there is no provision whatever, but in our opinion the privy (a public facility in the back yard) is in no case a sufficient provision for flatted tenements. It is never used, and cannot in the nature of the case be used by females, and seldom by children. The result is that every sink is practically a water-closet, and the stairs and the courts and roofs of outhouses are littered with deposits of filth cast from the windows."[46]

The dominant problem, however, was overcrowding. There were simply too few available houses for the people streaming into the city. In 1881, 14% of one-apartment houses, and 27% of two-apartment houses took in lodgers. In an 1891 example, noted on a Sanitary Inspector's night tour, a single room contained a labourer, his wife, two children, and the wife's brother, with 761 cubic feet of air-space. The labourer and his family lay on an old mattress on the floor of a recessed bed-space, while the wife's brother lay in a corner, with an old sack over him. There was an old table, a form, and a few dishes, while an old butter-butt full of dirty water completed the furnishings[47].

In the wynds and closes of the central area, furnished rooms or houses were let as lodgings on a weekly basis. In 1893, 204 of these existed, with cases reported of two to four couples sleeping in the same apartment[48]. The need to prevent such overcrowding led to the system of 'ticketed' houses, operated from 1866. Houses with less than three rooms had a metal plate fixed to the door, stating the number of occupants permitted, according to a ratio of 300 cubic feet of air space for every person over eight years of age. In 1896, there were c.25,000 such houses, the majority single apartments, and the night inspectors in that year found 3,686 cases of overcrowding, with 70-90 cubic feet of air per person instead of the new lower limit of 400[49]. By 1904, over 15,000 people were living in illegal conditions in ticketed houses alone, and pitiful attempts were made to deceive the night inspectors. The worst case found 11 adults occupying 880 cubic feet of space, and seven of them had hidden on an adjoining roof when the inspectors called. On several occasions two tiers of people were found, one under the mattress and one on top[50]. Officials were reluctant to prosecute such cases since expulsion would only produce overcrowding elsewhere, and alleviation of such conditions was only very gradually provided through the imposition of provisions of national and local Acts of Parliament (Table 6.vii). The 1892 Glasgow Buildings Regulation Act, enlarged upon by a similar act in 1900, provided some of the earliest firm guidelines towards improved living. The air-space limits of small houses were raised, from 900 to 1,000 cubic feet for one-apartments, 1,500 to 1,600 cu.ft. for two-apartments, and 2,000 to 2,400 cu.ft. for three-apartments. Raised ceiling heights, the practical elimination of enclosed beds, and the limitation on numbers of houses on a common stair, were all aimed at the fearsome mortality from contagious respiratory diseases[51].

Synchronously with enforcement of legislation aimed at existing and new accommodation, an assault was launched on the old city core, aimed at the wholesale removal of the worst slums. This ambitious surgery constituted an important milestone in the extension of municipal authority into the field of housing, since after the initial phase of demolition, new houses built remained in the ownership of the city corporation, beginning a process by which the majority of houses in the city were to come under local authority control. The scale of operation was also greater than in any other British city, including London. Between 1875 and 1888, slum clearance schemes in London displaced 34,693 people, c.0.9% of the capital's 1881 population[52]. In Glasgow, from 1866 to 1876, 28,965 people were displaced, representing 6.06% of the city's 1871 population. The first Glasgow Improvements Act of 1866, followed by Amendments Acts in 1871, 1880, and 1897, empowered a City Improvements Trust to schedule unhealthy houses for compulsory purchase followed by demolition, to purchase and lay out areas for new housing, and to provide accommodation for single homeless in municipally-run 'model' lodging-houses. Eighty eight acres of central slums containing c.51,000 people were scheduled for clearance (Pl. 6.x), but since compulsory purchase involved contacting property owners and agents in England, Ireland and the United States of America, the process of acquisition began slowly[53]. Descriptions of the first properties purchased demonstrated the need for clearance. Number 1 was a flat and attic, at 89 Gallowgate, on the west side of the court, with use of common ashpit and privy, while number 2, 17-19 Great Dovehill, was a front and back tenement with dungstead in the court[54].

The activities of the Trust may be divided into two broad periods. Between 1866 and 1889, demolition was the dominant process, leading to large-scale population displacement, and concomitant overcrowding in housing areas fringing Trust property. Various railway companies, anxious to secure central city facilities, played prominent roles in the disappearance of slums. The City of Glasgow Union Railway ran its lines through Gallowgate, Saltmarket, Bridgegate and Glasgow Cross, with the Trustees paying for the widening of spans to accommodate more spacious street layouts[55]. The Glasgow and South-Western, and North British Railways cleared away the old Boar's Head Close, the Vennels, and the Havannah to open a joint depot in the High Street, while the Caledonian Central Railway also cleared around Glasgow Cross[56]. Attempting to stimulate the private sector into provision of replacement working class housing, the Trustees were successful with the purchase and laying out of the estates of Overnewton, far west of the city centre towards Partick, and Oatlands, south of the river and east of Hutchesontown. However, the building slump of the late 1870s and 1880s (Fig. 6.iii.a) brought these efforts to a close, and the Trustees were obliged to embark upon a limited municipal building programme. By 1902, only 257 houses had been built, of which 112 were single apartments, and 145 were two-apartments. By

6.x   *1866 Improvements Plan; the shaded area was scheduled for demolition; the darker lines represent proposed new streets.*

1914 only 2,199 houses had been added to the city stock by the Trust, providing accommodation for c.10,000 people. Of these houses, only 273 were three-apartments or larger[57]. In the field of lodging provision for single homeless the Trust was more effective. The philanthropic Model Lodging Association had been formed in 1847 in an effort to combat the vile conditions within privately owned lodging houses. The high proportion of these latter in the areas to be cleared encouraged municipal venture and by the 1880s, the council owned and operated seven model lodging houses providing space for 2,430 people[58]. The standards set in these houses provided a yardstick for private enterprise and, together with the family houses built, marked the firm extension of municipal interest into the field of housing management. From these modest beginnings stemmed the twentieth-century development of housing management to embrace the larger proportion of the city's housing stock.

The glorious growth and burgeoning prosperity of Victorian and Edwardian Glasgow was not shared by all, and in the city's spectacular rise, fundamental weaknesses had either been ignored, or barely come to terms with. Considerable advances in public health were undermined by failure to grasp the nettle of housing, leaving this fundamental aspect of society to the vagaries of private sector provision. The dangers of an industrial monoculture, intensifying in its incest as its infrastructure and innovativeness progressively aged, lurked behind the demands of an Imperial economy. In many ways, the worst was yet to come.

REFERENCES

1. Phillips, Sir Richard (Common Sense), *Monthly Magazine*, Feb. 1811, pp.1ff.
2. Robertson, A. J., 1970. The Decline of the Scottish Cotton Industry, 1860-1914. *Business History*, 12, 2, p.118.
3. Census of Scotland. Enumeration Abstracts. 1861, 1891, 1911.
4. Gilfillan, J. B. S., and Moisley, H. A., 1958. Industrial and Commercial Developments to 1914. In Miller, R., and Tivy, J. (eds.) *The Glasgow Region*, p.173.
5. Lenman, B., 1977. *An Economic History of Modern Scotland. 1660-1976*, pp.179-180.
6. Strang, J., 1863. *Report on the Vital, Social and Economic Statistics of Glasgow for 1862*, p.33. Nicol, J., 1891. *Vital Social and Economic Statistics of the City of Glasgow 1885-1891*, p.193. Campbell, R. H., 1964. Scottish Shipbuilding; its Rise and Progress, *S.G.M.*, 80, 2, p.109.
7. Bremner, D., 1869. *The Industries of Scotland*, pp.68-71.
8. Lenman, B., 1977, *op.cit.*, p.173. Gilfillan, J. B. S. and Moisley, H. A., 1958, *op.cit.*, p.178.
9. Gilfillan, J. B. S. and Moisley, H. A., 1958, *op.cit.*, pp.183-4. Slaven, A., 1975. *The Development of the West of Scotland, 1750-1960*, p.133.
10. Nicol, J., 1885. *Vital, Social and Economic Statistics of Glasgow for 1884*, pp.80/81. Checkland, S. G., 1976. *The Upas Tree: Glasgow 1875-1975*, p.10.
11. Riddell, J. F., 1979. *Clyde Navigation. A History of the Development and Deepening of the River Clyde*, pp.229-232; 238-243.
12. Lamont, D. W., 1976. Population, migration and social-area change in Central Glasgow, 1871-1891. A study in applied factorial ecology. University of Glasgow; unpub. Ph.D. thesis pp.49/50.
13. O.S. 1:10,560, 1865. Sheet VI; J. Bartholomew, Plan of Glasgow and suburbs, 1:10,560; 1871 & 1886.
14. Simpson, M., 1972. Urban transport and the development of Glasgow's West End, 1830-1914. *Journal of Transport History*, N.S.1. 3, p.157.
15. Particulars and Plan of the Estate of Knightswood, 1885. S.R.O., R.H.P. 3339.
16. Best, G. F. A., 1968. The Scottish Victorian City. *Victorian Studies*, xi, pp.329-58.
17. Corporation of the City of Glasgow, 1914. *Municipal Glasgow, its Evolution and Enterprises*, pp.2/3.
18. Bell, J. and Paton, J., 1896. *Glasgow: Its Municipal Organisation and Administration*, p.xxii.
19. Census of Scotland, Enumeration Abstracts, 1861.
20. Cairncross, A. K., 1953. *Home and Foreign Investment*, 1870-1913, p.24.

21. Census of Scotland, Enumeration Abstracts, 1871, 1891.
22. Russell, J. B., 1886. *The Vital Statistics of the City of Glasgow*, p.74.
23. Lamont, D. W., 1976, *op.cit.*, pp.124/125.
24. Russell, J. B., 1886, *op.cit.*, pp.14, 20, 45; Census of Scotland, Enumeration Abstracts, 1851.
25. Glasgow Municipal Commission on the Housing of the Poor. 1904, Vol. I. Minutes of Evidence, p.4.
26. Lamont, D. W., 1976, *op.cit.*, pp.125, 136/137.
27. Gairdner, W. T., 1870. On defects of House Construction in Glasgow as a Cause of Mortality. *Proceedings of the Philosophical Society of Glasgow*, vii, p.249.
28. Russell, J. B., 1894. *Evolution of Public Health Administration in Glasgow*, p.205.
29. Russell, J. B., 1888. City of Glasgow Fever and Small-Pox Hospitals, Belvidere, p.3.
30. Gairdner, W. T., 1895. Memorandum for the Chairman of the Sanitary Committee, p.8.
31. Bell, J. and Paton, J., 1896, *op.cit.*, p.182.
32. McColl, D., 1914. 'Cleaning' p.154, in *Municipal Glasgow: its Evolution and Enterprises*, *op.cit.*
33. Flinn, M., 1977. *Scottish Population History*, p.26.
34. Nicol, J., 1891. *Vital, Social, and Economic Statistics of Glasgow, 1885-1891*, p.62.
35. Strang, J., 1861. *Report on the Vital, Social and Economic Statistics of Glasgow for 1860*, p.17.
36. Strang, J., 1859. *Report on the Vital and Economic Statistics of Glasgow for 1858*, p.7.
37. Chalmers, A. K., 1916. Health and Housing, p.15 (paper read at Scottish Housing Conference, Jan. 3rd., 1916).
38. Russell, J. B., 1887. The House in Relation to Public Health. *Transactions of the Insurance and Actuarial Society of Glasgow*, 2nd series, No.5, p.11.
39. Russell, J. B., 1888. *Life in One Room*, p.14.
40. Gairdner, W. T., 1870, *op.cit.*, pp.247/8.
41. Chalmers, A. K., 1916, *op.cit.*, p.3.
42. Butt, J., 1971. Working-class Housing in Glasgow, 1851-1914, in Chapman, S. D. (ed.), *The History of Working-Class Housing*, p.71.
43. Cairncross, A. K., 1953. *Home and Foreign Investment, 1870-1913*, p.20 in; Fluctuations in the Glasgow Building Industry, 1856-1914.
44. Chalmers, A. K., 1903. The Death-Rate in One-Apartment Houses. *Proceedings of the Royal Philosophical Society of Glasgow*, 34, p.137.
45. Gairdner, W. T., 1870, *op.cit.*, pp.255-257.
46. Presbytery of Glasgow, 1891. *Report of Commission on the Housing of the Poor in relation to their Social Condition*, p.12.
47. Presbytery of Glasgow, 1891, *op.cit.*, p.14.
48. Bell, J. and Paton, J., 1896, *op.cit.*, p.194.
49. Bell, J. and Paton, J., 1896, *op.cit.*, p.196.
50. Glasgow Municipal Commission on the Housing of the Poor, 1904. Minutes of Evidence. Vol.1, p.5.
51. Barras, G. W., 1894. The Glasgow Building Regulations Act (1892). *Proceedings of the Philosophical Society of Glasgow*, xxv, pp.155-169.
52. Yelling, J. A., 1981. The selection of sites for slum clearance in London, 1875-1888. *Journal of Historical Geography*, 7.2. Appendix p.165.
53. Manuscript Register of Notices for Properties to Owners, Life-Renters etc., by the Trustees under "The Glasgow Improvements Act, 1866". Issued 1870-1876. S.R.A., F.14.8.1.
54. Manuscript Register of property purchased under the provisions of the "Glasgow Improvements Act, 1866". S.R.A., F.14.3.
55. 29, Vic.cap, 1xxxv. The Glasgow Improvements Act, 1866. 1084.cl.10.
56. Bell, J. and Paton, J., 1896, *op.cit.*, p.229.
57. Butt, J., 1971, *op.cit.*, pp.62-3.
58. Laidlaw, S., 1956. *Glasgow Common Lodging-Houses and the People Living in Them*, pp.22-24.

7. BRAVE NEW WORLD

The Planned City: 1918-1982

Despite the intervention of a second global conflict, the period from the end of the First World War to the present may be seen as two closely related phases. Just as the Great War provided a major stimulus to the traditional industries of Clydeside in its demands for wartime supplies, and in the short-lived reconstruction boom which followed it, so the Second World War intervened to mask a picture of steady decline in industry, and in the fortunes of the people dependent upon it. No longer an area of increment, the population of Glasgow did not rise significantly after the boundary extensions of 1912, and in the post-Second World War period, entered upon a dramatic decline. The dynamism of the city and its region, symbolised by its burgeoning population and expanding Victorian industry, and manifested on the ground by the outward growth of its urban fabric, spearheaded by new industrial units and the successful middle classes, ended in 1914. A fossilised Edwardian central business district marks the strand-line of commercial success, while the urban sprawl of inter-war and post-war times consists of monolithic public housing estates, with few exceptions, stark manifestations of failure, and of desperate public attempts to deal with a legacy of inner-city decay ignored in the heady climb to industrial fortune. Discrimination against private housing led to suburban growth in areas such as Bishopbriggs, Bearsden and Newton Mearns, and induced middle-class emigration from the city.

As the star of heavy industry waned, and as housing became a strong political issue, so local authorities moved towards a larger scale of planning within the urban fabric, markedly after the Second World War. The configurations of the city came to reflect a range of vision, from far-sighted to expedient, distantly removed from the integration and intimacy of a more vigorous past. National government planners identified two strands in their approach, inter-woven in reality, but separated as much by their respective aims and requirements as by the varying emphasis placed on them over time. Between the Wars, a socially-directed strand of planning concentrated on the provision of housing for the working classes, while industry was largely left to generate its own salvation. After the Second World War, an economically directed strand, aimed at the decentralisation of concentrations of traditional industry and the attraction of new growth industries, ran parallel with housing plans.

The decline of industry

By 1918, the economic base of Glasgow still rested squarely on a complex of ship-building, marine engine production, and heavy engineering, so interlocked in their relationships as to exclude the possibility of diversification on any reasonable scale[1]. This grouping formed the major growth point of the Scottish economy, but was dangerously vulnerable to world demand. Reductions in orders from British shipping lines affected national production levels, but the specialisation in passenger liners and naval vessels typical of the Clyde rendered it susceptible to fluctuations of an intensity far in excess of anything experienced before the Great War. Admiralty contracts were extremely profitable, giving Fairfields, for instance, not only their highest profit ratios, but providing 34% of the total value of all ships produced between 1920 and 1929, and 41% between 1930 and 1938[2]. However, not all yards obtained naval contracts, and international agreements on reduction in naval strength made orders uncertain. Falling demand induced internal rationalisation of the industry, with a reduction in the number of yards, and the rise to dominance of a small number of large firms, thereby rendering the structure even more brittle than before[3]. In the Glasgow yards an inflated wartime workforce of over 43,000 men in 1919 shrank to 29,000 in 1930, and much lower during the great depression, when no records were kept. The 1936 figure of c.16,000 employees represents an increase on previous years, but although the trend continued, by 1939 only c.24,000 men were working in the yards[4], despite government measures to stimulate demand. The demands of re-armament and the placing of the Queen Mary contract had limited effects, and full production awaited the outbreak of war.

The peculiar structure of shipbuilding cast a shadow far beyond the confines of the yards. In an effort to ensure supplies of steel, certain yards purchased several Scottish steelworks, thus intensifying the already fragmented character of the Scottish steel industry and hindering vital integration and relocation[5]. Their industrial stranglehold prevented the movement towards diversification typical of the U.K. as a whole, and while nationally, ships and mechanical engineering accounted for 29% of production in 1924 and only 26.5% in 1935, in Scotland, where production was concentrated on Clydeside, the comparable figures were 54% and 57.7%. Conversely, in the newer and vital fields of cycles, motors and electrical engineering, Scotland's production levels of 4.9% in 1924 and 7% in 1935 were overshadowed by 24% and 33.3% for the U.K.[6] In the Glasgow area, some limited motor manufacturing, and the efforts of one firm in aircraft construction could make little showing against heavy engineering, in which even locomotive building suffered from lack of overseas markets[7]. This industrial pattern was at the root of the great severity of the 1930s depression in Glasgow, in comparison with most other British towns, and led to sustained levels of 30% unemployment through the period[8], with shipbuilding experiencing a level of 76% unemployment in 1932[9].

Government intervention in the direction of industry began with the 1934 Special Areas legislation, which designated Clydeside, but excluded the City of Glasgow, where unemployment was not as severe as in the surrounding area. However, this new initiative of slowing the drift to the south, and bringing work to the workers, was responsible for the creation of the Hillington industrial estate in 1938, sited outside, but immediately adjacent to, the south-western boundary of Glasgow, to make full use of the city's power of industrial attraction. By 1939 the estate had attracted 87 firms, but only 5,000 new jobs, and the outbreak of the Second World War brought a six-year confirmation of the old industrial pattern, with artificial full employment based on the heavy manufacturing industries, producing ships, locomotives, tanks, guns and steel plate for the war effort. It was only with the 1945 Distribution of Industry Act, based on the 1940 Report of the Royal Commission on Industrial Population (the Barlow Report) that there was a return to government encouragement of industry away from successful concentrations in the south, and into the new Development Areas. The City of Glasgow was included in the Central Scotland Development Area. At the same time, another crucial initiative was introduced by the Clyde Valley Regional Plan of 1946, and reinforced by the Town and Country Planning Act of 1947. This involved the twin aims of diversifying the top-heavy industrial structure of the region into the modern growth manufacturing industries, and at the same time, breaking up the spatial concentrations of industry and associated population, and creating regional centres of growth on industrial estates and in the anticipated New Towns. Table 7.iv (p.162) summarise the series of national and local planning Acts and reports which continued this policy.

A short-lived period of success appeared to follow the introduction of this early post-war legislation, but really represented only the continuing impetus of the wartime boom, and within a few years, spatial and structural variations became apparent. Of 17 industrial estates established on Clydeside, only the five largest were in or immediately adjacent to, Glasgow, at Hillington, Thornliebank, Craigton, Queenslie and Carntyne, an unfortunate imbalance for the city, since the new estates quickly demonstrated their polarising influence, acting as growth points in the region. They attracted the bulk of the immigrant light industries[10], and crucially seduced from Glasgow an important proportion of a badly-needed diversifying element. In this way, while the overall regional picture until the late 60s and early 70s was one of decentralisation and partially successful diversification, this was achieved by peripheral elements of the conurbation at the expense of the city core, where the traditional industries continued their decline. The 1946 Clyde Valley Regional Plan had been rightly pessimistic about the future of shipbuilding, predicting stabilisation below the employment level of the worst inter-war year, and the closure of some yards[11]. The series of amalgamations and closures including the collapse of Upper Clyde Shipbuilders had an inevitable effect on associated heavy industries, with steady decline becoming even more rapid after 1968. The spatial concentrations of these industries, and other residuals, meant higher concentrations of job losses in the relevant area employment exchanges. The banks of the Clyde west of the city centre contained the greatest number of large firms, and between 1954 and 1957, Partick and Govan exchanges lost 5,600 jobs, while away from the river, Springburn lost 10,000 jobs, many of them in its traditional locomotive engineering industry, with thousands more lost in the metal manufacturing concentrations of the East End[12]. At the same time, the city's redevelopment policy, based on 29 Comprehensive Development Areas, contained dire warnings to firms about disturbance and difficulties of expansion and 107 firms moved out between 1958 and 1968[13]. Perhaps more serious in its consequences was the death of hundreds of small enterprises whose low levels of capital and low overheads, in brick backyard or railway viaduct premises destroyed by demolition, denied them the possibility of relocation. The net result of these processes was accelerated industrial decline, and the maintenance of unemployment rates which from the early 1970s rose well above the Scottish levels.

Table 7.i.		Central conurbation employment forecasts		
	1974	1983		Uncertainty Range
		Upper	Lower	
Primary	2,000	2,000	1,800	200
Manufacturing	158,600	149,700	119,800	29,900
Construction	33,100	34,000	23,500	10,500
Services	289,600	305,700	274,900	31,700
TOTAL	483,300	491,400	420,000	72,300

Source: Adapted from, *Strategic Issues for Strathclyde: a Survey Report 1976.* Table 2.1.6, p.147.

The poor performance of existing industries, the reluctance of new industry to enter the area, and the failure of the service sector to compensate by expansion for job losses in the manufacturing sector, were enshrined in the main theme of the 1973 West Central Scotland Plan — 'Uncertainty'. Table 7.i demonstrates the level of that uncertainty in employment forecasts for the central conurbation. Continued failure to attract new growth industries to the city combined with structural change in industry, and the contractions and closures of the economic recession of the later 1970s and 1980s, to produce a virtual industrial desert. Almost 40,000 jobs were lost in Glasgow between 1978 and the end of 1981[14], and the term 'post-industrial city' comes readily to those who discuss Glasgow's problems and predict her future. It may be that Glasgow is fated to spearhead the exploration of yet another path of urban development, however unasked-for or forbidding, as the downward spiral of de-industrialisation continues.

Strongly linked to the fortunes of industry, changes in the port of Glasgow followed the same pattern of decline. Between the wars, despite the ravages of the depression years, the government-sponsored Unemployed Grants Committee funded the construction of the huge King George V dock at Shieldhall. Opened in 1931, it proved invaluable during the war years in its capacity to handle very large cargo vessels and troop transporters[15], but its location well downstream of the main concentration of port facilities pointed the way to future developments. The post-1945 period witnessed a downstream transfer of port facilities, slow at first, but gradually increasing in tempo. Attempts to inject life into the upper reaches, above the Kelvin confluence, were short-lived. Iron ore-handling facilities, opened at General Terminus Quay in 1958, and designed to provide a short-haul feed to the steelworks at Ravenscraig, could only handle ships up to 28,000 tons, and even these had to be towed backwards down the river after unloading. The opening of the deepwater ore terminal at Hunterston on the Ayrshire coast in 1979, with its capacity for 350,000 ton vessels[16], rendered the Glasgow location obsolete, and its apparatus was demolished in 1981. This was a clear demonstration of the unfavourable site of the inner port of Glasgow, at the head of an estuary with a narrow approach channel unsuited to the requirements of modern ships[17]. The Broomielaw and wharfages upstream were closed in 1947, apart from landings of road salt and road metals, and although trade remained relatively buoyant in the 1950s, the 1960s saw large-scale decreases in both foreign and coasting tonnages handled.

The creation in 1966 of a single body, the Clyde Port Authority, responsible for activities in the whole Clyde estuary, heralded a rationalisation, not just of authorities, but of approach to the Clyde and its port facilities, in which the keynote was concentration of activities in deeper water downstream. Modern berthage at King George V dock and the adjoining Shieldhall Riverside Quay now accommodates most of Clydeport's break-of-bulk traffic, while Shieldhall has also been specially equipped to handle exports of steel coil and strip. The opening of the Greenock container terminal in 1969 diverted this type of cargo from Yorkhill Quay, and now the Meadowside Granary and palletised citrus fruit-handling facilities at Whiteinch remain as the only major port activities within the city limits[18]. Approach works for the Kingston Bridge closed Kingston Dock in 1967, and Queens and Princes Docks followed suit, being infilled during the 1970s with rubble from inner city demolition. On the north bank of the Clyde, a landscaped pedestrian walkway, destined to extend via the Kelvin to Maryhill, has replaced most of the cargo sheds, and dredging of the harbour above the Kelvin has virtually ceased. In a few decades, a complete reversal of the struggle and achievement of over 200 years has transformed the harbour of Glasgow (Fig. 7.i and Pls. 7.i & ii).

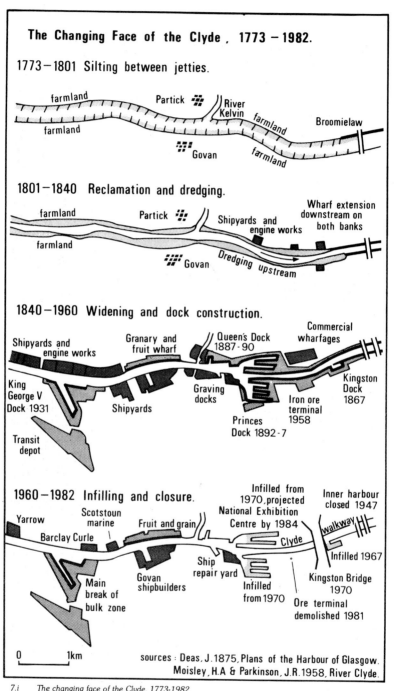

The Changing Face of the Clyde, 1773 – 1982.

1773 – 1801 Silting between jetties.

farmland — Partick — River Kelvin — farmland — Broomielaw

farmland — Govan — farmland — farmland

1801 – 1840 Reclamation and dredging.

farmland — Partick — Shipyards and engine works — Wharf extension downstream on both banks

farmland — Govan — Dredging upstream

1840 – 1960 Widening and dock construction.

Shipyards and engine works — Granary and fruit wharf — Queen's Dock 1887-90 — Commercial wharfages

King George V Dock 1931 — Shipyards — Graving docks — Iron ore terminal 1958 — Kingston Dock 1867

Transit depot — Princes Dock 1892-7

1960 – 1982 Infilling and closure.

Yarrow — Scotstoun marine — Fruit and grain — Infilled from 1970, projected National Exhibition Centre by 1984 — Inner harbour closed 1947 — walkway

Barclay Curle — Clyde

Ship repair yard — Infilled 1967

Main break of bulk zone — Govan shipbuilders — Infilled from 1970 — Kingston Bridge 1970 — Ore terminal demolished 1981

0 1km

sources : Deas, J.1875, Plans of the Harbour of Glasgow.
Moisley, H.A & Parkinson, J.R.1958, River Clyde.

7.i   The changing face of the Clyde, 1773-1982

7.i   *Queen's and Princes Docks, 1955*

7.ii   *Queen's and Princes Docks, 1982*

Interwar population and housing — the social strand

The opening of the twentieth century heralded change in the three major previous characteristics of the population of Glasgow, namely large overall increases, a substantial immigration component, and a horrific death-rate from communicable disease. Boundary extension and absorption of peripheral populations in 1912 had brought the city total to 1,008,487, and the censuses of 1921 and 1931 showed increases of only c.25,000 and 54,000 respectively. Such small increases, on such a large population base in which natural increase was relatively constant, and death rates gradually falling, indicated a consistent drift of population away from the city, and indeed, since 1901, emigration had greatly exceeded immigration. The great migrant streams of the past were over, and the city was now a net exporter of population, some to adjacent suburbs, but mainly to beyond Scotland altogether. There was no wartime census, but even taking into account over 9,000 war dead, the city lost c.120,000 people by migration between 1931 and 1951, predominantly young male adults of working age[19].

While the population may not have been expanding rapidly, it was gradually becoming healthier, and although tuberculosis and bronchitis continued to scourge young and old alike, they gradually succumbed throughout the interwar years to the continuation of the great struggle for public health initiated in the nineteenth century. Overall death rates per 1,000 dropped from 17.7 in 1911 to 14.2 in 1931, while infant mortality rates declined from 139 to 105 over the same period, though city averages disguised wide local variations, with overcrowded districts such as Whitevale and Townhead registering rates of 144 and 140 respectively, in stark contrast to Pollokshields' level of 50 per 1,000 in 1941[20]. Similarly, although the average density of population decreased from 60 per acre in 1911, to 54 per acre in 1921 and 36 per acre in 1931, extreme variation occurred between the high levels of those industrial wards grouped around the central business district, and the much lower densities of the largely peripheral residential wards, especially south of the river, where the proportion of the city's total population had grown from 25% in 1901 to 33% in 1931[21]. By that date, 700,000 people lived on 1,800 acres in and around Central Glasgow, averaging c.400 persons per acre, but with densely packed tenement dwellings giving levels of c.700 persons per acre in some parts[22].

The types of overcrowding identified and condemned by W. T. Gairdner in the 1870s still persisted after the Great War, with too many buildings crammed together, too many houses in each building, and too many people in each house. In 1921 63.5% of the population lived in one- or two-roomed houses, 55.7% of them at more than two per room, 27.9% at more than three per room, and 10.7% at more than four per room. Rising rates of household formation brought a sharp decrease in numbers of empty houses, and lack of accommodation, involving long, exhausting hours of travel to work was regarded as an important cause of industrial unrest[23]. There was an obvious and urgent need for action, but the sheer scale of the problem placed it well beyond the power of the local authority to cope. At the same time, while Glasgow's difficulties may have been greater in proportion, she was only one of a number of British cities with acute housing problems, and some initiative was required at a national level. The Royal Commission into Industrial Housing in Scotland, set up in 1912 and reporting in 1917, supported the view that private enterprise had failed to respond to housing demand, and only the State, acting through local authorities, could and should take responsibility. The direct result of this pressure was the Addison Act of 1919, which forced Scottish local authorities to submit proposals on working class housing schemes to the Scottish Board of Health, and in offering generous subsidies encouraged them to act quickly. Although poorly conceived in the way in which subsidy was made available, and for that reason a costly failure, the 1919 Act was a watershed in the acceptance by national government and municipal authorities of their responsibility to provide accommodation at decent minimum standards.

The subsequent interwar housing acts and their effects are summarised in Table 7.ii, with major contrasts apparent between the decades of the 1920s and 1930s. The Housing Acts of 1923 and 1924, in providing substantial subsidies for every housing unit built, not only gave a much-needed stimulus to the private building industry, but permitted extremely high standards of estate layout, building construction, and internal fitting. Spacious layouts, with broad, curving, tree-lined avenues, and semi-detached or four-in-a-block, two-storey houses set in extensive individual garden plots, were begun at Mosspark in the south-west of the city, and Riddrie in the north-east. They were quickly followed by much more extensive schemes at Knightswood, Scotstoun and Carntyne. Knightswood, built in several phases to house between 25,000 and 30,000 people, was provided with libraries, halls, parks and a limited number of shops and other facilities, and was the largest such development in Scotland, though lack of employment provision still necessitated travel into the city for work. These 1920s garden suburb houses still remain, especially after recent renovation, the most valuable and most desirable of the city's municipal housing stock, still commanding the high rent and rates levels which made them inaccessible to those sectors of the population most in need of such healthy accommodation when they were built (Pl. 7.iii).

Further laudable initiatives, such as the 1930 scheme aimed at slum clearance and area improvement, and which by providing subsidies on the basis of people rather than housing units, encouraged local authorities to rehouse larger and needier families, came to a halt with the onset of the Depression. Greatly reduced subsidies brought a lowering of standards of layout, construction and fitting, and a reversion to an older, more economic housing model, the tenement. Through the 1930s, a range of housing schemes of varying size was built, from a few closes on a gap site in cleared central slum areas, to more extensive developments of several thousand houses on peripheral sites such as Possil or Blackhill. The latter,

Table 7.ii. Interwar Housing Acts and Public Sector Schemes

LEGISLATION		GLASGOW'S INITIATIVE
	1916	Glasgow Corporation set up Commission to investigate working class houses. Corporation Housing Committee formed. Small housing development at GARNGAD.
1917 1919	1919	Royal Commission on Industrial Housing Report. *Housing, Town Planning etc. Act. (Scotland)* *(Addison Act)* subsidies for house-building. / Housing Department set up. Small number of temporary timber houses built.
	1920	Direct Labour Organisation set up — started work at DRUMOYNE.
1923		*Housing Act.* £6 — subsidy per house for 20 years — too low. *(Chamberlain Act).*
1924		*Housing (Financial Provisions) Act (Scotland)* *(Wheatley Act)* extended and increased subsidies.
	1925	City annexed 10,000 acres, incl. Lambhill, Carntyne, Nitshill, Cardonald, Knightswood, Scotstoun & Yoker. MOSSPARK & RIDDRIE schemes started, followed by KNIGHTSWOOD, CARNTYNE, SCOTSTOUN, in phased developments.
1930		*Housing (Scotland) Act,* (Greenwood Act) aimed at slum clearance & improvement.
	1931	Hogganfield & East Carntyne annexed. Onset of Depression & reduction in government subsidies. Cheaper tenement housing built on peripheral & inner-city gap sites. BLACKHILL, POSSIL, LILYBANK schemes.
1933		Subsidies assessed by *people* rather than houses. *Housing (Financial Provisions) (Scotland) Act* ended subsidies to private builders and reduced local authority subsidies from £9 to £3 per unit.

1935	*Housing (Scotland) Act.* Minimum overcrowding standards — extended assistance beyond slums.
1938	*Housing (Financial Provisions) (Scotland) Act* subsidies scaled to size of house to encourage building of larger houses.
1938	10,000 acres annexed in Easterhouse, Darnley, Penilee, Drumchapel, Summerston, Cathkin and Castlemilk — the foundation for post-war housing expansion.
1916/1944	54,361 houses completed (42,773 by private contractors, 5,998 by contractors & Direct Labour Org., 5,590 by D.L.O.)

Source: City of Glasgow District Council, 1975. *Farewell to the Single End.* Cramond, R. D., 1966. *Housing Policy in Scotland, 1919-1964.*

7.iii   *Inter-war local authority housing, Cardonald*

7.iv   *Derelict post-war houses, Easterhouse*

with c.1,000 houses in three-storey tenements, has become a byword for the worst possible living conditions in the city, developing this reputation virtually from the date of its completion. The fault did not lie in the type of housing, but in the choice of site, the lack of amenity provision, and a punitive housing management policy. No shop, library, hall or any other facility graced this drab scheme, virtually hemmed in by a canal, railway lines, gas-works, and polluting industry including a sulphur works. The fact that Provan gas-works and a small forest of industrial chimneys lay in the path of the prevailing westerly winds which carried their noxious odours directly to the Blackhill houses, bears witness to the lack of thought in site choice, and many of the inter-war tenement schemes were blighted from conception by proximity to industry. The low rents which these houses could command placed them squarely within the purse of the poorest sector of the city's population, and subsequent housing management policy exacerbated the concentration of social inadequates and disruptive tenants in parts of the scheme. For 40 years, the grey tenements of Blackhill and the solid, garden cottages of Riddrie faced one another in uneasy truce over the polluted ditch of the Monkland canal, each acutely aware of a social gulf between two public sector housing schemes, yawning far more widely than the few hundred yards of their physical separation.

Post-war population and housing

The development of Glasgow's population characteristics in the post-war period increasingly owed more to national and local government planning policies than to the operation of 'natural' processes. In spatial distribution, age and socio-economic structure, the present population may be seen as an artifact of government policy aimed at reduction and decentralisation, but running out of control, falling below what may be considered to be the optimum level and, because of its selectivity, leaving an aged and unskilled population in an exhausted city. The logic underlying directed migration from the city was clear enough. The housebuilding programmes of the interwar period had done relatively little to diminish the intense concentration of population within the city, and although some inner areas such as Cowcaddens, Gorbals, Hutchesontown, Govanhill and Woodside showed decreases of 18 to 24% between 1931 and 1951, this still left horrifyingly high inner city densities, while outer areas like North Kelvin and Pollokshaws recorded increases of 15 to over 50% in the same period[24].

The Clyde Valley Regional Plan of 1946 proposed a limit on further peripheral growth of the built-up area, with c.250,000 people to be absorbed between existing city limits and the inner edge of the proposed green belt, while a further 250-300,000 were to be located away from the existing conurbation[25], in expanded existing towns, and in specially created new towns. This 'overspill' of population was delayed in the face of opposition by the local authority, personified by Robert Bruce, the Master of Works and City Engineer, who believed that the 316,000 new houses which Glasgow would require by 1986 could be sited at appropriate densities and with a suitable proportion of garden space, within the city boundaries. The Corporation at first opposed the designation of East Kilbride, but by the 1950s had accepted its role, and agreed to the designation of Cumbernauld New Town. Work proceeded on the construction of huge peripheral housing estates while agreements on overspill of Glasgow's population were made with existing towns (Table 7.iv).

Table 7.iii. Population change 1931-1987

	Totals	% change on previous base	
1931	1,088,524	—	
1951	1,090,000	+ 0.2	
1961	1,065,017	− 2.3	
1971	898,848	−15.7	
1981	763,162	−15.1	*(N.B. loss rate 1981/7*
1987	740,563 (est.)	− 3	*estimated at much lower*
			rate of c.5,600 per
			annum, but may increase
			greatly if there is no
			economic improvement.)

Sources: Census Enumeration Abstracts 1931-71.
Strathclyde Regional Council 1981. *1980 Base projections to 1987. Populations, Households, Housing*, pp.12/13.

Table 7.iii shows the swift post-war decrease in Glasgow's population and it should be remembered that these figures take into account the population acquired by boundary extension in 1975. Allowing for natural increase as a constant process, it is obvious that there has been massive outmigration, averaging 11-12,000 people per annum between 1951 and 1961, and increasing in tempo to over 20,000 per annum as the huge city redevelopment scheme gathered momentum in the 1960s. Halting of wholesale tenement destruction by the mid-1970s slowed the outflow, and future projections estimate a greatly reduced flow of c.5,600 per annum to 1987. If population loss had been evenly distributed through the age cohorts of the city's population pyramid, and through the categories of employment, then less concern might have been expressed about the maintenance of social and physical services on greatly lowered population thresholds. However, a high degree of selectivity has operated in both cases, with migrants being concentrated in the more mobile professional, skilled, and semi-skilled working age categories, leaving the city with a high dependency ratio of young and old, and an employment (or unemployment) structure unbalanced towards the unskilled end of the spectrum. There has also been large-scale internal change in population distribution and density, with most of the large percentage decreases occurring in inner city zones, especially those undergoing redevelopment, such as Anderston and parts of the East End, while construction of peripheral housing estates has increased densities outwards. Increases have also occurred on infill sites near the city centre, such as Sighthill, and in low quality housing areas such as Blackhill[26].

The high post-war population densities in inner-city districts appear even higher when expressed as residential densities, taking into account the amount of land given over to industry, services and recreation. Residential densities varied from Hutchesontown with 564, and Cowcaddens with 514 persons per acre, to Langside and Cathcart with 71, and Craigton and Pollokshields with 64 persons per acre in 1951. Thus within an overall city density of 163 persons per acre, these wide variations reflected enormous inequalities in housing standards, in particular in levels of overcrowding and numbers of small houses[27]. The dominant housing type in the city was still the pre-1914 tenement, of red or grey sandstone, but the tenement facades concealed houses ranging from the 'single-end' of one room, and the 'room-and-kitchen' of two rooms, to spacious flats of five, six, and more rooms, purpose-built for the middle classes and once containing their own servants quarters. The relative spatial concentrations of these opposing types, and those tenement flats in the middle of the spectrum, strongly conditioned local levels of overcrowding. In 1951, 307,833 families lived in 295,472 houses, indicating a basic shortfall of 12,361 houses, without consideration of housing conditions[28]. In fact, 86,592 people were living in single apartments, and a further 350,739 in two-apartment flats, and these small dwellings continued to exercise their baleful influences on health and well-being, just as they had done over the last century. In 19 of the city's 37 wards, more than half of all houses were of one or two rooms, with proportions as high as 88.8% in Hutchesontown and 82.7% in Dalmarnock, while in more fortunate areas of the city, such as Craigton and Langside, the corresponding proportions were only 2% and 9.8% respectively. 130,435 houses, or 44.2% of the city's housing stock, were judged to be overcrowded, with the worst levels concentrated in the smallest houses crammed into the inner city wards. Apart from overcrowding, the tenement stock displayed an appalling lack of amenities, with over 50% of all houses having no bath, and 37.5% having only shared W/C facilities[29].

On the basis of these figures alone, the scale and urgency of Glasgow's housing problems was obvious, and even more so in comparison with cities such as Birmingham and Manchester, whose net residential densities of 48.1 and 77.4 persons per acre in 1951 fell far below Glasgow's 163. To compound the difficulties, the time-lag between recognition of the problem and appropriate remedial action made itself apparent by the increasing number of houses entering the overcrowded or unsuitable categories through lack of basic repairs or simply age deterioration, while necessary demolition of dangerous or sub-standard property simply removed more houses from the pool. Between 1945 and

Table 7.iv. Planning Initiatives and the Post-war City

Year			Decentralisation of industry and population
1945	Distribution of Industry Act	1946	Bruce Plan (Glasgow) opposed overspill
1946	New Town Act: Clyde Valley Regional Plan		
1947	Town & Country Planning (Scotland) Act / East Kilbride New Town designated	1948	City of Glasgow Development Plan Committee Planning on 'community area' basis.
1948	Glenrothes New Town designated (not for Glasgow overspill at first).	1951	City of Glasgow Development Plan approved.
1951	Clyde Valley Advisory Committee (revived by Glasgow Corporation).	1953/5	Glasgow Housing & Works: Architecture & Planning Departments re-organised. 23 new housing dvpt. areas proposed, including Drumchapel, Pollok, Castlemilk, Ruchazie/Garthamlock: c.27,000 houses in peripheral schemes. Royston, Govan, Hutchesontown to be redeveloped. (15,600 houses to be reduced to 5,100).
1956	Cumbernauld New Town designated.	1957	Comprehensive Development Area plan: Gorbals/Hutchesontown first — 28 others follow.
1957	Housing & Town Development (Scotland) Act, incentives for overspill.	1958	Moss Heights, Cardonald — multi-storey beginnings.
1958	Glenrothes agrees to take 1,000 Glasgow families.	1960	Easterhouse & Nitshill peripheral schemes begun.
1959	Overspill agreements with Haddington, Kirkintilloch, Hamilton, Johnstone & Irvine.		
1962	Livingston New Town designated.		
1963	Central Scotland Report: growth & development, 57 overspill agreements signed.		
1965/6	Irvine New Town designated.	1965/7	Glasgow Central Area report & Highways Plan: Greater Glasgow Transportation Study; Springburn Study; Red Road High-Rise flats finished — highest reinforced concrete domestic structures in Europe.

1972/5	Stonehouse New Town designated. Local Government Reform Act: Housing (Scotland) Act, 1972/5. West Central Scotland Plan.
1976	Strathclyde Region/Glasgow District. Stonehouse New Town de-designated. Strathclyde Regional Report.
1977	Action to terminate overspill agreements.
1978	Strathclyde Structure Plan (draft).
1981	Strathclyde Structure Plan approved.

1972/5	Housing action areas (small-scale clearance & improvement) C.D.A.s suspended. Housing Associations set up. Planning reports on Housing, Population, Employment, Shopping, from Glasgow District Planning Department.
1976	G.E.A.R.: 8-year plan for East End.
1977	City Housing Plan.
1978	First Local Plan (Kelvin). (by 1980 – 48 local plans).

Building and Demolition 1945 – 1979

Municipal houses built, 1945 – 79 : 119,544 ———

Houses demolished, 1954 – 79 : 76,914 – – –

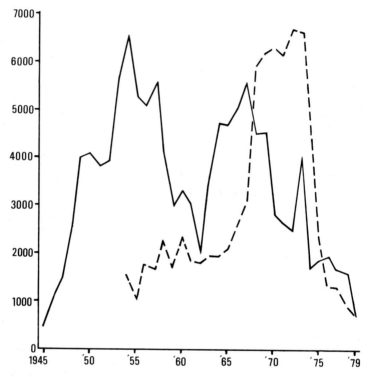

sources : Glasgow District Council; Housing management department,
Annual Report 1968, p 16 & 1979, pp 12 & 15.

7.ii   Building and demolition, 1945-1979

1961 the local authority completed over 62,000 new houses (Fig. 7.ii), but this success was dwarfed by a housing waiting list which had stood at almost 90,000 families in 1949, and had grown every year since. Glasgow's overcrowding level by 1961 (more than 1.5 persons per room) stood at 34.3% of all houses, in comparison with 10.7% in Birmingham, and only 6.4% in Manchester[30]. In 12 of the city's 37 wards, one- and two-room houses accounted for over 60% of stock, while in 15 wards over 60% of houses had no fixed bath or W/C[31], with both concentrations lying in the inner city. A drastic situation required drastic remedies, and the series of housing initiatives undertaken from the 1950s onwards must be viewed in the light of the pressing urgency of the problem. Planning experience is hard-won, and the decisions of the 1950s and 1960s may have laid the foundations of as many social problems as they were intended to solve, but they were conceived of necessity on a scale to match the challenge.

The attentions of the planners of the 1950s and 1960s may be seen as focused on four concentric zones of activity. The innermost zone comprised the central business district and its fringe, where business and commercial interests interdigitated with industry and housing. The second zone, or inner fringe, consisted of the densely built-up Victorian and Edwardian housing areas of the city, with their integral industry and local services. The River Clyde acted both as a southern boundary between the zones, and as a westward-elongating agent for the second zone. The third zone formed a penannular belt of land, absorbed by the city in the interwar period (Table 7.ii), with cottage-style municipal housing schemes dominating the land use on its inner portions, while its outer reaches awaited the construction of new housing. Beyond these zones of the city proper, a fourth area of activity stretched to Wick in the north, and Stranraer in the south, containing urban centres large and small, existing and proposed, destined to receive Glasgow's surplus population.

Zone 4 — Overspill

As part of the effort to relieve dense overcrowding in Glasgow, the 1946 Clyde Valley Regional Plan proposed an overspill of 250,000-300,000 people from the city, with c.200,000 to be accommodated in new and existing centres within the Clyde Valley and on the Ayrshire Plain, and the remainder to migrate beyond the region altogether[32]. Glasgow's opposition to this proposed loss of population has already been mentioned, and it was not until the demands of slum clearance made themselves felt that the attitude of the local authority changed. Of the 100,000 new houses required for the population displaced by comprehensive redevelopment, only 40,000 could be re-sited in the inner zone of demolition, while housing in the third zone had already crept up to the inner edge of the green belt, using up all the available space in the city[33]. At the same time, re-appraisals of the necessary scale of population loss predicted high levels of natural increase and diminishing rates of undirected emigration from the city, necessitating a shedding of 4-500,000 rather than the 2-300,000 envisaged[34]. Table 7.iv charts the rise and fall of the overspill programme, gathering momentum from the 1956 designation of Cumbernauld New Town, almost purely for Glasgow families, and the 1957 Act whose overspill incentives assisted the signing of 57 overspill agreements by 1963. The process reached its peak in the designation in 1972 of Stonehouse as a New Town, to be built and managed under the aegis of the East Kilbride Development Corporation. Four years later the damaging effect of sustained overspill was realised and Stonehouse de-designated. However, this was due less to official decentralisation of population, which only accounted for c.22% of the 1961/72 loss, than to the engine of a deteriorating economy, driving the socially mobile to seek opportunity elsewhere. At the same time, a new policy of conservation and rehabilitation removed the need to use overspill as a displacement safety valve.

Zone 3 — Peripheral housing schemes

For those who could not, or would not, migrate beyond the Glasgow boundary, even when compulsory purchase of their slum tenements provided an inducement, the outer parts of zone three were used, from the early 1950s onwards, to provide new housing areas. The City of Glasgow Development Plan Approval Order of 1954 listed 23 housing areas, some of them phases of schemes already under way, with the greater part of building to be completed by 1960[35]. Apart from the Milton, Barmulloch, Balornock group, huge housing estates were constructed at the four corners of Glasgow. In the north-west, Drumchapel, in the south-west the Pollok-Nitshill group, in the south-east Castlemilk, and in the north-west the Ruchazie, Garthamlock, Cranhill, Barlanark and Easterhouse complex (see Figs. 7.iii and 7.iv and Table 7.v) had accounted for over 60% of all municipal houses built by 1979[36]. The vast majority of these houses were three- and four-storey tenements, with small groups of pensioners' houses, and five-apartment terraced houses for large families interspersed. In the desperate race to provide houses, virtually no amenities, of even the most basic kind, were provided. For the first few years in Castlemilk for instance, children of school age had to walk to collection points, in all weathers, to be bussed back to schools in the old city core. As a temporary measure, converted tenement houses were occupied by the 5-12 year-olds as schools, but purpose-built primary and secondary schools were delayed for a further five years. Public halls, churches, cinemas and recreational facilities were either similarly delayed, or have never materialised. Until the late 1960s, shopping facilities were limited to a few small groups, whose high rents meant equally high prices, and in Drumchapel and Castlemilk, free shoppers' buses now take housewives to the new Clydebank town centre, or to a 'superstore' in Cambuslang, to provide the services which their schemes lack. Planners ideals of fresh air and natural green recreation space mean little to those above primary school age, and from the first arrivals in the 1950s, a kind of 'culture shock' gripped many families removed from the comforting, familiar, sooty womb of the tenement slums. The incidence of applications for transfer, and of illicit moonlight 'flits' or departures, is highest on the rural/urban interface at the peripheries of these schemes. High public transport costs impose a frustrating exile on thousands whose incomes are too low to permit journeys to the bright lights of the city, while higher than average unemployment rates and minimal industrial estate provision mean that for many there is not even an escape to work.

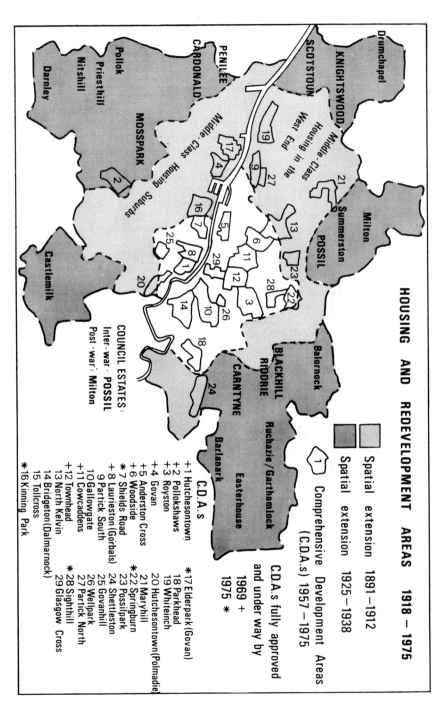

HOUSING AND REDEVELOPMENT AREAS 1918 – 1975

Spatial extension 1891–1912

Spatial extension 1925–1938

Comprehensive Development Areas
(C.D.A.s) 1957–1975

C.D.A.s fully approved
and under way by
1969 +
1975 *

C.D.A.s

+ 1 Hutchesontown
+ 2 Pollokshaws
+ 3 Royston
+ 4 Govan
+ 5 Anderston Cross
+ 6 Woodside
* 7 Shields Road
+ 8 Laurieston (Gorbals)
9 Partick South
10 Gallowgate
+ 11 Cowcaddens
+ 12 Townhead
13 North Kelvin
14 Bridgeton (Dalmarnock)
15 Tollcross
* 16 Kinning Park

* 17 Elderpark (Govan)
18 Parkhead
19 Whiteinch
20 Hutchesontown (Polmadie)
21 Maryhill
* 22 Springburn
23 Possilpark
24 Shettleston
25 Govanhill
26 Wellpark
27 Partick North
* 28 Sighthill
29 Glasgow Cross

COUNCIL ESTATES:
Inter-war: POSSIL
Post-war: Milton

Drumchapel

KNIGHTSWOOD

SCOTSTOUN

Middle Class Housing West End

Middle Class Housing in the West End

Summerston

Milton

POSSIL

Balornock

BLACKHILL
RIDDRIE

CARNTYNE

Ruchazie / Garthamlock

Easterhouse

Barlanark

PENILEE

CARDONALD

MOSSPARK

Middle Class Housing Suburbs

Pollok

Priesthill

Nitshill

Darnley

Castlemilk

7.iii   *Housing and redevelopment areas, 1918-1975*

A recent report by the City of Glasgow Housing Department on the Kingsridge and Cleddans areas of Drumchapel highlights the environmental awfulness of such schemes.

"The Kingsridge and Cleddans neighbourhoods of Drumchapel, located on the North-West boundary of the City consist of 2,021 dwellings, predominantly of the four-storey tenemental type. The present housing stock is imbalanced, with a heavy concentration of three and four apartment flats. The steep gradients combine with poor lay-out and narrow streets to produce a generally unattractive, uninspired and often oppressive environment. Open space, such as it is, largely derelict and trespass through closes and between buildings has become a serious nuisance. This has led to lack of privacy and security which in turn has resulted in residents feeling alienated from the surrounding environment. . . . The many problems of the area include high unemployment, a large percentage of one-parent families, high child densities, low income, delinquency and vandalism. . . ."[37]

Table 7.v.	House completions in peripheral schemes to 1978		
	1958	*1968*	*1978*
Castlemilk	7,926	9,578	9,747
Drumchapel	7,926	9,845	10,345
Easterhouse	3,569	12,997	14,959
Pollok	5,278	11,395	11,566

Source: Glasgow District Council: Housing Management Reports 1968 and 1978. City Architect's Department personal communication.

Surroundings of such Orwellian bleakness are neither easily improved nor outstandingly exceptional in peripheral housing schemes (Pl. 7.iv), though extensive portions of many of them are well maintained by their tenants, and are regarded as fairly desirable living areas. The generally low area densities, though higher than in most other cities, make rational location or centralisation of facilities difficult, while high rents for purpose-built shops, uncertain profits and lack of attachment to the area by shopkeepers produce a dependence on outside retailers. The response to localised high child densities is selective demolition of some tenements and conversion to community uses of others, but in some cases this is insufficient to eradicate the problem, and whole groups of houses, numbering in the hundreds, have been demolished after only 15 or 20 years of use. Often located on the peripheries of schemes, or even in detached situations, these groups of houses developed a low perceived status from an early stage. Concentration within them of 'problem families' brought increasing repair and maintenance costs, until the existence of a clearly defined social blot encouraged the idea of a fresh start on a cleared site. The new Pollok shopping centre was constructed over the fossil street-pattern of one such small scheme, while a cinder field marks the site of the Ranza Place scheme near Blackhill, demolished before the interest on its building loan was paid off.

Zone 2 — Destruction and renewal

House construction in zone three could proceed at any rate judged possible by the local authority given the financial and other constraints under which they had to work, since they were operating on green-field sites, but in zone two, the inner periphery, existing unsuitable structures had to be demolished before replacement could begin. Fig. 7.iii indicates the extent of this zone, comprising the expansion area of the city during the nineteenth and early twentieth centuries, and including the absorbed residential and industrial police burghs such as Pollokshields and Govan. Some indication of housing conditions in pre-First World War tenements has already been given, and since this zone contained the great bulk of the city's stock, housing renewal was obviously required. The 1946 Bruce Plan had envisaged related programmes of house-building on the outer periphery, clearance and renewal in the inner area, and a revitalised road and rail transport system linking the component units. A gradation of residential densities from 120 persons per acre in an inner zone, through 75 per acre in an intermediate zone, to 50 per acre in an outer zone, with corresponding proportions of flats to houses with gardens[38], proposed a radical departure from existing densities and spatial arrangement of housing types.

Once the implications of overspill had been recognised, the necessity for, and the possibilities of, Bruce's integrated plan were embodied in an ambitious programme of comprehensive redevelopment. Beginning with Hutchesontown — Gorbals in 1957, 29 Comprehensive Development Areas (C.D.A.'s) were outlined, covering one-twelfth of the total city area, and a substantially higher proportion of the inner peripheral zone. Figure 7.iii shows clearly the concentration of C.D.A.'s around the central business district, and the westward elongation of their distribution into the industrial areas north and south of the river. Clearance was to focus on working-class housing areas with their associated industry, while middle-class residential zones were to be largely undisturbed. 97,000 dwellings in the 29 areas either needed immediate clearance or were liable to degenerate shortly, and the decision was taken to demolish at a rate of 4,500 per annum until 1980. However, clearance was not evenly spread throughout the 29 C.D.A.'s, since their operation was envisaged as a twenty-year programme, and long delays were incurred in detailed preparation, plan submission and approval, and complicated compulsory purchase procedures. Thus by 1969, only nine areas had received formal approval from the Secretary of State for Scotland, and the bulk of the 63,000 demolitions carried out by this time was therefore strongly concentrated in those C.D.A.'s. By 1975, five further C.D.A.'s had reached the approval stage, and the total of demolitions in the city had reached over 95,000[39] (Fig. 7.iii).

It was at this stage that the full social cost of this physical destruction was realised, and the C.D.A. programme was rapidly terminated in its original form, all or part of seven C.D.A.'s being absorbed in new Local Plan areas, with another five being partially implemented under Housing or Education powers. The 'bold conception'[40] of the plan had swept areas clean of their houses, shops and factories, but more importantly, of their people. Table 7.vi shows the enormous population reductions experienced by some wards between 1961 and 1971, with the peak of displacement and demolition yet to come (Fig. 7.ii). Density reductions from c.450 to c.160 per acre meant two thirds of these people were to be displaced permanently, while for the remainder, the long time-lag between compulsory purchase, demolition and reconstruction meant prolonged exile in peripheral holding areas, all the more unsettling because of its temporary and uncertain nature. Whole territorially based communities, with deep historical roots, were destroyed as the massive C.D.A. onslaught tore the heart out of the city, and eventually the destruction and desolation of vital areas in Govan, Partick and Springburn brought the programme to a halt in September 1974. Since then, a slowing of the flow of central government funds for reconstruction has left the city with a legacy of too-numerous gap sites, some of enormous proportions, and the resemblance to bombed-out Continental cities after the Second World War is a parallel drawn by many Glaswegians.

Table 7.vi. Ward population decreases 1961-1971

	1961	1971	% decrease
Gorbals	23,428	7,445	68.3
Kingston	19,508	1,189	94
Anderston	21,457	9,265	66.9
Townhead	26,484	12,196	54

Source: Census Enumeration Abstracts 1961 and 1971.
   N.B. Ward boundaries do not necessarily coincide with boundaries of
        C.D.A's of same name.

From the early 1960s, continuing rapid decay in tenement fabric and the scarcity of building sites within the city boundary combined to exacerbate problems for that section of the city's population which was not to be subject to overspill. The successful example of the Moss Heights in Cardonald, built to a height of 10 storeys in 1957, and the example of other local authorities who were adopting a high-rise approach as a partial solution to their housing problems, making the most economic use of techniques of pre-fabrication and rapid assembly of sections, encouraged multi-storey building in Glasgow. The low densities of inter-war housing estates of the cottage type made them ideal sites for the first blocks, though they were soon diffused to post-war municipal schemes, and then to virtually any available site in the city. By 1968, 120 blocks had been constructed, but the main phase was yet to come, and in 1982, the total reached 321, of which 58 are managed by the Scottish Special Housing Association.

Table 7.vii. Population concentration in Glasgow District Council high-rise blocks

	No. of blocks	% of total	No. of houses	% of total	% of houses by apartment			
					1	2	3	4
8-11 storeys	78	30	3,142	12	7	12.5	9	22
12-19 storeys	61	24	5,042	20	12	22	23.5	–
20-31 storeys	123	46	17,193	68	81	65.5	67.5	78
			Total Houses		874	9,597	13,674	1,102

Source: Glasgow District Council: Housing Management Department. Annual Report 1979, pp.113-123.

Block heights range from eight to 31 storeys, containing houses of one-, two-, three-, or four-apartments, and Table 7.vii shows clearly the intense concentration of larger houses, with larger families, in the higher block range, producing extremely dense population groupings on the ground. Designed at first to house families without young children, at least above the fourth floor, sheer pressure on the housing authorities forced compromise, and with rising numbers of young occupants came gradual disillusion with multi-storey dwelling as a way of life for all but a limited sector of the population. Elderly people and young childless couples might find them suitable, if there were some guarantees that internal systems, especially elevators, would remain operational, but for others, the social costs are too high. Overall, the incidence of psychoneurotic disorders is twice as high in flats as in houses, and the incidence increases as the height of the flat increases. Isolation leads to social withdrawal and confinement and ultimately ill-health, in young and old[41]. Useless open spaces and lack of amenities breed crime and vandalism, indeed a French survey in 1978 of the most constantly occurring criminal type profiled a young man of 15-18, living in a city of over 200,000 people, on or above the sixth floor of a block of high-rise flats, tortured by noise and indifference in the harsh environmental surroundings.

Recognising the social evils latent in these structures, both the Scottish Special Housing Association and Glasgow District Housing Management Department have adopted new approaches, often involving conversion of blocks to community facilities or other special uses. One S.S.H.A. block at Anderston Cross has been converted to sheltered housing, with alarm call systems, two social work wardens and a caretaker, and is to be followed by five others in Hutchesontown, Govan and Partick. After a frightening fire in one of the notorious Red Road 31-storey blocks in Balornock (Pl. 7.v), tenants were evacuated, and a new tenant mix is being attempted, with shared tenancies of elderly and/or single persons on the first three floors, through 11 floors of council tenants, with children under 16 restricted to a total of 60, through 14 floors of student accommodation, to three floors of luxury penthouse apartments.

For an interim period, C.D.A.'s remained the favoured approach, but rebuilding within them took the form of two- or four-storey buildings rather than multi-storeys. The later phases of Townhead, Kinning Park and Govan, and to a degree Bridgeton/Dalmarnock, were characterised by low-rise housing, and no new high-rise were built other than those for which contracts already existed. By the early 1970s, recognition of the desolation of peripheral decanting schemes and of the fearsome cost of the C.D.A. blitzkrieg, had encouraged the development of a series of finer threads in the approach to urban renewal. The Town and Country Planning (Scotland) Act, 1972 and the Local Government (Scotland) Act, 1973 required District Councils to prepare Local Plans for all parts of their districts, and where these are adopted they will supersede existing Development Plan proposals, taking into consideration wider policies such as Strathclyde Region's Structure Plan and Transport Policy, and District Council Housing Plans[42]. Glasgow by 1980 had 48 Local Plan areas, for three of which, Kelvin, Camlachie, and Parkhead, the plans had been adopted, while another eight had been finalised or were in draft, and work had started on preparing 22[43]. Implicit in these Local Plans is closer co-operation with the people of the area within which the Plan is designed to operate, and the reaching of mutual decisions on retention and renovation of elements of the urban fabric, including housing, which would have been swept away under C.D.A. policy. To aid conservation and rehabilitation, the 1974 Housing Act empowered the Housing Corporation to provide financial assistance for local Housing Associations, and 1975 marks the real beginning of these groups' activities, as well as a total change in attitude to the tenement and its people. Important tenement renovation and rehabilitation schemes have been undertaken all over the city, ranging in scale from a few closes to several hundred houses, and in scope from stone cleaning and back-court modernisation, to complete gutting of the sandstone shell, and the creation therein of larger, better equipped flats. At the same time, enormous municipal programmes of modernisation and environmental improvement are re-vitalising inter-war and post-war housing schemes.

The new consultative and conservationist approach to urban renewal waxed as the overspill policy and the development of new towns waned, but it was realised that the experience of large-scale urban planning and management could embody all of the finer threads of the new philosophy. The east end of Glasgow, it was decided, was just the kind of area which could benefit most from an integrated, multi-purpose, large-scale planning initiative, and in May 1976, the Glasgow Eastern Area

7.v   *Red Road flats, Barmulloch*

7.vi   *New housing in the G.E.A.R. area, Bridgeton*

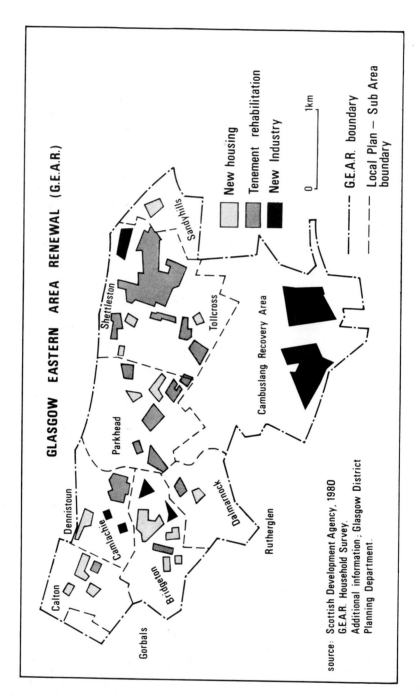

GLASGOW EASTERN AREA RENEWAL (G.E.A.R.)

New housing

Tenement rehabilitation

New Industry

0   1km

— · · — G.E.A.R. boundary

— · — Local Plan – Sub Area
        boundary

Sandyhills

Shettleston

Tollcross

Cambuslang Recovery Area

Parkhead

Dennistoun

Camlachie

Dalmarnock

Rutherglen

Bridgeton

Calton

Gorbals

source: Scottish Development Agency, 1980
G.E.A.R. Household Survey.
Additional information; Glasgow District
Planning Department.

7.iv   Glasgow Eastern Area Renewal (G.E.A.R.)

Renewal (G.E.A.R.) project was set up as part of a national initiative directed at inner cities. Capital commitment to the scheme from 1977 to 1982 was to be £156 million, and a group of participating bodies was set up under the overall co-ordination of the Scottish Development Agency[44] (Table 7,viii). It faced a daunting task. The 1,600 hectare area comprised a densely built-up inner zone, covering Bridgeton, Dalmarnock, Parkhead, Calton, and Camlachie, and a less congested outer zone consisting of Shettleston, Tollcross, Sandyhills and the Cambuslang recovery area (Fig. 7.iv). A major focus of Glasgow's nineteenth century industry, this was an area where textile works, forges and metal manufacturing concerns had been densely interwoven with tenement housing. The surgical operations of five C.D.A's in the 1960s and early 1970s had removed a great part of this already decayed industrial legacy, embodying in the process a rundown in population from 145,000 in 1951 to 82,000 by 1971, and by the time the project was fully under way in 1978, only 45,000 people remained in the area.

Table 7.viii.   **Participants and Responsibilities in G.E.A.R.**

		Capital Commitment
Strathclyde Regional Council;	social work, education, police, fire, transport.	£13m
Glasgow District Council;	housing, baths, parks, libraries, museums, halls, markets, environmental protection.	£52m
Scottish Special Housing Association;	housing.	£37m
Greater Glasgow Health Board;	health centres.	£ 3m
Housing Corporation;	rehabilitation by local housing associations.	£12m
Scottish Development Agency;	land assembly, derelict land clearance, environmental improvements, factory building and investment.	£39m
Manpower Services Commission;	employment, re-training, work experience.	—

Source: Scottish Development Agency 1978. *The Future for G.E.A.R.*

This population contained high levels of aged persons, single homeless, and other groups requiring special facilities, such as the handicapped, present in 30% of all households, compared with a level of 20% for Strathclyde Region. Only 31% of households included children, compared to 41% in the Region, and the proportion of unskilled heads of households was 50% higher than in the Region as a whole. A very high proportion of low income households, allied to the other aspects described, clearly indicates the low perceived status of the area, inhabited mainly by those with the lowest levels of socio-spatial mobility[45]. Obsolete industrial buildings of all sizes posed enormous problems of conversion and renovation, all the more urgent since, despite extremely high local levels of unemployment, the area employs a large workforce from the rest of the city. Removal of the support population needed to maintain a vigorous and varied retail sector had induced decay in retailing. Shops occupied the ground floors of tenements, and tenement destruction removed most of the area's rundown shopping facilities as well as other services.

A vigorous programme of combined action involved new house construction and existing house renovation, and by 1980, Glasgow District Council and the Scottish Special Housing Association had spent £26 million on building 782 houses for rent, with a further 1,300 planned by 1983, and on the modernisation of almost 2,000 houses, with another 4,600 planned by 1983 (Pl. 7.vi). Together with Local Housing Associations, they have spent £8 million on the rehabilitation of over 800 tenement flats, with another 2,000 in the pipeline. Landscaping of derelict areas has improved the environment, and the encouragement of private house building to create a more diverse social admixture has been surprisingly successful. By 1980 the S.D.A. had built 71 factory units, including small, badly-needed workshop units, while the British Steel Corporation provided 77 small workshop units at the former Clyde Iron Works, creating 500 jobs in what is now known as Tollcross Industrial Village. Training and work experience schemes for local residents, nursery schools and children's homes, play areas and recreation facilities, hostels, sheltered housing, and geriatric facilities have all been created to improve the quality of life. Preservation and rejuvenation of shopping cores in Duke Street and Shettleston Road, with linking shoppers' buses will provide a focus for area identity[46]. Inevitably, economic recession means lack of vital funds to complete projects of all kinds, and incomplete schemes are difficult to assess, but if commitment and dedication to a task count at all, then there is still hope for the east end.

Zone 1 — The central area

The innermost zone comprises the Central Business District and its fringe, lying north of the river, and having an irregular boundary with the surrounding residential/industrial zone (Fig. 7.v. & Pl. 7.vii). Distribution of land values and their reflections in land use and building height permits internal sub-division of the zone into a strongly defined commercial core, showing strong segregation between the competing land uses of shops, offices, hotels, wholesaling, warehousing and transport, a concentric multi-purpose zone of low commercial segregation, and a periphery of low levels of central area functions[47]. The attitude of planners towards this central area has not been a concerted one, possibly because of greater needs elsewhere in the city fabric, and change has therefore been of a highly variable character.

In the inner sector, or C.B.D. proper, invasion of the eastern portion of the residential Blythswood estate initiated a commercial development culminating in the concentration of highest land values and buildings in a business office grouping of 15-20 street blocks, with discontinuous tails southward to the river and westward through Georgian residential suburbs to an outpost in Victorian Park Circus[48]. Shopping developed from two socially polarised nuclei, namely a working-class orientated shopping area along Argyle Street and Trongate, historically linked to the ancient market core of the city, and in the west, a 'carriage-trade' middle class shopping area based at first on Buchanan Street in the 1870s, but losing its primacy to Sauchiehall Street in the 1880s and 1890s as the middle-class tide flowed west. Tramway routes reinforced this division, with those serving the east end running along Argyle Street/Trongate, and those serving the west end running along Sauchiehall Street. A linking zone of high-quality shops and places of entertainment developed north-south to form an elongated 'Z' pattern. East of the upright of the 'Z', and north of the Argyle Street/Trongate axis, land use was dominated by wholesaling, and industrial residuals such as small-scale watch-makers and jewellery manufacturers, and more importantly, clothing manufacturers, making up 46% of all factories in the area[49]. Three main-line railway stations, Central, St. Enoch, and Queen Street, had intruded into this core, with Buchanan Street in a slightly more peripheral location to the north of the area, together reinforcing the centrality of the C.B.D., which in its shopping functions alone, on at least a weekly visit basis, serviced a catchment area of 720 sq. kilometres, with a population of 1.8 millions[50].

In the commercial core and surrounding multi-purpose zone, fabric change has been limited. A short-lived office boom of the 1960s possibly reflected more of developers' perceptions of the financial incentives and restrictions of the 1960 Local Employment Act, and the 1964 Labour Government's ban on large-scale office development in south-east England, than any inherent dynamism in the commercial system[51]. Steep rises in rents further dampened demand, leaving the central area over-provided with office space. A 1971 report on the declining role of the C.B.D. forecast further contraction, especially in shopping[52], and the demise of a number of the more fashionable stores, especially in the western section of Sauchiehall Street, bore out this prophecy. The process of decentralisation of retailing from the C.B.D., to other areas within the city, together with the development of discount warehouses on industrial estates reduced the flow of city shoppers to the centre. At the same time, the development of East Kilbride town centre, and the redevelopment of town centres such as Paisley, Motherwell and Clydebank, drew off a proportion of the previous conurbation catchment.

7.vii   Central Glasgow: the partially completed Kingston Bridge with its approach works — can be seen on the left of the photograph, with the swathe of destruction in advance of Inner Ring Road construction, outlining the regular grid of Georgian New Town streets.

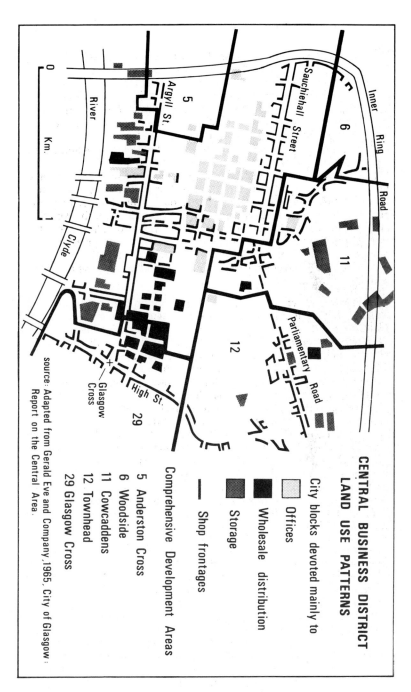

7.v   Central Business District land use patterns

Pedestrianisation of portions of Argyle Street, Buchanan Street, and Sauchiehall Street has highlighted a greatly reduced shopping provision, despite the construction of the Sauchiehall Street Centre. Of the railway stations, Buchanan Street is now occupied partly by British Rail offices and partly by a re-sited northern bus terminal, while St. Enoch, demolished in 1977 after service as a car park, still awaits development. Some distance west at Anderston Cross, a complex of 33 shops, two department stores and a 60,000 sq. ft. supermarket, with a hotel, restaurants and public house, built by the Taylor Woodrow Group, had not been a success, being too far removed from the main shopping centre, while the bus station and multi-storey flats incorporated in the development have suffered badly from drunks, vandals, and down-and-outs, who find refuge and concealment in the poorly lit wasteland around and under the Kingston Bridge approach ramps. As in other sectors of Glasgow's life, much of the vitality has ebbed from the centre, but the creation of conservation areas around Exchange and Blythswood Squares, and the protection afforded a wide range of architecturally splendid listed buildings, reveals a positive benefit.

In complete contrast to the core, change on the periphery of the central area has been swift and sweeping, where the inner boundaries of five Comprehensive Development Areas, those of Anderston Cross, Woodside, Cowcaddens, Townhead, and Glasgow Cross, intrude into the fringe, very deeply in the case of Cowcaddens and Townhead (Fig. 7.v). The familiar C.D.A. pattern of complete clearance removed the range of largely obsolete industrial, residential and commercial buildings characteristic of this zone, although the existence of an ambitious new transportation infrastructure plan may have hastened the demise of perfectly good buildings along its path. Severe traffic congestion had been an unfortunate characteristic of the central area since the nineteenth century, when traffic destined for the wharfages and sheds of the port of Glasgow, located so close to the city core, had to use the same limited river crossings as business traffic, while necessary access to docks and shipyards downstream hindered construction of relief bridges[53]. The narrow grid-iron streets of the city centre are unsuited to modern traffic, although the electric trams managed to keep traffic flowing until their removal in 1962.

In concert with the projected Erskine Bridge, nine miles downstream, designed to bypass the city altogether, and the Clyde Tunnel, completed in 1964 between Govan and Whiteinch, carrying western commuter traffic, the Inner Ring Road, crossing the Clyde on the Kingston Bridge, was designed to remove central area congestion. The plan undoubtedly succeeded, and traffic can now speed from Glasgow Airport in the west, to motorway junctions leading to Stirling, Edinburgh, and Carlisle, without entering the city streets. There has, however, undoubtedly been a blighting effect along both sides of its route, with communities and functions cut off from their natural hinterlands. In the north-western angle of the inner ring road, the large middle-class tenement flats on Garnethill lost their attraction as their shopping and service centre of New City Road disappeared under the motorway, and the population rapidly moved out. Perhaps a more positive note is that these empty flats, ignored by building societies, were bought by a section of the community able to generate its own capital, and became a major reception area for young, single Asian migrants, living in consortia in the large flats, before migrating westwards across the physical and status barriers of the Ring Road and the River Kelvin as success permitted them to bring their families to Glasgow[54]. Recognition of the blighting effect has been partly responsible for withdrawal of proposals for the Great Western Road, Crow Road, and Maryhill sections of the new road system, and the emphasis has changed to increased investment in public transport. A modernised Underground has been reopened and linked with surface commuter rail lines at several stations in the Transclyde system, but the city motorbus services, particularly to outlying schemes, badly need improvement.

People in the seventies — an overview

One hundred and five years after the City Improvements Act began the drive to improve the lot of Glasgow's working population, the 1971 Census provided a yardstick by which progress might be measured. On a national basis, at the spatial scale of Enumeration Districts, a range of measures of well-being, physical and social, was extracted and compared, and the worst 5% and 1%, containing c.4,700 and 870 E.D.'s respectively, examined. Although having only 4.3% of the total of E.D.'s in Britain, Clydeside demonstrated remarkably high concentrations of the worst, on severe overcrowding for instance, 43.9% of the area's E.D.'s were in the worst 5% category, while on male unemployment, 42% of Clydeside's E.D.'s were in the worst 1%. Adding overcrowding and unemployment together in spatial concentration gave Clydeside c.90% of the worst 1%, and the addition of other indicators brought the proportion to 95% demonstrating clearly the concept, and spatial concentration, of multiple deprivation[55].

Central government became aware of the scale and complexity of the problems of older urban areas, and the need to bring about rapid improvement, and the special government grant to Glasgow in 1971 of £5 million, to be supported by £2 million of municipal money, but to be spent within five years, prompted action. A survey, based on 22 physical, social and demographic variables identified one third of the city as being multiply deprived, and in spatial location, bearing little resemblance to the location of C.D.A.'s[56]. At the same time, the local authorities were trying to closely define these deprived areas on the ground, and achieve measures of their relative needs[57]. Local government reorganisation in 1975 passed the overall responsibility for progress to Strathclyde Region, and in 1976, 114 Areas for Priority Treatment were identified in the Region, 53 of which were in Glasgow, containing 68.76% of the city's population, or 519,127 people[58]. They were based on housing areas ranging from

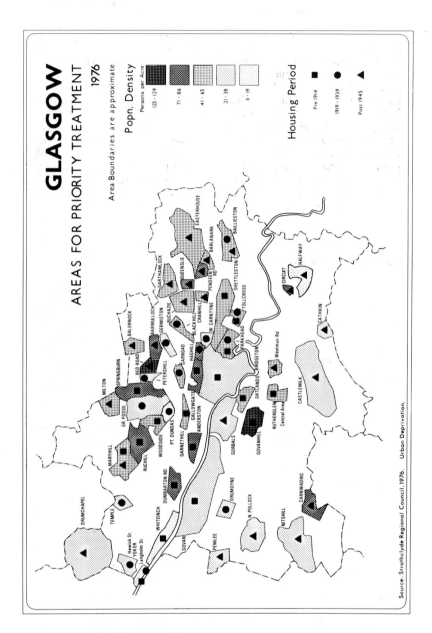

7.vi   *Areas for Priority Treatment, 1976*

nineteenth-century tenements to local authority housing schemes of the inter-war and post-war periods, and shockingly, the completed C.D.A. of Gorbals, containing 13,000 people in a newly built environment (Fig. 7.vi). Projects under way in seven (later eight) Regional Initiative Areas confirmed the main problems as: large proportions of children, inadequate housing, poverty, high unemployment rates, long term unemployment, low educational attainment, high shopping costs, and dependence on bus services[59]. On the basis of local variability of factors, two sets of policies were conceived, aimed at central, common initiatives, and special area approaches. The 114 Strathclyde A.P.T.'s were revised in 1982 to a total of 75, including some amalgamations and extensions, and 46 of these, including the G.E.A.R. area and the Maryhill Corridor, are in Glasgow[60]. When small area data from the 1981 census becomes available, some revision of detail may be necessary, but it seems likely that the A.P.T.'s will remain the spatial focus of activities through the 1980s.

From the late nineteenth century, three approaches to the living environment of the people of Glasgow may be discerned, beginning with a broadly based assault on sanitation and public health, and by the First World War, moving to the more localised scale of the house. From the 1920s, there has been an enormous improvement in physical housing conditions, but this is only one element of the problem. The search for solutions to housing problems, involving the construction of peripheral schemes and high-rise flats, has been successful in reducing indices of overcrowding, but at the expense of the general well-being of the community. Advancing rapidly into the 1980s, the emphasis is less on the house and more on its dwellers. The evolution of Community Councils, Housing Associations, and Tenant Management schemes, highlights the way in which people, looking after their own interests, have become the focus of improvement. It is obvious, however, that the new people-oriented philosophy in planning is going to have to work overtime to fulfil its promise to the two-thirds of Glasgow's population which wait, in trepidation or in apathy, for the next round of projects embarked upon in their name, and on their behalf.

REFERENCES

1. Checkland, S. G., 1980. The British City-Region as Historical and Political Challenge in Pollard, S. (ed.) *Region and Industrialisation. Studies on the role of the region in the economic history of the last two centuries,* p.288.
2. Campbell, R. H., 1980. *The Rise and Fall of Scottish Industry 1707-1939,* pp.138-139.
3. Buxton, Neil K., 1968. The Scottish Shipbuilding Industry Between the Wars; A Comparative Study. *Business History,* X, p.108.
4. Robb, A. M., 1958. Shipbuilding and Marine Engineering in Cunnison, J. & Gilfillan, J. B. S., (eds.). *The Third Statistical Account of Scotland: Glasgow,* p.200.
5. Campbell, R. H., 1980, *op.cit.,* p.127.
6. Campbell, R. H., 1980, *op.cit.,* p.149.

7. Orr, S. C. & J., 1958. Other Engineering; in Cunnison, J. & Gilfillan, J. B. S., *op.cit.*, pp.219-20.
8. Leser, C. E. V., 1958. The Industrial Pattern; in Cunnison, J. & Gilfillan, J. B. S., *op.cit.*, p.133.
9. Carter, C. J., 1972. Comparative Studies in the Post War Industrial Geography of the Clydeside and West Midland Conurbations, p.24. Unpublished Ph.D. Thesis, University of Glasgow.
10. Welch, R. V., 1974. Manufacturing change on Greater Clydeside in the 1950s and 1960s. *S.G.M.*, 90.3., p.176.
11. Abercrombie, P. & Matthew, R. H., 1946. *The Clyde Valley Regional Plan*, p.84.
12. Welch, R. V., 1974, *op.cit.*, pp.171-4.
13. Henderson, R. A., 1974. Industrial Overspill from Glasgow, 1958-1968. *Urban Studies*, II, p.64. Corporation of Glasgow, 1959. *Industry on the Move*, p.10.
14. Glasgow Herald, February 17th, 1982, p.7.
15, Riddell, J. F., 1979, *op.cit.*, p.253.
16. Clyde Port Authority, 1980. *Report and Accounts, 1979.*
17. Desbarats, J. M., 1972. Some geographical aspects of port modernisation: the case of Clydeport. *S.G.M.*, 88.3, p.186.
18. Clyde Port Authority, 1979. *Clydeport*, pp.6-13.
19. Robertson, D. J., 1958. Population, Past and Present in Cunnison, J. & Gilfillan, J. B. S., *op.cit.*, p.66.
20. Whyte, W. E., 1941. Planning for Post-War Glasgow. *Proceedings of the Royal Philosophical Society of Glasgow*, 68.1, p.6.
21. Robertson, D. J., 1958, *op.cit.*, pp.55, 53 and 74.
22. Grieve, R., 1954. The Clyde Valley — A Review, p.5. (Paper delivered at the Town and Country Planning Summer School held at the University of St. Andrews 1954 under the auspices of the Town Planning Institute).
23. Scott, W. R. & Cunnison, J., 1924. *The Industries of the Clyde Valley During the War*, pp.164-169.
24. Robertson, D. J., 1958, *op.cit.*, p.61, Table XIII.
25. Abercrombie, P. & Matthew, R. H., 1946, *op.cit.*, p.342.
26. Scottish Development Department; Census Research Unit, 1975. *Glasgow Change exercise.*
27. Robertson, D. J., 1958, *op.cit.*, p.55, Table IX.
28. Census Enumeration Abstracts, 1951.
29. Cunnison, J. & Gilfillan, J. B. S. (eds.), 1958. *The Third Statistical Account of Scotland: Glasgow.* Appendix part III2. Housing conditions, pp.867/9 and 873/4.
30. Census Enumeration Abstracts, 1961.
31. Census Enumeration Abstracts, 1961.
32. Abercrombie, P. & Matthew, R. H., 1946, *op.cit.*, pp.176/185.
33. Farmer, E. & Smith, R., 1975. Overspill Theory: a Metropolitan Case Study. *Urban Studies*: 12, pp.153 and 155.
34. Corporation of Glasgow, 1960. *First Quinquennial Review of the Development Plan*, p.8. Forbes, J. & McBain, I. D. (eds.), 1967. *The Springburn Study*, paras. 4.56 to 4.61.
35. Corporation of Glasgow, 1954. City of Glasgow Development Plan Approval Order. Written Statement, pp.7, 13, and 14.
36. Glasgow District Council, 1979. Housing Management Department: Annual Report, p.16.
37. City of Glasgow Housing Department, 1980. Kingsbridge and Cleddans: Environmental Improvement Brief, p.3.
38. Corporation of Glasgow, 1946. Second Planning Report, pp.9 and 15.
39. Glasgow District Council, 1979. Housing Management Department: Annual Report. p.12.
40. Miller, R., 1970. The New Face of Glasgow. *S.G.M.*, 86.1, p.9.
41. Scottish Development Department, Housing Development Group, 1975. The Social Effects of Living off the Ground. H.D.D. Occasional Paper 1/75, p.8.
42. Glasgow District Council: Planning Department, 1981. Possilpark Local Plan; Written Statement, p.1.
43. Development Plan Progress in Scotland: Bulletin 14, Winter 1980/81, p.2.
44. Scottish Development Agency, 1978. *The future for G.E.A.R.: Key issues and possible courses of action*, p.4.
45. Scottish Development Agency, 1978. G.E.A.R. Household Survey, pp.viii and ix.

46. Scottish Development Agency, 1980. G.E.A.R. The facts and the future (Information sheet).
47. Diamond, D. R., 1960. The Central Business District of Glasgow. Lund Studies in Geography, Series B. Human Geography No.24, pp.526 and 533.
48. Gerald Eve & Co., 1965. *City of Glasgow: Report on the Central Area*, Plans 9c and 11, pp.99 and 111.
49. Henderson, R. A., 1974, *op.cit.*, p.70.
50. Gerald Eve & Co., 1965, *op.cit.*, p.39.
51. Sim, D. F., 1976. Patterns of Building Adaptation and Redevelopment in the Central Business District of Glasgow. Unpublished Ph.D. Thesis, University of Glasgow, p.28.
52. Gerald Eve & Co., 1971. *Glasgow: Report on Aspects of Future Shopping Provision*, p.23.
53. Miller, R., 1970, *op.cit.*, p.11.
54. Kearsley, G. W. & Srivastava, S. R., 1974. The Spatial Evolution of Glasgow's Asian Community. *S.G.M.*, 90.2, p.114.
55. Holtermann, S., 1975. *Areas of Urban Deprivation in Great Britain*. H.M.S.O. Social Trends No.6.
56. Scottish Development Department, 1973. Summary Report of an Investigation to Identify Areas of Multiple Deprivation in Glasgow City. Central Planning Research Unit Working Paper No.7.
57. Corporation of Glasgow, Planning Department, 1973. *Areas of Need in Glasgow*.
58. Strathclyde Regional Council, 1976. *Urban Deprivation*, p.22.
59. Strathclyde Regional Council, 1978. *Monitoring the Seven Initiative Areas*.
60. Strathclyde Regional Council, 1979: *114 A.P.T.'s* and 1982: *75 A.P.T.'s*.

EPILOGUE

The city and the future

Reaching out for the year 2000, the planners will bend their intellects towards the equalisation of opportunity, the eradication of relative poverty, the easing of the bodies and spirits of the city's people. But the city is more than the people, or at least the present people. It is at once the sum of the achievements of all past people who lived in its caves and warrens, and the ideas of a few who never saw it in reality. It is the mind-child of some, and the womb and rack of multitudes. Its constituent elements and structural arrangements are the end results of processes as far removed from biology as the stresses which shaped the sandstone of its walls and the slates of its roofs. Its timescale lies between the geological and the biological, bewildering humans with the rapidity of inception of change, and the slow climb to a pinnacle of completion which will never be reached. The city is simply, and enduringly, the city.

INDEX